Praise for
The People and the Music . . .

"The Nashville skyline of today, with its overabundance of glass-laden skyscrapers, is vastly different than when I moved here in 1993, and the skyline which I first saw of Music City is, in the same way, quite removed from the skyline of the Nashville of the 60's. You could say that the Nashville music scene today is the same - pickers, singers, and songwriters that have been here for even 30 years are removed from the people, offices, and communities that helped forge "The Row" into what it became to the country music industry back in the 1960's through the 1980's.

Barbara Martin's book *The People and the Music* is a wonderful trip down her memory lane of the people whom she called friends as well as peers in the music business on Music Row in the 1960's. A time when almost every phone call was long distance, Rolodexes sat on every music business person's desk, and where the alleys and sidewalks of 16th and 17th Avenue (Music Row) were as much of a place to converse with friends as it was a place to do business.

The names of a great number of people in this book may be foreign to the reader, or at best jog a recollection for those fans of the old Nashville music scene. Other names will be easily recognizable as well. But in the end, they are individuals who, each in their respective ways, helped make up the often unseen side of the music business in Nashville in a time when things were much simpler and Nashville was more of a community on the Row than a corporate machine.

There's also stories and recollections of some of Barbara's longtime friends, which is particularly engaging. Barbara is one of the last folks still alive at the time of my writing who not only remembers, but also actively participated in a Nashville that time has forgot.

I hope you find reading this book as pleasurable and enlightening as I did. It made me long for a place in time in Nashville's music scene that I never knew. Perhaps this book will transport you to the times, places, and people in Barbara's memories as much as it has me."

—*Bob Minner*
Acoustic guitarist for Tim McGraw,
IBMA-nominated Songwriter, producer

"Barbara Martin Stephens new book, *The People and the Music*, offers a unique look at a side of the music scene most fans never see. With a sharp memory and a keen eye for detail, she describes her work as a booking agent in the 1950s and '60s during one of the most productive and influential eras of country and bluegrass music when artists such as Jimmy Martin, Patsy Cline, the Louvin Brothers, Loretta Lynn and others were running up and down the blue highways playing radio barn dances, country music parks, state fairs and political campaigns all over the country.

The People and the Music gets into the nitty gritty of booking shows for traveling musicians in the pre-digital age when paperwork, phone calls, personal connections, the US Postal Service and moxie got solid work for the artists that one represented. Barbara describes her own successful efforts as well as the work done by the other key industry people she introduces throughout the book.

Current readers might be surprised by the very personal, handshake world of country music in those days before the personal computer and social media. Mrs. Martin Stephens provides important documentation of those times as well as colorful anecdotes of the movers and shakers who inhabited Music Row. That said, she's not content to dwell on the past and the reader will be introduced to other figures who keep the flame for bluegrass and roots music burning brightly. Last, but not least, she closes the book with some favorite recipes that you can try at home. Good food and good music go hand-in-hand and there's nothing more country than a home made biscuit!"

—*John Fabke*
July, 2024

"Barbara Martin Stephens' latest memoir *The People and the Music* offers her unique perspective of some of the biggest stars as well as some of those often-overlooked people behind the scene. She takes her reader back to the early days of Nashville's historic Music Row, as well as behind the scenes at the Grand Ole Opry, Wheeling (WV) Jamboree, and the Louisiana Hayride. Her voice—sometimes full of admiration and other times marked by wry humor—rings true as she shares inside stories of friends and colleagues. Perhaps the most endearing character to emerge is Stephens herself."

—*Nancy Posey*
MA.Ed, EdD. Music journalist and songwriter

COUNTRY AND BLUEGRASS, THAT IS!

. . . .

BARBARA MARTIN STEPHENS

THE PEOPLE AND THE MUSIC
Country and Bluegrass, That Is!

Copyright © 2025 Barbara Martin Stephens

All rights reserved. No portion of this book may be reproduced, stored in a retrieval system, or transmitted in any form or by any means—electronic, mechanical, photocopy, recording, scanning, or other—except for brief quotations in critical reviews or articles, without the prior written permission of the publisher.

Email: fsunole65@aol.com

ISBN Print: 979-8-218-55388-3
ISBN e-Book: 979-8-218-55764-5

Cover Illustrations by Lindsey Martin Crumpley
(Lindsey took my ideas and brought them to life!)

Book Design by Mary Susan Oleson, Blu Design Concepts

Printed in the United States of America

Photos of Buddy Lee Rita and Buddy Lee courtesy of Donna Lee.

Photo of Hubert's house courtesy of Ruth Elkins.

Photographs of Wilma Lee, Stoney Cooper, Jerry Johnson, Peggy Gayle and the Leary Family courtesy of Bruce McGuire.

Photographs of Radio Dot & Smoky and Family — courtesy of Dave Heath, President, Wheeling Jamboree Museum Archives.

Photographs of Ronnie Reno and Family, courtesy of Ronnie Reno.

Photographs courtesy of Ginger Boatwright appearing in her chapter.

Contents

ACKNOWLEDGMENTS..11
CONDOLENCES..13
PREFACE 21

CHAPTER 1: Booking Agents, Managers, and Promoters....31
- The Louisiana Hayride...31
- Gene Johnson Promotions..37
- The Barbara Martin Agency 40
- Gra-Mar Talent Agency...48
- Buddy Lee Attractions 59
- Hubert Long Talent Agency 63
- Colonel "Buster" Doss 71
- The Jim Denny Agency...75
- Wil-Helm Agency..78
- The Bob Neal Agency 84

CHAPTER 2: The Women behind the Scenes....................95
- Betty Harford (wife of John Hartford) 95
- Joyce Jackson, personal secretary
  and assistant to Jim and Mary Reeves......................106
- Elizabeth (Libby) Griggs 115
- Corky Wilson..120

CHAPTER 3: Singers, Songwriters, and More 129
- Donna Darlene and Shot Jackson 129
- Jim Rushing, the Song Crafter..................................138
- Bob and Birdie Smith and The Station Inn 147
- Merle Kilgore 164
- Louisa Branscomb,
  Pioneer for Women and Songwriters......................170

- Grant Turner 190
- Carl Belew 194
- Wilma Lee & Stoney Cooper, Jerry Johnson Colmus & Peggy O'Leary 200
- Ginger Boatwright 217
- Jimmy Payne 231
- Billy Hunter 242
- Dottie Swan, the 901 Club 259
- Charmaine Lanham and Marty Lanham 264
- Johnny and Jeanette Williams 269
- The Nashville Musicians Union 276
- Ronnie Reno 280

Epilogue: The Music Business Today 299

My Memories of Three of the Greatest Banjo Players:
Sonny Osborne, Bill Emerson, and J. D. Crowe 309

Just Something Extra For Fun 324
"Little House" a poem by Barbara Martin Stephens 325

Recipes 326
- Ireland's Inn Steak and Biscuits 326
- Barbara's Biscuit Recipe 327
- Barbara's Marinade Recipe 328
- Barbara's Holiday Supreme Salad 328
- Barbara's Mexican Cornbread 330
- Barbara's Beef Stew 331
- Barbara's Best Gingerbread 332

Photo Memories 334

About the Author 345
Index 348

*This book is dedicated to my mother,
Willowdeen Farmer Gibson.
She instilled in me a passion
for reading and writing
before I started school.
She was born on the 4th of July
and was a real "firecracker".
I love her dearly.*

Acknowledgments

I WOULD LIKE to thank Joyce Jackson, Dave Barton, Patricia Ann Eaves, Don Cusic, Corky Wilson, Libby Griggs, Betty Harford, Jimmy Payne, Jeanette and Johnny Williams, Rita Faye Wilson, Ronnie Reno, Bruce McGuire, Dave Pomeroy, Katie and Eric Hogue, Ginger Boatwright, Billy Hunter, Charmaine Lanham, Art Malmin, my son James H. (Timmy) Martin Jr., Michelle Canning, Jeff Miller, and all those who talked to me about their lives in the music industry—including those who wouldn't return calls. Few of us are still living who worked in the industry in the '50s and '60s. My memory, while still very good, only goes so far. So, without them, this book would not be possible. Thank you, thank you, from the bottom of my heart.

A special thank you to my like-family friends, Katie and Eric Hogue. And, Mary Susan Oleson, my graphics designer and friend. Without you all, I couldn't have done it again.

I would also like to thank my granddaughter, Michelle Martin, who did the first couple of edits on this manuscript. Michelle has always been someone who excelled in the English language and loved to read. She is an excellent editor. And thank you to my editor, Nancy Cardwell Webster, who is the very best. Nancy also edited my first book, *Don't Give Your Heart to a Rambler, My Life with Jimmy Martin, King of Bluegrass*.

Condolences

We have recently lost three very dear people, good friends and long-time residents of the Nashville Music Community

GLORIA BELLE FLICKINGER LONG has been a member of the bluegrass community for over 40 years. She played bass, guitar, and sometimes banjo with Jimmy Martin and the Sunny Mountain Boys for many years. She and her husband, Mike Long, had a band and began touring following their marriage in the mid-1980s. Gloria Belle was a terrific entertainer with a smile that lit up her entire face, a very kind and loyal person.

Condolences

Gloria Belle lived with me and my family in Plantation, Florida, for over a year. Her mom and dad would come to visit, and I got to know them. They had a terrific, close-knit family, and Gloria Belle was a great roommate. I am so happy to have seen she and Mike Long, her husband, in February 2023. Gloria had Alzheimer's, so she didn't know me. But she kept her eyes focused on my granddaughter, Michelle, and kept smiling at her. I think she was remembering her from the time she was about seven years old. I told Gloria, "You still have that beautiful smile." She smiled even brighter. I will miss her.

JANE GLASER, wife of Jim Glaser (Tompall and the Glasers). Jane was such a beautiful lady, the mother of four children who fought a long, hard battle for many years with various health problems. As with most of the wives during the late '60s and early '70s, she worked hard to support Jim while he and his two brothers, Tompall and Chuck, were becoming known in the field of country music and to raise her family. She worked in their publishing company, anything to help the family.

My last memories of her are so vivid. We were at the Memorial Services for Jimmy Payne's wife, Jo. Jane was sitting near the back with Katie and Eric Hogue. As I neared where Jane was sitting, she reached out and grabbed my hand. She said, "I want to talk to you." I told her, "I want to talk to you too." A couple of days later, I called her and we talked about the old days for about 15 minutes. I called her more often after that but was only able to speak to her a couple of times. I wanted to feature her in this book, but between her health problems and a busy life, we were unable to get together.

JIMMY PAYNE was a songwriter and musician extraordinaire. One of the most honest, gentle, funniest people I have ever known, Jimmy was a terrific musician and loved his wife, Jo, and daughter, Amanda, and the Lord with every inch of his fiber. I never knew when he was going to call, morning, noon, or evening. We would talk about the old days in the music business and laugh and laugh and laugh.

Jimmy Payne

Rest in peace my friends. We will meet again.

THE CONDOLENCES CONTINUE

Since June 19, it has been a devastating nine days in Nashville and the field of Bluegrass Music. We have lost two of its greatest pioneers and one of the best bass players around.

Mark Kuykendall

MARK KUYKENDALL. I only met Mark Kuykendall one time in person and that was at IBMA in Raleigh, N.C. in 2018. Patricia Anne Eaves (Tricia) and I were sitting in the lobby of the Sheraton Hotel when Mark came in. He walked over to Tricia since he knew her and she introduced me to him. He grabbed both of my hands and said, "I have been wanting to meet you." We sat in the lobby and talked and he wanted to buy my book, *Don't Give Your Heart To A Rambler*. I gave him a copy, he insisted on paying for it and I wouldn't let him. From that time on, we were friends on Facebook. He was so kind to me. He worked for Jimmy Martin for several years but, I never knew him. I do know that Mark loved his family and was a deeply religious man. He also loved Bluegrass Music.

Mark passed away on June 19, 2023. He was 60 years old and suffered complications from diabetes for many years. We will all miss him.

Condolences

JESSE McREYNOLDS. I knew Jesse during the 1960s when I traveled with Jimmy Martin to the Bluegrass Festivals. I didn't book Jim & Jesse but knew Jesse personally. Then, in 2018 after my book was released, Nancy Cardwell, who was playing bass for Jesse, asked me to go to the Grand Ole Opry with her. That night, Jesse and I reconnected after over forty years. We talked like we had seen each other the day before.

Jesse McReynolds

After that first connection, I saw Jesse many times at the Grand Ole Opry either with Nancy or other people. I liked to tease him about being on the television show "Nashville" and not letting me come to the filming because I was in love (not really) with Deacon. I did meet and talk with Charles Esten who played Deacon but it was in the dressing room with Del McCoury. He was everything I thought he was on the television show and more. I just liked to tease Jesse about it.

I attended Jesse's 90th birthday party held in Gallatin, Tennessee at the home of Mike and Brenda Scott. They call their home, "The Grand Inheritance," and it is absolutely fabulous. Jesse, Roland White, and I took a picture that evening.

Condolences

*Two long time friends, fabulous musicians and me,
Jesse McReynolds, and Roland White*

Jesse's funeral was being held the day I found out Bobby Osborne had passed away. I was getting ready to go to Jesse's funeral when I received the call about Bob's passing. It was devastating news to come at such a difficult time.

Jesse McReynolds photo is courtesy of LuAnn Adams Smith.

• •

BOBBY (BOB) OSBORNE. I learned yesterday, June 27, 2023, Bob had passed away. I was devastated. I couldn't function. This is a man I have known since I was 17 years old. Our families lived together, traveled together, laughed together, cried together, first babies born 20 days apart, and loved for seventy years. I didn't think it could happen.

Condolences

Not right now when he had so many good things going on in his life.

I saw Bob when he played the American Legion in Inglewood, a suburb of Nashville, in January and February, 2023. He had three shows scheduled and each one had a full house. I didn't go to the show in March and regret that I didn't go. I had seen him the latter part of 2022 when he appeared at The Station Inn.

Bobby Osborne

His good friend and mine, C.J. Lewandowski was at the American Legion show and told me that he and Bob were going to California to cut an album together. C.J. had been spending a lot of time with Bob and they became best friends. I told C.J. I thought it was wonderful he was spending time with Bob. C.J. is great with older people and has always been good to me. Get Bob interested and out of the house. My exact words were, "Put him on the plane and have a great time." C.J. said, "I intend to do just that."

Bob had celebrated his 91st birthday on December 7th when he appeared at the American Legion in early January. He said on stage, "I am 91 years old and I am working on 100." I was rooting for you to make it, Bob.

Condolences

My memories are so long and vivid of things we have done, said, experienced and seen over the past seventy years, together and apart. I lost a person who was very dear to me yesterday, one I will never forget. The world lost the best tenor singer, mandolin player, and a standup person when they lost Bobby Osborne.

'Till we meet again Old Friends . . .

Preface

Moving back to Nashville in April 2019, it wasn't unusual for me to spend my days driving around looking at all my old hangouts, including what is now known as Music Row. There have been so many changes in just a few short blocks. The changes were something I never noticed when my husband, Chuck Stephens, and I visited Nashville, and I did my roaming.

Chuck and I came to Nashville three or four times a year to visit family. We stayed at my house off Indian Lake Road in Hendersonville. I worked online with my law office in Fort Lauderdale a couple of days a week. Working didn't leave much time to roam during my short visits. Moving back, retiring, and my husband deceased, I had a ton of time to ramble and think. My favorite pastime has been to sit in my car at my old hangouts and reminisce about the old days.

Chuck Stephens

But my reminiscing wasn't limited to Music Row, I would go around my old neighborhood, Centennial Park, and the place on top of the small viaduct on Charlotte Pike and 25th Street where I got my

The People and The Music—Country and Bluegrass that is!

first kiss. Those are very special places for me. It they weren't special, I wouldn't remember them so vividly 72 years later.

Living in Fort Lauderdale working as a paralegal/administrator/accountant full time, raising a family including my granddaughter, Michelle, keeping house, and taking kids to football games, dance classes, piano classes, and recitals didn't leave me much alone time. The music business and first kisses were not on my mind. I was busy at home with my family and at work.

Once I retired and my husband, Charles E. (Chuck) Stephens passed, I finished writing my book *Don't Give Your Heart to a Rambler, My Life With Jimmy Martin, King of Bluegrass* and sent it to the publisher. Finishing the book didn't stop me from thinking about the music business. I continued to think about the business conducted, the people, and things that went on in the 1950s and 1960s on what is now called "Music Row" or "Music Block" (includes 17th Avenue South as well.) During the time I was on the Avenue (it was known as either 16th Avenue South or 17th Avenue South), the music business occupied both streets for a couple of blocks.

Before the music business took over that area, it was all residential. My grandmother lived at 1614 McGavock Street. I have pictures of my son, Mike, sitting on the steps. My aunt, Jessie Wainwright Blackwell, lived two doors down. The entire area was residential until the early '60s when a few businesses started moving in.

I came home from Middletown, Ohio, to have my son, Timmy, and was staying with my grandmother and mother at the McGavock house in late August 1954. The day of Timmy's birth, August 28, 1954, I walked from 16th and McGavock to Walgreen's Drug Store at the Arcade on 5th Avenue North. I had a pimento cheese sandwich

Preface

with potato salad for lunch and walked back to my grandmother's. That night Timmy was born. The area is a huge part of my life, both personally and professionally.

I have now been in Nashville for three years, I continue to go out to Music Row, and sometimes I will circle the block several times just to reminisce. This is the area where I spent my time in the 1950s and mid-1960s. In the 1960s, it was a bustling place where we conducted the business of music. By this time, my grandmother's home was long gone, and it was a vacant lot. For years, though, the steps still stood there. I could go and sit and remember her green 1949 Ford parked at the curb. It was easier to park at the curb than in the back.

McGavock Street between 16th Avenue South and 18th Avenue South as it looked In 1957. Mother standing in front of my car parked in front of our house at 1614 McGavock Street about 1957

There are a couple of ways to get to Music Block from downtown Nashville. You can drive west on Broadway. At the Y, turn left onto 18th Avenue and enter the round-a-bout to 17th. You can also drive from downtown Nashville on Deaderick Street to Buddy

The People and The Music—Country and Bluegrass that is!

Killian Circle. There is a beautiful statute in the round-about entitled "Musica." Seventeenth Avenue South is now one-way going south, while 16th Avenue South is one-way going north. Taking the round-a-bout to 17th Avenue South, driving down the street, there are very few buildings that look exactly the same as they were in the mid-'60s. Some of those remaining are the firehouse and RCA Victor Studios on the left side of the street. Elvis Presley, Eddy Arnold, and Jim Reeves (plus many others) recorded at RCA. Chet Atkins was the head of A&R (Artists and Repertoire) at Victor.

The steps leading up to my old office on 17th Avenue are still there. You have to look closely to see them, sandwiched in between a monster building on one side and RCA on the other side. My office was located in a two-story, beautiful old house converted to offices. It was on the second floor, and I could clearly see the alley running parallel between 16th Avenue South and 17th Avenue South. I opened this office in association with John Denny in 1967. I don't know why the developers left that little strip of land, but I am glad they did. I can look at those steps and remember my office each time I drive down the street.

Memories of the building that formerly stood there are so vivid. I can still see John Denny coming into my office or see Dolly Parton standing in the alley. The alleyway was like a sidewalk—someone always walking down the alley or stopping to talk whenever they saw a friend, and you always saw someone you knew. John and Bill Denny's offices at Cedarwood were located directly behind my building on 16th Avenue South. I used the alley to go back and forth several times a day. I always ran into someone, and what was supposed to be a five-minute walk became a thirty-minute conversation. What good times they were!

Preface

My last office

Turning left from 17th Avenue onto Grand, I make another left turn onto 16th Avenue South. When I stop at the light at the corner of 16th Avenue and Grand, I look at the building that housed a five-and-dime store on the southeast corner and remember my cousin, Clyde Hines' wife, Willie Mae, who worked there for 25 years. Again, very few buildings remain from the '60s on 16th Avenue. One of those remaining is the Capitol Records Building. Hubert Long had his talent agency on the second floor, and I always think of him when I look at the building.

Across the street from Hubert was Cedarwood Publishing and the Jim Denny Artist Bureau, located at 815 16th Avenue South. I worked closely with the Denny Agency, including Lucky Moeller and

The People and The Music—Country and Bluegrass that is!

Jack B. Andrews, the entire time I was booking talent in Wheeling and Nashville. Tree Publishing was across from Dottie Swan's restaurant and bar, the 901 Club. Regardless of who owns it, I still see Dottie or her daughter, Little Dottie, behind the bar.

Tree Publishing was founded by Jack Stapp in the early 1950s. Before, he passed away, Buddy Killen became the president. The circle or round-about three blocks up the street is named after Buddy Killen. Tree Publishing has always been a major force in the publishing business in Nashville.

Decca Records is on the west side of the street, as is the Wil-Helm Agency and Cedarwood. It looks exactly the same, and I hope it stays that way. I never look at it without remembering Owen Bradley's and Harry Silverstein's offices. Both were on the second floor where the little balcony can still be seen from the street. Harry's office was on the left as you went up the stairs, and Owen's office was directly in front of the stairs. A highlight of my day was going across the street to Decca. Regardless of what Harry and Owen were doing, they would stop and come out to see me or motion me into the office. Not only did I love those guys, I respected and admired them as well.

My agency, Gra-Mar Talent Agency, was located across the street from Decca. Wil-Helm Agency was located next door to Decca. Wil-Helm is now an optician's office, and my building has been torn down and is a vacant lot. Before the building was demolished, it was in total disrepair. An awning had been added and it was falling down

There were other non-music-related businesses on the street, including the bar I mentioned earlier, operated by Dottie Swan (formerly Radio Dot and Smoky). But the buildings and the booking

Preface

Gra-Mar Talent was behind the big windows

agencies I mentioned are the offices I worked with most closely in my business.

Music Row (16th and 17th Avenues South) was a busy place in the 1960s. People were everywhere—people who worked there and people who were looking for a record contract, show dates, someone to record their song, or just to be seen. It was not unusual to see Brenda Lee, Mel Tillis, Jimmy Martin, Faron Young, Carl Belew, Eddy Arnold, Billy Walker, Billy Grammer, Doyle or Teddy Wilburn, Loretta Lynn and her husband Mooney, or even Elvis Presley just walking up or down the street talking to people. People were coming and going from all of the offices in the couple of blocks where the music business was conducted. The Glaser Brothers were

The People and The Music—Country and Bluegrass that is!

on the streets every day. Their offices were upstairs over Wil-Helm. As Jimmy Payne said to me when I was interviewing him, "It was like a circus. Everyone was out and about, happy and conducting business."

As you return to the Circle, look at the park on your left at the statue of Owen Bradley playing the piano. Nearby is where the guitar-shaped swimming pool Webb Pierce built in the '70s as a tourist attraction. It was directly across from the original site of the Country Music Hall of Fame. The City filled in the pool and it is no longer there.

Webb Pierce also built an exact replica of the guitar shaped pool at his home on Franklin Road in Nashville. He wanted the tourist to visit it and they did. Nearly 3,000 people visited the pool each week causing Ray Stevens, Webb's neighbor, to lead his neighbors to file a suit and ask Pierce to end the tours. They won the case. The pool was later sold to Spence Manor, which is now condominiums.

One day while riding around 16th Avenue, I decided to pull over and just sit in my car and look around. I thought about all the people I knew who tried their best to make it in the music business, who sold their songs to make a living for their families, or who had charted records but had no show dates. Some of those good, talented people gave up and went back home. The people working in the offices gave their all for very little money, and a lot of their work was for free. They worked diligently but were never recognized. These were good people, very talented singers, musicians and songwriters, and dedicated people. I thought, "How soon we forget those who worked behind the scenes, wives who stayed at home or worked a job to help their husbands try to succeed in the music business; and those whose luck ran out, gave up and went home."

Preface

Webb Pierce and his wife, Audrey

Then there were those that worked in the business as leaders or stars that have been forgotten—including the guys and gals that sold hit songs for $100 or less, but their names are not listed as writers. They all made a difference, but just mention their names now and most people don't know who they are or how much each of these people contributed to the music business as it is today. I knew these people and how hard they tried. It would take several books to write about all of them. Let us read some of their stories and not forget again.

CHAPTER 1:
Booking Agents, Managers, and Promoters

Without a booking agent who was aggressively looking for show dates for him or her, an artist was up the creek without a paddle. I booked my first show in Shreveport, Louisiana, when I was only 23 years old—not out of curiosity, but necessity. So, let's start there

THE LOUISIANA HAYRIDE
Shreveport, Louisiana | 1958 – 1960

In Shreveport, Jimmy Martin was a big star on the "Hayride," as it was known by the people who worked there. The Hayride paid its musicians and "stars" very little money for their appearances on Saturday night. I believe Jimmy was getting $100 for Saturday night. He had to pay Paull Williams and J.D. Crowe out of that. The acts expected to make money from their appearances on the road. Of course in order to do that, you had to have someone to book your act.

Jimmy's band in Shreveport consisted of Paul Williams (real name Paul Humphrey) and J.D. Crowe on banjo. We lived together in an apartment in a beautiful old house at 552 Egan Street in

The People and The Music—Country and Bluegrass that is!

Tillman Franks, Johnny Horton and Scotty Moore

Paul Williams, J.D. Crowe, Jimmy Martin

Booking Agents, Managers, and Promoters

Shreveport. Living together was the only way we could all survive.

Few people on the Louisiana Hayride in Shreveport had show dates or other places to appear. Out of all the people on the Hayride at that time, I didn't know anyone who was getting booked. None of the Hayride acts appeared in a night club in Shreveport, including Jimmy Martin, Carl Belew, Merle Kilgore, James O'Gwynn, the Browns, Margie Singleton, and others. Merle was a disc jockey and had extra income. Those who didn't have a wife, girlfriend, or husband working and helping to support them were up the creek without a paddle. They had to go home or starve.

Taken in Shreveport 1959

I worked at Reliable Investment Firm in the building that housed KWKH, the radio station that broadcast the Louisiana Hayride. Every day I would see Tillman Franks, the booking agent for the Hayride talent, go in and out of the building. I would also see Johnny Horton go in and out. But, unlike Tillman, Johnny would stop by my office and chat for a while before heading up to Tillman's office. I went up and spent my lunch hour with Tillman almost every day. I watched him wheel and deal on the phone, talking to various people. He didn't know it, but I was learning everything he was

The People and The Music—Country and Bluegrass that is!

doing. He probably thought I was just passing time. Tillman didn't mind me sitting in his office because when he was on the phone and needed pen, paper, or whatever, I would get it for him. I was listening and learning to do what he was doing…booking and promoting. I didn't think twice about what he might say if I did book a show, but I was determined to do it.

Jimmy and I were standing on the front porch where we lived, talking about money and how we had done so well in Detroit, but were barely existing in Shreveport. I was only making $30 a week, whereas in Detroit I was making $100 a week. Jimmy was working a TV show at CKLW-TV in Windsor, Ontario, weekly, and on the Barn Dance at 12101 Mack Avenue in Detroit every Saturday night. From those two gigs alone, he was making $200 a week. He was also picking up a bar gig a couple of times a month. I would go with him to the bars and pass the hat for tips. The tips were always good because I talked to people as I got their money. All that, plus his winnings from Snooker, made us comfortable as far as finances go. Add in the fact that Jimmy could squeeze a dime until it turned into a dollar was a plus. But in Shreveport, all that changed.

Tillman was only interested in promoting Johnny Horton and his new record, "The Battle of New Orleans." The rest of the people who played on the Hayride were just out of luck. As Jimmy and I were talking about not having any show dates, I said to him, "You know, I can do what Tillman does." Jimmy sort of looked around, like someone may be listening, and said to me, "If you can, do it." I asked him to go to the Musicians' Union and pick up some contracts. It was a political year in Louisiana, and I knew exactly what I was going to do.

Booking Agents, Managers, and Promoters

Jimmy brought the contracts home, and I read every line of the contract a couple of times, making sure I understood it. I wanted to know what I was dealing with since this was the first contract I had ever read. I told Jimmy I needed some brochures and records. He went to Tillman's office and picked them up for me. I was concerned Tillman's name was stamped on the brochures or the records. It wasn't. Then, I started doing some investigating. I knew Jimmie Davis was running for governor, and I also knew that Earl K. Long was running. Grand Ole Opry acts had been appearing for Jimmie Davis and were well publicized. Their appearances weren't surprising since Jimmie Davis was also a singer. (Remember his hit, "You Are My Sunshine.") My thoughts were, "Earl K. Long could use some music on his campaign." I contacted the campaign manager for Earl K. Long and sent him a couple of Jimmy's albums and brochures.

It only took a few days, and I heard from Mr. Long's campaign manager. He loved the idea of having a top act from the Louisiana Hayride appear on behalf of Earl K. Long. We negotiated and I booked a week of shows with him. Jimmy would appear in seven different towns in Louisiana and put on a show prior to Earl K. Long coming on stage to speak. Before I could receive the returned, signed contracts, Earl K. Long was admitted to a hospital. This didn't stop me. I was more determined than ever to book some shows for Jimmy.

I then contacted DeLesseps Story Morrison, the sitting mayor of New Orleans who had decided to run for governor after Earl K. Long dropped out. He and his campaign manager thought having Jimmy Martin and the Sunny Mountain Boys appear on the campaign trail would draw more crowds. I booked a week with them and caught the "booking" fever. I loved it and I was good at it. So,

The People and The Music—Country and Bluegrass that is!

WWVA Jamboree, Wheeling, West Virginia

Tillman Franks, thank you for starting me on this trail even though you told me not to do it again.

In February 1960, Jimmy decided to move to Wheeling, West Virginia, to become part of the WWVA Jamboree. I loved Louisiana and really didn't want to move. But where my family went, I would go. And, off we went.

The day we arrived in Wheeling, it was snowing, the skies were gray and overcast, and the houses were built on stilts (high up). I didn't know why the houses had to be so high off the ground. We moved into an apartment on the second floor over an empty store on Wheeling Island. When Wheeling Island flooded, I found out why the houses were built high off the ground! The Ohio River flooding was an annual occurrence and Wheeling Island was a perfect target for the flood. Flat!

GENE JOHNSON PROMOTIONS

Gene Autry visits Radio Station WWVA in the Hawley Building. Showing him around are: Gene Johnson, Lee Sutton, Joe Barker, and Gene Autry. Others unknown

Photo courtesy of Dave Heath, President, Wheeling Jamboree Museum Archives

A couple of days later, Jimmy was going to the radio station to check-in with Gene Johnson, who would be booking him. I went along to meet him, as well. Lucky for me that I did. Gene was looking for a secretary, and I happened to be looking for a job. He hired me and I started to work the next day. On our way home, I told Jimmy, "I am going to learn everything Gene Johnson knows about booking because I am going to become a booking agent."

I arrived at Gene's office the next morning and the first thing he did was show me his notebook of contacts. I have always been a

The People and The Music—Country and Bluegrass that is!

person who could read something a couple of times and memorize it quickly. This is what I did. Unfortunately, as I have aged, I am no longer able to do this. While my memory is still terrific, it is not the same as it was at 25. Regardless, Gene was amazed at how quickly I knew all the people we would be dealing with on a daily basis. I also knew their phone numbers. I thought, "If I get fired, I have the contacts."

Gene was very patient with me. He taught me all the ins and outs of booking. One of those things was how to make friends with people I didn't know but would be speaking to regularly. It was important for him, as well as me, to know these folks. I had lots of ideas to make more and more contacts, but I never shared them with Gene. In my heart I knew one day, and soon, I was going to be doing this for myself.

Gene was a jewel to work with. He was one of the kindest, smartest, nicest gentlemen I had ever known. If I made a mistake, he never yelled. He would merely show me how to correct it. And one of the best parts, we booked a lot of shows for Wilma Lee and Stoney Cooper and Hawkshaw Hawkins, three people I dearly loved. I had been friends with Wilma Lee and Stoney for years. So, I got to see them more often. I also loved "Hawk" and Jean Shephard. Hawk never came into the office, that he didn't bring me a candy bar. He never knew I didn't like chocolate. Seeing all the entertainers often allowed me to make friends with them and to earn their trust as Gene's assistant. (I had already graduated from secretary status to being his assistant.)

John Corrigan was director of the WWVA Jamboree. Within a couple of weeks, Gene had me working every day with John on the weekly schedule and discussing the guests that were available to appear on the Jamboree. After we discussed the available guests, I would go back to the office and book the act for an appearance on the Jamboree. I was also coordinating the nightly promos with Lee Moore, the all-night disc jockey at WWVA.

I had been working for Gene about six months when he came in one morning, locked the door, and told me he needed to talk to me. I thought, "Oh, what has Jimmy done now?" The last time I was called into an office I got fired because Jimmy hung around the bar where I worked every night. I loved my job and hoped something similar had not happened. However, Gene had a different objective. He wanted privacy when he told me he had purchased a radio station in Pittsburgh, Pennsylvania. He planned to move to Pittsburgh as soon as his licenses were all in place. I asked him about the business. He told me I could have it and knew I was fully capable of doing his job. He also told me he would teach me everything he knew about booking talent and would speak to John Corrigan on my behalf. Those words were music to my ears.

Over the next two months, Gene did exactly what he said he would do. He let me talk to the buyers and book the shows. He would critique my phone calls, proofread my correspondence, and look over the contracts. He wanted to make sure that I was doing everything correctly. One day, he told me I was an excellent booking agent and handled the clients and the entertainers wonderfully. I was excited. Now I was going to have a profession, and one that I loved. I thought I had died and gone to heaven. I was so proud of me.

THE BARBARA MARTIN AGENCY
WWVA Jamboree | Wheeling, West Virginia

The day Gene closed the office was both sad and thrilling. I loved working with Gene Johnson, but I was moving on with my life. Gene gave me the typewriter, all the office materials, and his contacts book. Even though I had memorized the book long ago, I was thrilled to have it.

I moved everything home. I didn't have room for a desk, so I used an end table. Jimmy and I, our son Timmy, and Paul Williams were living at 714 Euclid Avenue, Martins Ferry, Ohio. We had a small house with two bedrooms, one bath, and a kitchen just big enough to walk through to go out a door onto the teeny-tiny back porch and yard. But, to us, it was heaven. We paid a total of $5,800 for it: $5,000 in cash, and we financed $800. Our first house and NOW, my first office.

I set everything up in the living room and started to work. I joined the Musicians Union and became a licensed booking agent. I had several contracts (from Gene), and I started writing letters to people and agents letting them know that I would be booking the Jamboree talent and Jimmy Martin and the Sunny Mountain Boys.

Booking Agents, Managers, and Promoters

John Corrigan was the new Jamboree director. Gene and I talked to John, and he agreed my agency would book all the guest acts and any of the Jamboree acts that wanted me. In turn, my agency and the dates booked for each act would be broadcast nightly over radio station WWVA on the Lee Moore Show. Lee Moore, the all-night DJ known as "the coffee-drinking nighthawk," was also a member of the Jamboree. It would be quid-pro-quo. They would get Nashville talent for less, and my agency would get free publicity. We continued with this agreement long after I moved to Nashville and until the day in 1967 when I closed the doors of my office on 17th Avenue South.

John Corrigan

I held back on making new contacts while working for Gene—things I wanted to do to get more shows for Jimmy and the other people I was booking on the Jamboree. Now, I decided to talk to Jimmy and go for it. But before I talked to Jimmy, I did some investigating. We didn't have computers or ways to look up places and phone numbers. In those days, we used Information (411) for phone numbers and addresses.

I called the Musicians Union and asked them about fair conventions. They were more than happy to tell me about the ones

The People and The Music—Country and Bluegrass that is!

in Pennsylvania, Ohio, Michigan, and the national convention in Chicago. I immediately called information and got their telephone numbers and addresses. I sent letters to each of them, telling them I wanted to join their associations. This was my first step in securing new leads. Then I started talking to other agents about clubs they were booking. I worked closely with people like Will Groff from Harrisburg, Pennsylvania; Bobby Brown from Baltimore, Maryland; Billy Deaton out of San Antonio, Texas; Ramblin' Lou in Niagara Falls, New York; Jack Andrews in ,Nashville; Jim Godsey; Millie Ruton of Hillbilly Park; and many, many others. My phone was ringing constantly, and I couldn't have been happier.

As soon as I received the information from the fair associations, I joined each of them. Then I marked out the time for their conventions and started preparing to attend. I believed they would pay off and they did, in a big way. The first year at the Pennsylvania Fair Association, I booked 90 shows for Jimmy and the other entertainers on the Jamboree, as well as some acts from Nashville. This continued from convention to convention, and in Chicago at the National Convention I booked several package shows with Jimmy and acts from Nashville, plus many smaller venues. Jimmy attended each and every convention with me. He worked the table, handing out brochures, talking to people, and he did a good job. He was also beneficial in getting several of the delegates to book shows with me. The free advertising on WWVA certainly helped, as well as having a good roster of talent. Jack Andrews and Lucky Moeller, Smiley Wilson from Wil-Helm, and Hubert Long had all given me great talent and good prices, so I could add my 15 or 20% for the package shows.

My daily tasks probably would have been boring to the

ordinary person, but I was doing something I loved. Every day after Timmy left for school, I would sit at my typewriter, look through my notes and the calendars I kept for each act, and decide where I was going to try to book them that day. It took planning to schedule acts within driving distance of where they were playing the day before or the day after. You couldn't book an act too close to the town where they were scheduled, since it could take some of the audience away from that venue. I wrote a lot of letters, sent telegrams if time was of the essence, and called whenever necessary. In those days, telephone calls were expensive. So, I tried to keep my phone bill under $200 a month.

I had great success in Wheeling, booking shows throughout the eastern part of the United States and all over Canada and the Maritime provinces. I started booking USO shows in Wheeling. This was thrilling for me since my cousin, Wanda Rose Gibson, had been a dancer for the USO right after the War. I was also good friends with Jerry Johnson, who was the first female entertainer to go overseas with Roy Acuff. It meant a lot to me when I was finally able to book some USO Shows.

The D.J. Convention in Nashville rolled around in November 1962. Jimmy and I went, and we met with Bob Neal who was with the Wil-Helm Talent Agency. Jimmy wanted to be booked by a big-name agency. He never thought of me as a "real" booking agent, even though I was booking more shows for him than he had ever played before. I was also booking other people on a daily basis from the Jamboree and the Opry. Jimmy still wanted a big-name talent agency. He didn't think I had enough clout to get him on the Opry. He fantasized a "big" name agency could be his ticket to be invited to join the Grand Ole Opry. What he didn't understand it wasn't the booking

The People and The Music—Country and Bluegrass that is!

At the D.J. Convention held at the Andrew Jackson Hotel at the Ca. 1968.

agent's name that was keeping him off the Grand Ole Opry, it was his mouth and actions and he wouldn't listen to anyone.

Jimmy going with another talent agency meant I would probably have to go with that agency as well. After talking to Bob Neal, Bob wanted me to come onboard as an agent and, in turn, they would take on the booking of Jimmy Martin and the Sunny Mountain Boys. I agreed to bring my sources into the agency with me. They would not be for the use of anyone other than me. I would continue my role with WWVA as its booking agent.

BARBARA MARTIN AGENCY
224 Jacksonian Drive | Hermitage, TN

Jimmy, Timmy, and I moved to Nashville in March 1963. Timmy was in the third grade, and I planned to go to work for the Wil-Helm Agency on 16th Avenue South. I had mixed feelings about the move. My agency was doing well in Wheeling, and I loved working from home. It was comfortable for me, and I could pursue any avenue

Booking Agents, Managers, and Promoters

I wished to book shows. I did plan on getting additional talent to book, but I laid those plans aside to go to work for Wil-Helm.

It took about a week to find a house, buy it, and move in. The house was located at 224 Jacksonian Drive in Hermitage. Bob Neal lived at 3982 Bonnavista Drive, about one-half block from our house.

After settling in our house, Jimmy and I went to Decca to visit Harry Silverstein and Owen Bradley. We told them what was happening and then went next door to see Bob Neal. I needed to find out when they wanted me to start to work. We visited Bob at his house several times during the short time we had been in Hermitage but never discussed business. Sitting across from Bob at his desk and without blinking an eye, Bob informed Jimmy they were not going to be able to book him. But they still wanted me to come to work as a booking agent for Wil-Helm. Bob didn't give us any reason for the change with Jimmy but said, "He welcomed me to the fold."

I said to him, "If you're not booking Jimmy, I can't work here." Jimmy and I left. We went home, set up the typewriter in the living room at my desk (by now, I had a desk), and the next morning, The Barbara Martin Agency was back in business.

I continued to operate my business and it thrived. I booked a few shows for Loretta Lynn, who had become a friend. She didn't have any work and lived close by. I also booked Melba Montgomery, Freddy Hart, the Vandergrift Brothers, Betty Amos and the Rhythm Queens, Grandpa Jones and Ramona, and many others. I didn't specialize in bluegrass music since Jimmy was my bluegrass group, but I did book a couple of dates for Don Reno. I still have the contracts. I liked booking country acts and had plenty from

The People and The Music—Country and Bluegrass that is!

Wheeling. I was booking Betty Amos and the Rhythm Queens, the Vandergrift Brothers, and Onie Wheeler in clubs featuring country music. The Vandergrift Brothers were my staple act for clubs and small venue shows in the Northeast and Canada, while Betty Amos was loved in Texas and the Mid-west.

I booked guest acts for the WWVA Jamboree at least once a month and sometimes more. My agency continued to be advertised nightly on the Lee Moore Show on WWVA. Business was booming, and I was booking more and more shows every day.

This was a time when the Musicians Union was on top of everything. If you booked a Union act, you had to file a copy of the contract, together with a surcharge, for each show date. If an act failed to pay his/her dues to the Union, the Union knew it immediately and remember, there were no personal computers around at that time. That's how connected the Union was to everything. I was a member of the American Federation of Musicians and a licensed booking agent, so I had to abide by all the rules.

In November 1963, I received a letter advising a complaint had been filed by Local 619, A F of M, saying I had failed to file a contract and I was in violation of Article 17, Section 17 of the By-Laws. Believe me, I sent that contract and the $12.00 surcharge for the date via Air Mail the same day. I vowed never to let that happen again.

The next complaint from the Union said I was booking non-Union acts while being a licensed Union Booking Agent. This was also against the rules. The act was the Vandergrift Brothers. They had let their dues lapse and I didn't know it. That was a tough one to prove since I was booking shows for them every week. I called Don Vandergrift to find out what was going on, and they immediately

Booking Agents, Managers, and Promoters

brought their dues up-to-date. The Union closed its case after several letters back and forth. I still have the letters.

In the fall of 1963, Billy and Ruth Grammer invited Jimmy and me to their house for a fish dinner. I was thrilled. I loved Ruth and respected and liked Billy. I had met them at the Opry (as in Grand Ole Opry), a couple of months earlier. Ruth and I hit it off immediately, and I knew she was going to become a good friend.

Billy and Ruth Grammer's house was on Old Hickory Boulevard in Brentwood. From the moment we arrived, the conversation flowed, and the night was magical. After dinner, Billy suggested that we form a talent agency together. I would be in charge of booking the talent, and he would be in charge of obtaining new talent for us.

We would rent space on 16th Avenue South. We worked out the details and agreed to start on this right away. Stupid me! I didn't even stop and think that I had a thriving business already, and now I was going to share it. Again, Jimmy thought this might be a step toward making him a member of the Grand Ole Opry. So, he encouraged the move.

Billy and Ruth Grammer

GRA-MAR TALENT AGENCY
16TH Avenue South | Nashville, Tennessee

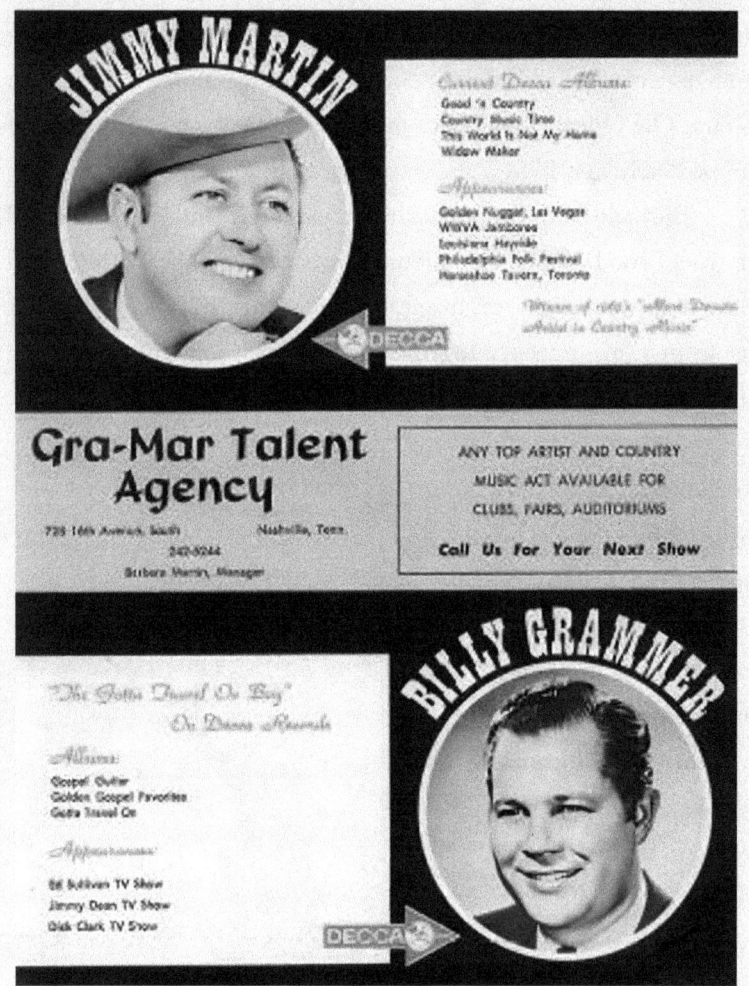

Billy Grammer and I rented space across the street from Decca Records and the Wil-Helm Agency. It was a large room facing 16th Avenue South. Until a year or so ago, it had an awning out to the sidewalk and was quite run down. It had a big window in front, and Billy washed that thing nightly. Billy had night blindness, and I always asked him how he could do the windows so well at night. He would just grin.

Cowboy Jack Clements, Happy Wilson, Stan Hitchcock, and Don Light who was the manager for *Billboard*, were all in the building with us. I became friends with all of them, and I began booking Stan Hitchcock. I thought Stan was very talented and quite a good looking, young man. I pushed him hard. As he once said to me at a ROPE luncheon, "you ran me all over the country." (Reunion of Professional Entertainers)

Cowboy Jack Clements country music industry. He was a singer, a producer, he appeared on the Grand Ole Opry numerous times, and he was a publisher/writer. Cowboy was extremely likeable and would wander back and forth across the hall to visit us a couple of times a day. The day I packed, labeled, and wrote cards for Jimmy's new Decca record, "Widow Maker" to over 1,000 disc jockeys, Jack was right there along with Happy and Don Light to load all my mail bags into my little Renault (car). I was nine months pregnant and couldn't lift anything heavy.

Cowboy Jack Clements

Happy Wilson was born in Haleyville, Alabama and named Eugene Burnett Wilson. By the time he was 15, he was huffing and

The People and The Music—Country and Bluegrass that is!

Happy Wilson

puffing to get on a radio station and play music. Later known as Happy Wilson, he and his Golden River Boys were tops in Alabama and traveled throughout the state with their road show. He married Marian Worth while appearing in Birmingham, Alabama, and the two of them moved to Huntsville, Alabama, where they appeared with the Slim Lay Show on WBHP. Marian Worth was a big part of their show, and the audience loved her. While in Huntsville, Happy and Slim started promoting Marian and eventually signed her to Columbia Records. When they moved to Nashville, Happy was the main guy for a large music company and he was also in charge of the Capitol Record operations in Nashville for a very short while.

Happy's office, across the hall from my office, primarily published and produced records. Happy also wrote and published songs. One of the songs he wrote was, "Sleeping at The Foot of The Bed," which was a big hit for Little Jimmy Dickens. He wrote songs recorded by Webb Pierce and Hank Thompson. Unlike Jack, Happy didn't wander over to our office very often. But if I needed him, he was there. I never asked him if he booked Marian Worth. He was a jolly fellow, tall and very slim. And quiet! I never saw Marian come to his office.

Booking Agents, Managers, and Promoters

Don Light   *Stan Hitchcock*

My friend, Don Light, was one of the nicest people I think I have ever known. Don's office was upstairs with Stan Hitchcock. He was in charge of *Billboard* magazine's Nashville office. He also wrote music for various publishing companies, one of which was Glaser Music Publishing. Don opened, "Don Light Talent Agency" in 1965. He was booking gospel groups including The Oak Ridge Boys, The Chuck Wagon Gang, Governor Jimmie Davis of Louisiana, The Rambos, the Lewis Family, and so many, many others. Don and I would talk about booking, sort of like banjo players or mandolin players talk about instruments, making them and maintaining them.

In 2018, I was returning from Nashville to Fort Lauderdale. While waiting for my luggage this lady was sitting next to me, and she was talking to one of the skycaps. She had a serious Southern accent. I said to her, "Where are you from?" She said, "Nashville." We started talking and exchanged phone numbers. A few weeks went

The People and The Music—Country and Bluegrass that is!

Sonja Light Maxwell

by, and I heard from her again. This time, we met for lunch. Her name was Sonja Maxwell, and she turned out to be the ex-wife of Don Light. She presently lives in Melbourne, Florida, and she is one of the sweetest people I know. We are always in contact with each other, and I love her dearly. She has nothing but kind words to say about Don. She blames their divorce on the fact that "she wanted to fly," and fly, she did. She worked and retired as a flight attendant.

The other person I mentioned in our building was Stan Hitchcock. Stan was a super-talented and a nice guy. He was also good looking, which didn't hurt when I sent his photo to the clubs using country music. I loved booking Stan. I knew he would be at the venue on time, there wouldn't be any problems, and the people would love him. That was just him....pure professional. Until his death in January 2023, Stan and his wife, Diane lived in a Nashville suburb. He was one of the founders of CMT television and headed the organization for quite some time. In later years he partnered with Ronnie Reno at Americana Television based in Branson, Missouri and Blue Highways Television, in Nashville.

Life on 16th Avenue was certainly different. We had people

Booking Agents, Managers, and Promoters

dropping in all the time. Mel Tillis was one. Most of the time, he brought his daughter, Pam, with him. I adored little girls, and at the time I only had sons. I would stop what I was doing and talk to Pam. She probably doesn't remember our fun little talks. I loved spending time with her because I was pregnant at the time and was hoping for a girl. Sure enough, it was my daughter, Lisa.

I typed my fingers to the bone every single day, sending out letters, talking on the phone constantly while tuning out the visitors or drop-ins as I called them. I would type and talk on the phone at the same time. Billy thought we needed to hire a secretary. We did. It only lasted one day, and I fired her after she dropped my precious typewriter on the floor. Her name was Dixie Dean. It was lucky for her that she was fired. She went on to marry Tom T. Hall and become well-known in the music business as a songwriter, publisher, and record label owner. In fact, she was inducted into the Bluegrass Music Hall of Fame located in Owensboro, Kentucky

In making this move with Billy Grammer, I became the first and only female booking agent on 16th Avenue South (now called Music Row). I didn't think about this at the time, but now that I am an old lady I think about it. I was also the only female booking agent at the WWVA Jamboree. I had the guts to begin a booking career in the first place, but business was my passion and I knew in my heart, I could do it. Being on Music Row gave me lots of opportunities. The guys on 16th and 17th Avenue had been doing business with me for several years primarily on the phone. I was never treated differently as a female in person.

One of those opportunities was attending the meetings held at the Jim Denny Artist Bureau with Lucky Moeller, Jack Andrews,

The People and The Music—Country and Bluegrass that is!

Hubert Long, Connie B. Gaye, Bob Neal, and Smiley Wilson. Connie B. Gaye, a well-known country music disc jockey, businessman, and promoter, was trying to get a nationally televised country music television program off the ground from Nashville. He had worked with Jimmy Dean (the sausage man), Roy Clark, Patsy Cline, and many others. He was brilliant in promotions and country music. There were lots of meetings, but the show never materialized. I was hoping it would come to pass and gain national attention for all of us.

I also attended a meeting held at Ireland's Inn about the startup of the Wilburn Brothers TV show. I went with Loretta Lynn. The meeting was quite interesting and lasted approximately three hours. After the meeting, we picked up the first stage dress she ever had made for herself from the tailor.

Many discussions later, Billy and I decided to go into the promotion business. At the time, what they called "telephone rooms" were making lots of money. The way it worked, you found a sponsor such as the American Legion, VFW, or other such organization. You went into that town or city, signed a contract with them, and they received 25% of the money earned for ads in the program book and sale of tickets after expenses. We sat up a room at their club and telephones were installed. Volunteers from the sponsor's entity would make phone calls to businesses and members to sell advertisements in the program book and tickets for the show. They promoted the show. In our case, the show would be Jimmy Martin and the Sunny Mountain Boys and Billy Grammer. Sometimes we used a comedian and a girl singer, as well. When the logistics were worked out, I immediately found sponsors in Keokuk, Iowa and Springfield, Illinois. Our first two shows would be an easy drive from each other, but far enough apart to attract crowds from each town.

I wanted to be able to give the sponsor an accounting at the end of every week with an outline of money received and expenses incurred. That way, we all knew where we were and what we had to do to further raise funds for the show.

I contacted my sister, Betty Taylor to work the shows in Keokuk and Springfield. At the time, Betty was living and sharing an apartment with Shot Jackson and Donna Darlene. She worked as a cashier at the local Piggly Wiggly grocery store. When I called her, she didn't have a second thought about leaving and going with us. I told her I wanted her in charge of handling sales of tickets and advertising for the shows, and also in charge of making sure the funds were collected and deposited. Billy and I decided to hire Cedric Rainwater (a/k/a Howard Watts) to go with Betty and help her. Cedric was a comedian who worked on the Grand Ole Opry for several years and traveled on the road with many well-known entertainers. I knew Cedric and his wife well. I thought he could be trusted.

The first couple of weeks in Keokuk things went smoothly. Betty and Cedric were established in a hotel with adjoining rooms. Then Betty called me one evening and said Cedric was not giving her the money he was collecting and refused to discuss it with her. I told her not to tell him, but I was on my way. I called Billy Grammer and told him what was happening. I got a flight out of Nashville that night. I would surprise Cedric the next morning.

I arrived in Keokuk and Betty picked me up. She sneaked me into her room. The next morning when Cedric knocked on the door to go to breakfast, we were ready. I opened the door and said, "Get all your books and the money you have collected and let's go over them."

The People and The Music—Country and Bluegrass that is!

You could have knocked him over with a feather, but he complied.

The three of us went down to breakfast, and I sat in a corner where I started going over the receipts and the sales, advertisements, and tickets. The cash didn't match the sales. I asked Cedric where the rest of the cash was. He told me he had used it for promotional purposes. I advised him he didn't have the authority, and any cash used had to be approved by Betty, and then by Billy or me. I told him I wanted the rest of the money then, or I was calling the police to arrest him for theft. He finally relented and gave it to me. I fired him and he made his own way back to Nashville. That was the last I saw or heard of Cedric Rainwater, a/k/a Howard Watts. My trust was short llived.

Despite this setback, the shows were a tremendous success. But, by the time Jimmy and Billy played the shows, they were not speaking. They never acknowledged each other in either Keokuk or Springfield. They played the shows like robots. Billy and I had no problem with each other, so we could converse and carry on business as usual. The problem was between Billy and Jimmy. It was a "rift" that would never be healed. However, this meant the end of Gra-Mar Talent Agency.

A word of explanation about the "rift." Prior to the shows in Keokuk and Springfield, I booked package shows for Jimmy Martin and the Sunny Mountain Boys and Billy Grammer in California. The night before the final show in Oakland, we went to a Hawaiian themed restaurant owned by a friend of Billy's. We had a fun night. Then, as we were leaving, Jimmy made some smart remark to Billy. Billy's friend, the owner of the restaurant, heard Jimmy and sucker punched him in the kidney. Jimmy's kidney was badly bruised, and he was bedridden for several days. I took him to the hospital, and the doctor put him on bedrest. He was unable to stand and, therefore, unable to perform in Oakland.

Jimmy was worried about not being able to make the show. I told him not to worry. I went on stage in his place in order to have the contracted number of people for the show. All I have to say is, "Thank God for Vernon Derrick!" He helped me through it. From that day forward, Jimmy and Billy never spoke again. Upon our return to Nashville, I moved my agency back home and, once again, The Barbara Martin Agency, was back in business. Gra-Mar Talent was closed.

I continued to book acts from the WWVA Jamboree and bought and sold acts from the various agencies in Nashville until September 1966. I left Jimmy for the final time and felt my life as a booking agent was over. Had I thought about it, I could easily have gone to work with one of the agencies on 16th or 17th Avenue. I was well-respected as a booking agent, and someone would have hired me. I never asked.

A couple of months after I left Jimmy, I ran into John Denny. John offered me a chance to open my agency again. He had an office I could use on 17th Avenue, and we could share. I was happy to be booking shows again, but a new problem arose.

I had a good roster of talent, talked to John Corrigan and continued to book the acts for the WWVA Jamboree. The problem with my roster was they were very good entertainers, but not well known. I was booking lots of country music nightclubs where a solo act was getting $100 a night or $290 for a weekend. The acts with bands were making more. But, when it came down to it, 15% of

The People and The Music—Country and Bluegrass that is!

$100 was $15.00. That was split between John and me. I had kids, and I couldn't take care of them on the money I was bringing home. I made more as a waitress. So, I finally closed the Barbara Martin Agency down forever in 1967. My last show was in Guelph, Ontario, Canada with Hank Williams, Jr. and Willie Samples.

Moving forward to mid-September, 2019, Louisa Branscomb, Jeanette Williams, Katrina Kimbrough-Brake, Patricia (Trish) Eaves, and I were all sitting around my dining room table having a long, leisurely breakfast talking about every aspect of the bluegrass and country music fields. We were discussing booking shows, and someone asked me if I ever thought about booking. A few minutes later, I said, "Yes," I think I can still do that." So, I decided I would get back into it. I immediately contacted the Pennsylvania Fair Association and joined. I knew their meetings would be coming up in January. I put together a brochure with five acts on it, made a poster, started contacting people online, etc. I was working regularly and then, on December 16, I had an auto accident. While recuperating, I realized booking was boring to me. It wasn't the same, personal way I had done business. Everything was handled on the internet. You talked to no one. Contracts were sent and signed by email. Boring, boring, boring! I just wanted to write my books and songs. I got out of the booking business as quickly as I got in. Let the young people handle it!

BUDDY LEE ATTRACTIONS

In 1964, my friend Audrey Williams dropped by my office at Gra-Mar Talent Agency. She told me she and Buddy Lee were opening an office down the street and it would be known as Aud-Lee Attractions. Of course, they were going to be booking Hank Williams, Jr., Audrey's son. I was thrilled my friend, Audrey, was going to have an office close by. A few days after that, Jimmy Martin was in my office, and we walked down to the Aud-Lee office and met Buddy Lee. George Jones was there that day as well. Of course, Jimmy had to get pictures. Somewhere a camera appeared, and pictures were taken. George left, and we went back to conversing with Buddy and Audrey. Buddy invited Jimmy and me to his house.

After meeting Buddy, Jimmy and I learned that Buddy Lee and his wife, Rita, were previously professional wrestlers. A week or so later, Jimmy and I stopped by to see Buddy and Rita Lee at their home in Donelson. This was my second time meeting a professional wrestler even though my grandparents, my mother, my sisters, and I attended the wrestling matches at the Hippodrome Skating Rink every Tuesday night. Hollis would have been salivating, just knowing I was in that house.

Rita and Buddy Lee

Rita Lee was beautiful with long, black hair and a great personality. She certainly did not look like a female wrestler. She was simply too petite and cute. Rita was cooking when we came into the house and immediately invited us to stay and eat with them. She made these amazing fried potatoes. She fried diced potatoes and onions in olive oil and then seasoned the potatoes with oregano, salt, and pepper. I never heard of using Oregano for anything other than spaghetti sauce. Olive oil was not in my vocabulary. When I took a bite, they were the most delicious potatoes I had ever eaten. I was addicted to them from that day to now. After that, I started using Oregano in other things and frying in olive oil. To this day, I keep trying to duplicate Rita's potatoes. I come close, but in my mind they have never been as good as Rita's. Whenever I ate the potatoes at Rita's house through the years, I savored every bite. I never tired of them. Mine come pretty close, but you know what they say about "close." It only counts in horseshoes. Donna Lee, their daughter, told me she makes potatoes like her mother. I haven't been invited to try them. But, one can only hope.

The latter part of 1965, I left Jimmy again (one of the many times). Prior to leaving him, Rita asked me to move close to them. She would watch Lisa for me while I worked. Buddy Lee wanted me to come to work for him. By then, Aud-Lee Attractions had closed, and Buddy worked from the basement in his home. He was continuing to represent Hank Williams, Jr. This was before he opened another office on Music Row. I rented an apartment within walking distance of Buddy and Rita and moved everything on a weekend when Jimmy was out of town.

Monday morning, I started working for Buddy in the basement, and Rita took care of Lisa upstairs. I was able to watch him work every day. I came to know his tactics to book shows which, by the way, were far different than mine. While I was more personal,

The People and The Music—Country and Bluegrass that is!

Buddy was more of a "good ole boy" with the guys, but more gracious with the ladies. Nothing wrong with that. He was very successful.

I only worked for Buddy Lee about two weeks. Timmy and Ray kept skipping school and going back home to Jacksonian Drive. Jimmy would bring them back to the apartment. Finally, I moved back and that was the end of working for Buddy Lee. I was back to working at the Barbara Martin Agency. I continued to stay in contact with Buddy and booked acts from his roster.

Buddy opened Buddy Lee Attractions on Music Row. I have read that he was one of the people personally responsible for getting the career of Garth Brooks off the ground and for promoting the very first Farm Aid with Willie Nelson. Buddy Lee Attractions became one of the biggest talent agencies on Music Row.

Buddy and Rita remained friends until I married Chuck Stephens in 1971 and moved to Florida. To my sorrow, I never saw either of them again. My son, Buddy, is named after Buddy Lee. Buddy's real name (my son) is Lee Ease Martin, and we called him Buddy from the day he was born. When my Buddy had a son, he called him Little Bud. The name lives on. Timmy and Ray continue to be friends with Buddy and Rita's children, Joey, Donna, and Regina.

Buddy Lee was selected Agent of the Year in 1980 by the Nashville Association of Talent Directors. He passed away September 24, 2000, of respiratory failure at the young age of 65. His wife, Rita Lee, passed away on July 27, 2012. Their surviving daughter, Donna Lee, became CEO of Buddy Lee Attractions and finally closed its doors on September 11, 2018.

HUBERT LONG TALENT AGENCY

Hubert Long with Bill Anderson

Hubert Long was one of the finest gentlemen I have ever known. From the day in 1953 when Doyle Wilburn introduced me to Hubert, we were friends. I admired and respected him very much. He had a terrific sense of business and was an excellent conversationalist.

The latter part of 1953, early 1954, one, sometimes two, evenings a week, a group of people would meet at Hubert's house on Moss Rose Drive and just talk. It was usually people from the Opry or just friends. My girlfriend, Jean Armstrong, and I were invited. Neither of us owned a car. Doyle Wilburn always picked us up and took us to Hubert's house. Jean Armstrong later married Don "Suds"

Slayman, a fiddle player for Marty Robbins, and Suds would come with us. Jimmy was never invited.

It was such a pleasure, sitting around with Hubert, Doyle, and a few others, talking about various things including business. Even though I was not in the music business at the time, it was a learning experience. It was an innocent gathering, and we usually drank Cokes. One or two of the guys may have had a beer, but it wasn't the norm. The get-togethers were a lot of fun and informative.

Jimmy and I left Nashville in March, 1954. I wasn't in contact with either Doyle or Hubert after that. The Disc Jockey Conventions began at the Andrew Jackson Hotel in Nashville, and Jimmy and I attended. I would see Hubert and Doyle at the Convention.

In August 1954, Jimmy and I moved to Detroit, Michigan. Jimmy and the Osborne Brothers were playing Casey Clark's 12101 Mack Avenue Barndance, and Doyle and Teddy Wilburn made guest appearances. I looked forward to Doyle and Teddy Wilburn, Faron Young, Skeeter Davis, and Webb Pierce coming to the barn dance. They were my friends, and they found time to have conversations with me even though I was only involved in the music business through Jimmy.

I finally became a booking agent in Wheeling, West Virginia when we were with the WWVA Jamboree. Then I began having extensive contact with Hubert Long for talent. At the time, he was booking Bill Anderson, Tammy Wynette, George Jones, Jim Ed Brown, Melba Montgomery, and many others. We used them on the Jamboree as well as other shows nearby. Melba Montgomery was a favorite of people in the WWVA listening area and those attending the Jamboree.

Booking Agents, Managers, and Promoters

I think I was only in Hubert's office one time. I booked one of Hubert's acts and needed the promotional materials that day. I decided to walk down to his offices in the Capitol Records Building to pick up a package. I remember Hubert coming out of his office to meet me. We talked for a few minutes, and I returned to my office. Most of the time when I booked a show, I spoke to Shorty Lavender.

Shorty (Grover) Lavender worked as a booking agent for Hubert. Shorty was well known as a fiddle player and worked with Ray Price and the Cherokee Cowboys. In those days, pay for a sideman was not much. If they were lucky, they were paid $25 a day. They needed a second job to support their families. Shorty went to work as a booking agent.

Louie Dunn and Chuck Meese also worked with Hubert Long Talent Agency as booking agents. Then in September 1969, Dave Barton joined the fold. Dave had been working for Jim Ed Brown as

Shorty Lavender

The People and The Music—Country and Bluegrass that is!

Dave Barton

a road manager/musician (bass player) since he left The Nightbeats. Jim Ed recommended Dave to Hubert. Hubert immediately hired Dave and sent out a letter on September 29, 1969, to all the people he did business with, introducing Dave and enclosing a brochure of the talent associated with the Hubert Long Agency.

Dave was from Bradenton, Florida and teamed up with some friends to form a band playing rock 'n' roll. They called themselves "The Nightbeats." They were playing five nights a week around the Bradenton/Tampa/St Petersburg area. Then they got a call to audition from Artists Corporation of America, a talent agency in the old Milwaukee hotel in downtown Milwaukee, Wisconsin. Dave and the rest of the band members were an average age of about 23 years old, wild, and crazy. They loaded up in two cars and drove to Milwaukee to audition. They had the rock 'n' roll uniforms, changing costumes every set, in a high energy rock show. Artists Corporation put them to work. They worked every week and were never out of a job. They worked so much, they had to ask for a vacation and Artists Corp would mark two weeks off the calendar. They worked non-stop for three years, and on their vacation they would go home to see their families in Florida.

Booking Agents, Managers, and Promoters

In October 1964, Dave told the band he no longer wanted to do rock 'n' roll. He always liked country music. He couldn't see himself standing on a stage, shaking his butt and dancing to the music when he was 35 years old. He was getting out while the getting was good. He left the group, and The Nightbeats broke up. He moved to Nashville, got married, and started playing country music.

It wasn't long before Dave joined Jim Ed Brown. He worked with Jim Ed until he joined Hubert. He had a conversation with Jim Ed and told him he was tired of the road. Jim Ed knew Hubert Long and spoke to Hubert about Dave. Dave wanted to be able to work a regular job and spend more time with his family.

When Dave went to work for Hubert as a new agent with the firm, Dave got all the phone calls who didn't ask for someone specifically. This was standard practice whenever a new agent would come to work for Hubert. Each of the agents was paid a salary and at the end of the year if the business had been good, a bonus was given to each employee.

Hubert had a large stable of talent including Bill Anderson, George Jones, Tammy Wynette, Jeanne Pruitt, Dottie West, Ferlin Huskey, and many more. He worked with Mervin Kahn in taking country music acts to England. Mervin put on a festival in England once, sometimes two times a year, where he had 25 to 30 country music acts in England appearing at the festivals. Mervin came to the United States, sat down with Hubert and other booking agents, and booked his acts for each festival.

Booking was not the only music business entity Hubert owned. However, it was the catalyst for his publishing companies. He owned Moss Rose Publishing Company, named after the street where he

The People and The Music—Country and Bluegrass that is!

lived. Being the thinking-outside-the-box person he was, he had an ingenious idea for any new talent signing with his agency. When he signed a new act to his roster, he would tell them, "Let's you and I start a publishing company. I will get Shirley to run it and put $1,000 into the bank and open a checking account. You publish any songs you write in the publishing company. Then when you record a song, we will have the publishing rights and put it in our company." He did this with every act, and he had as many as 20 publishing companies at any one time.

Hubert had Kris Kristofferson on a draw on the publishing side. He told Dave one time that he had to let Kris go because he owed him $8,000. But, Hubert said, "If he ever writes a big hit, I will get my money back. At the time, Hubert and Marijohn Wilkin owned Buckhorn Music and published, "Sunday Morning Coming Down," "For the Good Times," "Bobby McGee," and others, all written by Kristofferson. Buckhorn had seven songs in one album entitled, *Silver Tongue Devil*, written and recorded by Kristofferson. Marijohn Wilkin also recorded a couple of big hits published by Buckhorn. All of it, the booking agency, the talent, the songwriting, and the publishing, worked hand-in-hand to form one powerful company. I believe Hubert got his money back from Kris.

Hubert was a genuine businessman. Every Monday afternoon, all the booking agents would gather in Hubert's apartment (which was now all in the same building), have a cocktail, and dinner prepared by the cook. Following dinner and cocktails, they went to the conference room. Each agent brought his notebook and contracts for the week. Hubert read and went over every agent's book to confirm every date was listed. He read every page of each contract, and he made sure

Booking Agents, Managers, and Promoters

every contract for each artist was signed by the agency for the week. If a pickup date was needed for any of the acts, the next morning you had to get on the phone to the local disc jockey in that area and see if anyone was buying talent, get their name and phone number, and call them. Then if a matinee was scheduled for any show, the next morning you called the artist to let him/her/them know they had a matinee show and when and where it was happening. He wanted to make sure every contract was complete and there were no surprises for the artist or the firm. In other words, don't come yelling, "I didn't know." He made sure they knew.

Tuesday was the day Hubert and the employees met for lunch in Hubert's apartment and discussed the publishing companies. He talked about who was recording next week or next month and sent songs out. The record companies regularly sent out a blue sheet to all the publishing companies to let them know who was recording and when, on what label, what kind of songs they were looking for, and the name of the studio where they were recording. Hubert went over every blue sheet with his group and discussed possible songs for each person who was recording. If one of the artists recorded a song published by one of Hubert's publishing companies, it could mean a big payday for his company.

The agency and the publishing companies were good places to work. The employees were treated well. Hubert had a lady that came in every day and prepared lunch. If you were invited to lunch at Hubert Long's apartment, that was a big deal.

Dave worked for Hubert three years before Hubert was diagnosed with a malignant brain tumor that went straight across his forehead. Dave's wife, Mary Lou, worked for the doctor who operated on Hubert. The doctor told Mary Lou the type of tumor Hubert had was very aggressive. He also told Dave, "You might want to start looking for a job. Hubert had surgery and chemotherapy, but within three to four months the tumor returned with a vengeance. Dave continued to work for Hubert until he passed away.

Hubert was an extraordinary success story. He was born in Texas and joined the Navy after high school. Following the Navy, he worked briefly in a record shop in Texas and then for a short time with Decca and RCA Victor. His turning point came when he met Colonel Tom Parker and became interested in the promotion part of the business. I have often heard Hubert was partially, if not fully, responsible for getting Eddy Arnold's career off the ground. He opened his own agency when he moved to Nashville. Hubert was very involved in the formation of the Country Music Hall of Fame, and I believe he was one of the first to be elected as president. He had extensive real estate holdings on Music Row and throughout the city. I have never read anything about Hubert going to college after being discharged from the Navy. I never heard him say anything about college. In his case, he didn't really need it. He had the "smarts" and proved it.

Hubert was a very good friend. He was probably 10 or 12 years older than me. When I didn't have a car and was working until midnight every night at the Pancake Pantry on 21st Avenue South, Hubert came, picked me up and gave me a ride home. In all my years of knowing him, he never made a sly remark or a pass at me. He was just a down-to-earth, kind person. He passed away on September 7, 1972, from a very aggressive brain tumor. He was only 48. The old saying is, "Only the good die young." Hubert Long was definitely one of the good people. Fame and fortune never affected him.

COLONEL "BUSTER" DOSS

I was on my way to see Jack Andrews, and I ran into Billy Walker coming out of Cedarwood. Billy and I both stopped to greet each other, and he said, "Barbara, when you get a few minutes, stop by Buster's office and I will introduce you." At the time, I had not heard of "Buster," but I would go and meet him. Buster Doss' office was located on the corner of 17th Avenue South and Horton Avenue, about a block away.

    A week or so later, I was at Cedarwood to pick up some brochures and decided to walk over to Buster's office and meet him. I was having a slow day on the phone and Billy (Grammer) was manning the office. I knew Buster was booking some dates for Billy (Walker) but didn't know who else he was handling. Most of the offices on Music Row were in old semi-mansions (two-story houses). Buster's office was on the second floor of an old house. There was no air conditioning, and the windows were open. Billy Walker was sitting in the window getting some air. Billy saw me coming and waved. It was a hot spring day in Nashville. Billy was waiting when I walked up the stairs and came to greet me.

    Billy took me into Buster's office and introduced me. I sat down in one of the chairs in front of his desk, and Billy sat in the other.

The People and The Music—Country and Bluegrass that is!

Billy Walker

I thought, "Buster looks like a tall General Custer with his goatee and his rugged looks." Today, I would say "Colonel Sanders," but the Colonel wasn't around back then. Buster was a nice, congenial guy and I liked him right away. We talked about booking, and he gave me some pictures and brochures of the acts he was handling, including Billy Walker. I told him I would stick something in the mail on my acts.

Billy walked me downstairs and told me Buster owned several radio stations. He said, "You should get Jimmy's records to him." He also said Buster had been a child actor in the old medicine shows and had trained with Bud Abbot and Lou Costello, Gene Autry, Red Skelton, and Roy Acuff. He didn't tell me why he was called "Colonel," and I never found out.

I probably saw Buster a dozen times after that first day. My office was on 16th and his was on 17th. I rarely had business on 17th. I booked Billy several times but always through the Denny Agency. Billy Walker was one of my favorite people. In my book, *Don't Give Your Heart to a Rambler, My Life With Jimmy Martin, King of Bluegrass*, I tell the story about the last time I saw Billy. Billy and I remained friends until his death. Billy and his wife, Betty, are both buried in Spring Hill Cemetery. I visit them whenever I am there.

I found out a little bit about Buster much later. He joined the Navy right out of high school and while in the Navy, he produced shows in 1945 to entertain troops. When he got out of the Navy, he was invited to join the Louisiana Hayride as an entertainer. He produced and recorded his own record before becoming a member of the Hayride. Joining the Hayride meant he became part of an elite group of entertainers such as Hank Williams, Kitty Wells, Webb Pierce, Faron Young, and Johnnie and Jack, who all went on to become members of the Grand Ole Opry. Buster moved to Nashville and became an agent. He was also quite an entrepreneur, having owned as many as seven radio stations at one time while still producing records, writing songs, and producing shows.

Buster founded a record label called Wizard Records in Missouri. When he brought the label to Nashville, it became the first independently owned record label on Music Row. He was known around town for being the person behind the largest telephone promotion unit (phone rooms) in the country promoting Grand Ole Opry Shows. In fact, Buster told me how the phone rooms worked and how I could do it. After mulling it over for a couple of days, Billy and I discussed it and agreed to try it. That is when we booked the Keokuk, Iowa and Springfield, Illinois shows. They were both successful shows.

Buster continued to be active in the music business until his death in 2008 at the age of 81. The few times I saw him, he was always very interesting. He never lacked for a new topic of conversation. I remember Buster coming with Rusty Adams to my house in Parkview. We all sat at the kitchen table and just talked for a couple of hours.

Buster is buried in Franklin County, Tennessee.

THE JIM DENNY AGENCY

Lucky Moeller *Jack B. Andrews*

When I think of The Jim Denny Agency, Jim Denny does not come to mind. I think about the two most important people to me in the agency, and they were Lucky Moeller and Jack B. Andrews. Lucky's son, Larry, also worked there. I never spoke to Larry more than a few times. But from 1960 to 1967, there was not a day during the business week that I didn't speak to either Jack or Lucky, or both. It was not unusual for me to speak to either, or both, of them five times a day—especially when we were booking our spring and summer packages. The phone was ringing constantly, and if it wasn't, I usually walked down to their office.

We were all busy booking shows on the telephone every day. The majority of the business was done by phone. Of course, there were a lot of letters going back and forth as well—packages with photos, records, and brochures. If time was of the essence, we hand delivered whatever was needed and if it was out of town, it went air

Booking Agents, Managers, and Promoters

mail. The goal was to get the shows under contract and get a retainer! Those things were important. You always needed to make sure you had enough to cover half of your act's fee on deposit. It was a necessity to get part of the money up front because, in those days, some of the promoters were known to cry "poor mouth"—all out of money. The favorite line of one promoter, especially, Carlton Haney, was, "We just didn't have enough people to pay everyone." I have heard Carlton say that a hundred times not just to me but other booking agents and entertainers. He only pulled this with me one time and that was at his first bluegrass festival in Fincastle, Virginia. When I told him I could be paid with his typewriter and other office equipment, I got the money. He never pulled the poor mouth act on me again. He knew I would take his typewriter.

I first spoke to Lucky and Jack when I went to work for Gene Johnson at the WWVA Jamboree. Jack was my favorite, and if he wasn't busy, I always talked to him. Jack was younger than Lucky by many years (still several years older than me), and maybe that was why I related better to him. But they were both fantastic business people, and they were always ready to do business with me.

I bought lots of talent from Jack and Lucky, and they, in turn, booked quite a few shows for Jimmy Martin—mostly package shows. I booked primarily fairs, clubs, small auditorium shows, nightclubs, and fire carnivals, but I also did package shows. I had someone say to me, "I don't know what a fire carnival is." I explained, "A fire carnival is a carnival put on by a local fire department to raise funds for equipment." They are extremely popular in the Northeast, particularly in Pennsylvania. I booked hundreds of them over the years.

Jim Denny was a super-talented businessman. He worked his

way up the ladder at WSM and became manager of The Grand Ole Opry. Jim Denny started Cedarwood Publishing with Webb Pierce. I don't know if Webb was also a partner in the talent agency. Webb was also an astute businessman. Knowing Webb, I believe he would have jumped at another business opportunity. Unfortunately, whenever I saw Webb outside, we didn't discuss business or who was involved with what. We usually discussed what was going on in the world, other people, etc.—just personal, everyday conversation.

Shortly after starting the publishing company and the talent agency, Jim left his position as manager with the Grand Ole Opry due to a conflict of interest. When Jim passed away at the young age of 52, The Jim Denny Agency and Cedarwood Publishing Company were taken over by his sons, Bill and John Denny. They assumed the leadership role over the agency and the publishing company, following in their father's footsteps, The Denny Agency and Cedarwood became the largest talent agency and publishing company on Music Row, or as it was known back then, 16th Avenue South. Rightfully so, Jim is in the Country Music Hall of Fame. He was a powerful man on the Nashville music scene.

Jim's son, Bill, is a chip off the old block. In 2016, Bill was the namesake and inaugural recipient of the CMA's J. William Denny Award. The Award was for his lifetime of dedication, distinguished service, and meritorious contributions to the Country Music Association's board of directors. The award is an honor that can only be presented once a year, and its recipient can be living or dead.

Bill first joined the board at CMA in 1961. He later served as president in 1966 and chairman in 1975. He has since served on numerous committees and has been credited with the growth of the organization.

Music was not the only career Bill excelled in. He was also

Booking Agents, Managers, and Promoters

president of Nashville Gas in 1998 and served on the board of Tennessee Natural Gas Lines from 1978 until 1985. At that time, Tennessee Natural Gas was sold to Piedmont Natural Gas. Bill retired as president of Nashville Gas in 1998.

John Denny was a force in his own right on Music Row. He was the vice-president of Cedarwood Publishing. John, a songwriter as well, started Dollie Records, a spinoff of Cedarwood. Cedarwood was sold to Mel Tillis in 1983.

John produced singles for Carl Perkins on his Dollie Records Label including "Country Boy's Dream" and "Shine, Shine, Shine." Both songs made the charts in the mid-'60s. He also signed and produced records for Diana Duke, Johnny Wiggins, Marti Brown, Gene Wyatt, and Johnnie Bailes.

John formed his own business, Denny Music Group, in 1965. A music publishing company he had under the group registered 422 titles with BMI. The majority of his songs were recorded by independent artists.

From 1965 to 1980, he founded JED Records which were his initials (John Everett Denny). He had his own recording studio called Denny's Den. John received a Lifetime Achievement award from R.O.P.E. (Reunion of Professional Entertainers). He was one of the organization's founders together with Gordon Terry, a well-known fiddle player.

Jim's son, Bill's brother, and my partner, John Denny, passed away on July 21, 2020, after a long-fought battle with diabetes and Alzheimer's Disease. John was a gentle soul and a person that I will always remember as a good guy. As of the writing of this book, Bill Denny is still living and in his 90s.

THE WIL-HELM AGENCY

*Front row: Teddy Wilburn, Smiley Wilson, Doyle Wilburn
Standing front: Staff. Back row: Lester Wilburn,
Leslie Wilburn, and Don Helms*

The Wil-Helm Agency was located on the southwest corner of 16th Avenue South and Edgehill Avenue, right next door to Decca Records. The building was a former residence and is two-story. The agency was started by Doyle and Teddy Wilburn and Don Helms, one of the finest steel guitar players around. They formed Sure Fire Publishing Company at the same time. Parking was in the rear, and there was a stairway leading to the upper floor. The Glaser Brothers and Jo Walker, who was just starting the Country Music Association, occupied the offices on the upper level. Later Ric Records would be located on the second floor, as well.

Booking Agents, Managers, and Promoters

Doyle Wilburn was my favorite of the Wilburn Brothers. He was definitely one of the nicest people I ever met. He never lost his Arkansas charm. He was friendly, a good entertainer, and an excellent businessman. I first met Doyle backstage at the Grand Ole Opry when I was dating Jimmy Martin. I didn't talk to many people, but I could talk to Doyle. He was five years older than me, but still closer to my age than Jimmy was. The first thing I did when Jimmy and I arrived at the Opry on Friday and Saturday night was talk to Doyle. It was friendship. Sometimes, when Jimmy would leave me at Tootsie's while he ran over to play the set with Bill Monroe, Doyle would come in and we would sit and talk. Jimmy was a little jealous.

When Jimmy and I moved to Nashville, I was supposed to go to work as an agent for Wil-Helm. I talked about this in the section dedicated to Bob Neal, so I will not repeat it here. I often wonder how it might have turned out, had I become an agent with Wil-Helm.

Bob's departure from Wil-Helm left a void, and Wil-Helm asked Smiley Wilson to join the firm as a booking agent. Smiley and his wife, Kitty, and their daughter, Little Rita Faye, had been entertainers in the country music field for many years. They appeared on the early morning television shows in Nashville, including *Eddie Hill and Country Junction.* Smiley made cowboy movies with Red Barry and Lash LaRue, and he and Kitty recorded with Martha Carson, The Louvin Brothers, Jean Shepard, Bill Carlisle, Marty Robbins, and their daughter, Little Rita Faye. There were many others they recorded with, as well. The family was well-known in country music.

Smiley and Kitty Wilson were working the road as the opening act for Ferlin Huskey when Smiley became ill. Smiley was busy on the road, handling and making sure the equipment was ready

The People and The Music—Country and Bluegrass that is!

Smiley Wilson

for the stage show to begin and taking it down after the show, appearing on the show with Kitty and as the master of ceremonies. He had been having severe pain in his back and was advised by a doctor to come off the road. He needed to be on bed rest for six weeks, and he knew this was going to be life-changing. He was later diagnosed with a debilitating kidney disease.

Smiley was born in Attalla, Alabama in Etowah County, and he was given the name, Hamilton Knowles Wilson. He was named after his father, and he always despised the name. Despite his dislike, some of the people in his hometown used to call him, "Little Knowles from Attalla." He was a happy kid and always smiling. It wasn't long before the people from Attalla soon renamed him and he had a new nickname, "Smiley." His beautiful smile was contagious, and the nickname would go with him throughout his life. Smiley was a very gentle person. I don't think I ever heard anyone say anything derogatory about Smiley or his wife, Kitty. Kitty was related to Johnny Johnson, who played guitar on the Grand Ole Opry with Roy Acuff, Hank Snow and others. Johnny was married to Jerry Johnson (later

Colmus), who played stand-up bass for Roy Acuff, Bill Carlisle, and Cousin Jody.

In mid-1963, God opened the doors for Smiley when the Wilburns offered him a job, and he became president of Wil-Helm Talent Agency. Smiley would take over Bob Neale's position. This would be a good move for Smiley and for Wil-Helm.

Once Smiley took over the agency, he soon brought his daughter, Little Rita Faye, into the office as a receptionist. He also took over the management of Loretta Lynn, who was under a five-year contract with Wil-Helm. Later when that contract was almost ready to expire, he signed a 20-year contract on April 12, 1966 with Loretta for exclusive booking and management. He became the person responsible for developing Loretta's career. Smiley booked her on national TV shows, obtained commercials for her with big name companies, and guided her. Teddy Wilburn assisted Loretta with choices from wardrobe to counseling. He and Smiley became the ones she depended on. At the same time, Smiley also booked a roster of talent including the Osborne Brothers and the Wilburn Brothers,

The agency enjoyed many successes during Smiley's leadership, including the *Wilburn Brothers TV Show* and the promotion of Loretta Lynn's rodeos. But in 1967, Doyle Wilburn began drinking alcohol excessively. He was a nasty drunk and became verbally abusive and foul-mouthed. He didn't care where he was; he would start yelling or cursing, vomiting, or pass out. He was an embarrassment not only to himself, but to anyone near him.

Teddy Wilburn left the TV show because of his brother's alcoholism and verbal abuse. He moved to California. Smiley Wilson became Loretta's go-to person and Smiley tried his best to counsel her, but he just wasn't Teddy.

Despite Doyle Wilburn's drinking and ranting, Smiley continued to try to do his job. But when Loretta decided she had enough, she cancelled her contract with the agency for non-performance. The Wilburns sued Loretta for breach of contract and Loretta, in-turn, counter sued for non-performance. Some of the allegations in that lawsuit shown in the appeal include: (1) insulting the producer of the *Johnny Carson Show* while there to close a deal for Loretta to appear on his show; (2) drunkenness on the part of Doyle Wilburn while on the stage acting as master of ceremonies; (3) actually disturbing Loretta during performance; (4) the telling of sacrilegious jokes on Loretta's show in Boston, Massachusetts; (5) drunken vomiting on the dinner table at a post-performance party given for patrons, promoters, disc jockeys, and their wives; (6) drunkenness during most of a tour in England; (7) drunkenness during the time Loretta was preparing jingles for the Coca Cola ads; (8) getting drunk and passing out during the signing of the Glo-coat contract; (9) being so drunk while emceeing Loretta's performance at a rodeo that he fell off the stage; (10) drunkenness when taping Loretta on the *Ed Sullivan Show*; (11) insulting the black musicians while on the *David Frost Show*; (12) being drunk on practically every road trip, interfering with Loretta's need for rest on the bus, ignoring instructions of airline personnel while on flights, and generally being an obnoxious drunk in the presence of people upon whom the success of the artist depended. This conduct was all carried on while Doyle Wilburn was acting as Loretta Lynn's representative for the agency.

Adjudication by the Courts for Loretta Lynn was rendered on June 29, 1983. An appeal by Wil-Helm to the Supreme Court was denied. Loretta was released from her management contract with denial of their appeal. Wil-Helm's claim for damages for breach of contract by Loretta and her claimed damages were declared as being equal. Neither received any monetary damages, and no money was exchanged. However, Sure Fire Publishing still had a contract for the publishing of her songs.

Loretta continued her relationship with Sure Fire Publishing until October 7, 2000, when she filed a lawsuit in Davidson County Tennessee Chancery Court to regain the copyrights to her songs including "You're Looking at Country," "You Aint' Woman Enough," "Fist City," and her top hit, "Coal Miner's Daughter." The lawsuit was dismissed by the Court and suit was filed in the District Court. District Court ruled for Loretta Lynn. Sure Fire appealed and after a hearing by the Appellate Court, the lawsuit was remanded to State Court. I could find nothing further on the case as to whether it was actually refiled in State Court.

Smiley Wilson left Wil-Helm Agency in October, 1970. He joined Haz Jones, who owned a talent agency on Two-Mile Pike in Goodlettsville. Smiley lived in Ridgetop, making his commute to the office much shorter. He stayed with Haz Jones a short while and then opened the Smiley Wilson Agency. He continued to work for himself until his health deteriorated so badly he sold his business and retired. Smiley passed away from kidney failure in May 1988. His wife, Kitty, passed away on June 9, 2000. They are buried side by side in Goodlettsville, Tennessee. Their only daughter, Little Rita Faye, is active in the community, healthy, and lives in Ridgetop, Tennessee. Her son, Earl Sinks, Jr., sings and has recently recorded an album. Rita Faye is no longer involved in the music business.

THE BOB NEAL AGENCY

Bob Neal

I first visited the offices of Wil-Helm Agency in March 1963, and Bob Neal was the booking agent (probably the managing agent.) He had been Elvis Presley's manager in the early days *before* Colonel Tom Parker. Bob's story would not be complete without a look back at his career with Elvis.

Bob Neale was born in 1917 in the Congo. Back then, we called it, "The Belgian Congo." His parents were missionaries. He didn't start in the broadcasting business until after his graduation from college. Radio Station WMPS in Memphis, Tennessee, was just getting off the ground around the same time he graduated. They offered Bob a job as a disc jockey, and he was on his way.

Booking Agents, Managers, and Promoters

Bob was a disc jockey at WMPS in Memphis the day Sam Phillips gave him a new record by Elvis Presley. It was Elvis' first single record, "Blue Moon of Kentucky." I remember Bobby Osborne, Jimmy Martin, and I were on our way from Nashville to Mayfield, Kentucky. Jimmy and Bob were going to appear on the radio station in Mayfield and let the D.J. know they had just signed a contract with RCA Victor. On the way there, the disc jockey played, "Blue Moon of Kentucky" by this new kid, Elvis Presley. Bob and I both loved Elvis' version. We were rocking to the song in the front seat while Jimmy sat in the back seat, seething. He thought it was terrible for some kid to ruin Bill Monroe's beautiful song.

Got off the track there for a minute, but getting back on, Elvis was already appearing on Saturday nights at the Louisiana Hayride in Shreveport, and he was getting some show dates. Scotty Moore, Elvis' guitar player, was Elvis' manager. It was during this time Elvis decided that he needed a manager, and he wanted a person from Memphis (or, as we from Memphis call ourselves, "Memphians"). Bob Neal came to mind since he had already been working with the group. Elvis and Sam Phillips met with Bob, and they signed a management contract in December 1954. The one-year contract became official on January 1, 1955.

Bob and Helen, his wife, were going on shows with Elvis almost every day. During this same period of time, Bob was booking Jim Ed, Bonnie, and Maxine Brown on Elvis' shows. In addition to the Hayride, they were appearing in Mississippi and Arkansas, and sometimes in southern Missouri. Helen would drive and let Bob and Elvis sleep. When they arrived at the show, Helen would sell tickets, and Bob would take up tickets and cash from whomever had not gotten

The People and The Music—Country and Bluegrass that is!

Bob Neal wih Elvis Presley

there in time to buy a ticket. When he closed the ticket booth, he would run to the dressing room, get ready to M.C. the show, and run on stage. Then, back in the car and back to Memphis to do the same thing over again the next day. The routine of driving all night to get back to Memphis, doing the radio show, resting for a couple of hours, and jumping back in the car got old. Bob and Helen were both worn out. About this time, Colonel Tom Parker came onto the scene.

Booking Agents, Managers, and Promoters

Colonel Tom Parker was a mystery man. He was aloof, claimed to be born in West Virginia, and had a terrible temper. His reputation preceded him. He was named an honorary "Colonel" by Jimmie Davis, governor of Louisiana, for his political services to the governor—sort of like being a "Kentucky Colonel," a "Louisiana Colonel" instead. He carried this title for the rest of his life and was always known by "Colonel." It was later discovered that Tom Parker was not really Tom Parker but had been born in Breda in the southern part of The Netherlands. His real name was Andreas van Kuijk-Dries. He was linked to a murder in The Netherlands, but never questioned. He left Breda the night of the murder and never returned to visit his mother, sisters, or brothers, or for his parents' funerals. He never held a U.S. passport.

Colonel Tom Parker

Elvis never played in Europe or outside of the U.S., not even Canada. No one ever knew why Colonel Tom didn't book him in any of these lucrative locations. The reason was Colonel Tom wasn't a citizen of the United States and didn't hold a passport. If he went outside the borders, he couldn't get back in. He couldn't book Elvis outside the U.S. without telling him why he couldn't go. Knowing he was wanted for questioning in The Netherlands, he wasn't going

The People and The Music—Country and Bluegrass that is!

to say anything to anyone.

Bob Neal never said, that I know of, when or how he met Tom Parker. But it is well-known in the industry that before Bob's contract with Elvis expired, Bob and Colonel Parker were maintaining a 40% commission agreement on all of Elvis' proceeds. I never heard how long this agreement was in effect.

Bob continued to be Elvis' manager until their contract came up for renewal in December. But In November 1955, RCA Victor purchased Elvis Presley's recording contract from Sun Records. Bob and Colonel Parker split Elvis' commissions and Colonel Parker was now in charge—future commissions and all.

I think Bob Neal was the most gifted booking agent, promoter, and businessman on Music Row, as well as one of the most considerate people I ever knew. He came to Nashville in early 1963, shortly before we moved from Wheeling. He was in Shreveport and was managing Johnny Cash in 1958. Jimmy Martin was also there at that time. He met Bob and got to know him quite well while in Shreveport. Since I was in and out of town the first year we lived in Shreveport, I didn't meet him until the D.J. Convention in Nashville in November, 1962.

Bob had proven himself as a perspicacious businessman before he moved to Nashville. While with Elvis, he started Elvis Presley Enterprises. He had an office in Memphis on Union Street. Helen, his wife, was the receptionist, and they designed and obtained merchandise for Elvis to sell on the shows. He also owned a record shop and later a radio station in Shreveport. In Memphis, he started Stars, Inc., a talent agency. He was able to sign just about everyone who recorded for Sun Records and some who weren't, including Johnny Cash, Jerry Lee Lewis, Carl Perkins, Roy Orbison, Johnny

Booking Agents, Managers, and Promoters

Horton, and Faron Young, plus others.

Bob worked diligently to make sure he got information about his acts to the newspapers, *Cashbox, Billboard*, and any magazine featuring country music with the details on what they were doing, a new record, and always with his name implanted firmly in the article. With all this information about publicity and how valuable it was, he started Music City News Service in 1966. This service offered news of the country stars and taped interviews to the radio stations playing coutry music. He knew what he was doing, and he was doing it long before anyone else.

We arrived in Nashville in March 1963. Jimmy and I were looking for a house to buy and had been invited to Bob and Helen Neal's home in Hermitage Hills. I was hoping to get some indication as to when Bob wanted me to start work at Wil-Helm. Unfortunately, we never got around to that. When we told them we were looking to buy, they told us about a house that had just gone up for sale at 224 Jacksonian Drive. Jimmy and I left almost immediately, told Bob we would see him at Wil-Helm, and rushed to see the house.

Once at the house, we called the agent, and he came out and let us in to see it. We were thrilled. It was the most beautiful house we had ever seen, with three bedrooms, one and a half baths, kitchen, living room, and hardwood floors. Coming from a two bedroom, one bath, with a teeny tiny kitchen in Martins Ferry, this was a mansion. We had never had a bathroom connected to a master bedroom, so this was going to be a luxury. I decided I was going to have my office in the living room. Jimmy and I talked about where the boys were going to watch TV and get their homework. One of the bedrooms was paneled, and we thought this would make a good TV room.

The People and The Music—Country and Bluegrass that is!

Bob and Helen Neal's house at 3982 Bonnavista, Hermitage

Our home at 224 Jacksonian Drive

Booking Agents, Managers, and Promoters

Looking back now, since we had Timmy and Ray and always a banjo player, a mandolin player, or someone else living with us, we really needed a larger house. Paul Williams lived with us until he married Edria, Jimmy's sister. We were thrilled with the house and the fact that we would be around the corner from Bob and Helen Neal.

We bought the house for $10,000 and moved in. It was time to go to the Wil-Helm Agency and find out when Bob wanted me to start work. We first went to Decca, next door to Wil-Helm, and told Harry Silverstein and Owen Bradley we had bought a house and where. After sitting and talking to Harry and Owen for an hour or so, we then went next door to Wil-Helm. I have already told you what happened in the section about the Wil-Helm Agency, so I won't go into that again. My firm belief is that Bob Neal left Wil-Helm over that situation. Bob was an ethical man, and I don't think he liked the way things were handled.

Getting on to Bob's next venture, he opened the Bob Neal Agency on Music Row. He brought in his son, Sonny Neal, to work with him. Sonny was a gifted booking agent and had been raised in the industry. Bob's office was actually on 17th Avenue South, but they call it Music Row. I always wondered why they didn't call it, "Music Block" (now, they are), since it actually covered a city block, plus some. Bob always had the best in talent on his roster. In 1966, he was representing Carl Belew, Stonewall Jackson, Sonny James, Johnny Paycheck, Warner Mack, Connie Hall, and Jimmy Martin. I was very happy Bob listed Jimmy and was always thrilled to work with him. We spoke often on the phone, and I used some of his talent as guest artists on the Jamboree and dates in the Northeast.

In 1973, after the death of Hubert Long, Dave Barton, joined

Behind the Scenes

Bob Neal and Dave Barton

the Bob Neal Agency as a booking agent. Dave loved working for Bob. At the time, Helen, Bob's wife, and Sonny, their son, were also working there. Helen was involved with all aspects of running the business. She was not a booking agent. Sonny was learning the business. Dave worked for Bob as an agent for about six months or until he could no longer stand the office politics. He returned about a year later when Dick Blake went back to work for Bob as the office manager. Everything was good around the office and Dave stayed there for a couple of years.

After I left the world of country music and closed my office in 1967, I was very busy trying to make a living and going to school. I didn't get the opportunity to see either Bob or Helen, or even Sonny. Jimmy and my sons, Timmy and Ray, continued to be friends with

Booking Agents, Managers, and Promoters

Bob, Helen and Sonny.

Something that bothers me, and still does, is the fact that Bob is rarely given credit for having been Elvis' manager. I was at Graceland one time and after touring the mansion, I asked one of the employees why Bob Neal was never mentioned, or his wife Helen. They both did so much for him. They started his TCB (Taking Care of Business) Enterprises, designed and obtained things for him to sell, and were there driving him back and forth to shows in the early days. Bob and Helen Neal were two of the best people anyone could ever know. They were honest, loyal, ethical people. It would have been a different ending for Elvis with Bob and Helen at the helm.

Bob continued to be a force in country music. He was a director for the Country Music Association in the '70s and in 1977 (the same year Elvis died), he was named Man of the Year by the National Association of Talent Directors. He passed away on May 9, 1983, at the young age of 66. The following year, he was inducted into the Disc Jockeys Hall of Fame. His wife, Helen, lived to be 91 years old and passed away on March 1, 2014. Bob and Helen had five children, Sonny, Tony, Bobby, Sean, Kevin and one daughter, Tobi. His son, Sonny Neal, continued in the music business until his passing on June 10, 2007.

CHAPTER 2:

The Women Behind the Scenes

BETTY HARFORD, *wife of John Hartford*

John and Betty Hartford, 1968

The first thing one notices when seeing the names Betty Harford and John Hartford, side by side, is the spelling of their last names. Chet Atkins was the person responsible for the change of spelling. He thought the general public and people in the industry would remember John's name more easily if it was changed to "Hartford." So, John changed his name and added the "T" to become Hartford. Betty and their daughter, Katie, kept the original spelling. They remained Harford. Betty and John's son, Jamie, who is a very talented musician in his own right, uses the

The People and The Music—Country and Bluegrass that is!

Hartford spelling. I never knew John by anything other than John Hartford.

I first met Betty Harford when John brought her to my house in 1965. At the time, we lived on Jacksonian Drive in Hermitage. She and John had only recently moved to Nashville and their son, Jamie, was a baby. I thought Betty was very pretty, but I didn't have much time to just sit around and talk. I was booking shows and working in my living room. I liked Betty immediately and thought she was a neat lady. We were both tall and skinny and had long, dark hair, so we had things in common. I just didn't have time for socializing.

The next time I saw Betty was at IBMA's World of Bluegrass week in Raleigh, North Carolina in September, 2018. I walked up to the John Hartford Booth and Betty was standing there talking with a customer. I waited and then said to her, "You probably don't remember me." She said, "Yes, I do. You're Barbara Martin, and I have not seen you since 1965." We re-connected, and it was like we had never been apart. It was 1965, all over again. The only difference was now I had time to get to know her, and get to know each other, we did. Since that day, we have seen each other and been together whenever we could. We rode in the car together from Seattle to Nashville during COVID. Nothing was open and when we did find a restaurant, we laughed and acted like teenagers. It's not unusual for us to talk on the phone two or three hours or more at one time, or to sit up until two or three in the morning talking. We never run out of things to say. She is my friend for life. Now, I want you to know her as I do.

Betty Harford is a terrific singer. She has that old-style glamour, sophistication, and awesomeness in her voice and stage presence. I told her, "You should have been the one to pursue your career," but, like all of us "in the day," we had to let the men follow their dreams. We (women) stood in the background.

Born in Missouri to a large, close-knit family. Her mother was the oldest of 12 (an even dozen) children. Her grandparents, with whom they lived, were dirt-poor, tenant farmers. Sometimes there wasn't food to eat, but Betty and her uncle, Jimmy Payne, could sing, and they would entertain the family together. It made the hunger pains go away when she was entertaining.

Her uncle, Jimmy Payne, was her mother's brother. He was one of the youngest of the brothers and sisters, and only four years older than Betty. The two of them grew up and related to each other as if they were brother and sister. They continued to do so until his death May 15, 2023, at the age of 87.

Betty was born singing. Her first recollection of entertaining the family was singing "The Dearest Friend I Ever Had" when she was five years old. She has that voice that can go from a high soprano to a low alto. Church choirs love her. She can sing any part. I have stood next to her in church when people all around us turn to look to see who is singing. I don't open my mouth to try to sing, especially next to Betty with that beautiful voice.

She was the oldest child of Bertha and William Thomas Beck. They had one younger son. Her mother, Bertha Viola Payne, was a seamstress. She could sew or do alterations better than anyone. Having little to no money, Bertha made their clothes. They lived with her maternal grandparents. Betty's life with her grandparents and all her aunts and uncles was a happy place, although extremely

The People and The Music—Country and Bluegrass that is!

difficult. Food was scarce, but they made do. A nickel for an ice cream cone was non-existent. The one thing they each had was a voice. The singing could be heard all over the fields and pastures when they were picking cotton. Betty and her Uncle Jimmy worked all day in the fields picking cotton. When they returned home they ate supper, and the entire family gathered in the living room. For Little Betty, it was time for her to sing.

Betty's father, William Thomas Beck, was a handsome devil, 6'2" tall, with fantastic hair, and people compared him to James Garner. He was an alcoholic, and he loved the ladies, and they chased him. He left the family when Betty was three years old. After that, he would return maybe once a year and continued to do this until Bertha divorced him. The last time Betty saw him was when her daughter, Katie, was about eight years old. She never had a real relationship with her father because of his alcoholism and not being there for her and her younger brother. He died in 1985 because of injuries sustained in an automobile accident.

Her mother found out her daddy was leading a double life. He had a second family in Michigan while he was married to her. Betty was grown when she found out about her father's extra family: three children, two girls, and a boy. The boy was adopted at birth, and Betty has no knowledge of him. She is in touch with both girls, and they have written three books about their father. Betty has read the books and, as she puts it, "the girls have a different opinion of their father than she does." Her father never married the mother of these children, and in turn, the sisters never married. The mother passed away early in life. Betty still sees her half-sisters on occasion.

Growing up in a strict household who kept a tight rein on

The Women Behind the Sceness

the kids, it was surprising when she was allowed to sing outside the house. Betty was only 14 years old when she and her Uncle Jimmy Payne hosted a gospel show on KTCB-Malden in Malden, Missouri. Betty's singing versatility came in handy and helped to make the show a tremendous success with listeners in the area. They remained on the station for several years. She and Uncle Jimmy performed everywhere anyone asked them, at grand openings, churches, and country gospel festivals. They had one microphone at KTCB, and they would gather around it and sing. They were very popular in the area but were never paid for their work.

Betty's high school years were perfect. She was involved in the Glee Club and academically, she was at the top of her class. She wanted to become a nurse. When she told her mother what she was going to study in college, her mother said, "What college? You are not going to college." That's when Betty changed all her classes and took secretarial courses. She knew she could make a living being a secretary. While taking the classes, she kept telling herself, "I have to do well in these classes. They are going to support me when I leave home." Her plan was to leave home as quickly as she could after graduation.

In 1956, Betty graduated from high school and immediately moved to St. Louis, where she stayed with her aunt. The following day, she interviewed and was hired at Hussman Refrigeration. This was her first job interview. All her studying and the skills she had obtained to be a secretary were going to come in handy. But life never goes smoothly, and for Betty this was true. Three weeks later, her mother and brother showed up at the aunt's house where Betty was living. Betty was appalled that her mother and brother were

The People and The Music—Country and Bluegrass that is!

there. When Betty asked her mother what she was doing in St. Louis, her mother replied, "I have taken care of you all these years. It's your time to take care of me." From that day forward, she took care of her mother for the rest of her life.

Betty worked at Hussman three years. She was then offered a job at the Downtown YMCA in St. Louis as an administrative assistant. By then, Uncle Jimmy was also in St. Louis. He had continued to sing and play music after Betty left the farm. In St. Louis, he was meeting people and playing more music. Betty loved Jimmy being in St. Louis and thought she could get back to singing with him.

On Thanksgiving Day, 1961, Jimmy asked Betty to attend an event at Radio Station KSTL. This decision, unbeknownst to her, would change her life forever. It was there she met John Harford, a local D.J. She wasn't that impressed with John, but he was certainly attracted to her. He immediately started pursuing her, and they eventually started dating.

After meeting John and getting to know him, the two of them began recording songs (demos) John had written. John liked Betty's singing and harmonizing. They would continue to sing together and do demos for themselves and others throughout their life together.

Betty and John were married on February 9, 1963. Betty didn't know when she married John she was beginning a nomadic life. For the next two years, they were constantly moving from Missouri to Illinois and back again. In each place, John would work as a disc jockey. First at WCLW in Clinton, Illinois, where he was also part of the Gray Brothers Band. Then, on to KFAL in Fulton, Missouri, where he was a disc jockey. Betty discovered while they were in Fulton, that she was pregnant with Jamie, their first born. Once

The Women Behind the Scenes

again, it was time to move. They moved to Malden, Missouri, where John continued to work as a disc jockey for KFTL. On the side, he was appearing with Jerry Foster and Bill Price around the local area. At each stop along the way, Betty found a secretarial job. Some of the jobs were short-lived since they didn't stay in one place very long. All of this moving around happened in a span of two short years.

Not too long after John's stint at KFTL, Jerry Foster and Bill Price moved to Nashville, and John decided they were also going to try their luck there. Son, Jamie, was born, and they were now a family of three. John told Betty to pack up; they were moving to Nashville.

Betty's uncle Jimmy had introduced John to Jim Glaser. Jimmy and Jim were in Special Services together in the Army and knew each other quite well. Jimmy was living in Nashville and associating with people in the music business. Naturally, on Jimmy's recommendation, the first thing John did when he arrived in Nashville was contact the Glasers.

Chuck, Tompall, and Jim Glaser owned Glaser Publications and Glaser Sound Studio where they did demos. They had offices upstairs over Wil-Helm Talent Agency. The entrance was from

Jim Glaser with his wife, Jane

the rear to their second floor offices. John was a terrific song writer, and he became part of the roster. Betty was an excellent administrative assistant, and Chuck Glaser immediately hired her. Added to that, she could sing on demos. Betty became the "go-to girl" for the Glaser organization. She did everything from typing contracts and obtaining copyrights, to singing with John or whoever on the demos.

Betty worked at Glaser Publications and became friends not only with the guys, but also with their wives. Their families played together, worked together, and sang together. The women continue to be friends to this day.

After taking his wife to the movies to see *Doctor Zhivago* one day, John came home and wrote, "Gentle On My Mind." He played it for the Glaser Brothers the next day, and they immediately took him to see Chet Atkins at RCA Victor. RCA was only across the alley from Glaser's offices. Chet loved the song and set about getting John in to record it. The Glasers' company would be the publisher. Life was just about to go ballistic for John and Betty.

Betty and John remained with the Glasers until their move to California in March, 1968, after John's "Gentle On My Mind" became a multi-platinum seller. John became a part of *The Smothers Brothers Show* and was under contract to Kragen & Fritz, and later to William Morris Agency in California. Betty was an integral part of John's career. John would never sign a contract and/or appear anywhere unless Betty reviewed the contracts. John trusted her like no other person in the world. That business relationship continued even after they were divorce.

Life in California was unlike life in Nashville. John was such a huge success, and the California atmosphere was drawing him

The Women Behind the Sceness

Unknown celebrating wth Betty and John Hartford

from one place to another. His life seemed to no longer be his own. John was on the *Smothers Brothers Show* and part of their writing staff. He was on the *Johnny Carson Show*. Life changed. He was riding in limos rather than driving; he was idolized, and he loved it. John and Betty were not the couple they once were because of the demands on him by others outside of his own family. In 1969, Betty decided she could no longer live the California life and filed for divorce.

The divorce was granted in 1970, and Betty and her two

The People and The Music—Country and Bluegrass that is!

children returned to Nashville on January 1, 1970. John and Betty remained friends until his death from cancer on June 4, 2001 at the age of 74.

Once in Nashville, Betty bought a house for herself and her children. She enrolled in Trevecca College and pursued the college education she had wanted and waited for so long. Betty graduated from Trevecca with a degree in Human Resource Management.

At the time this book was written, Betty Harford was living in Nashville, where she was doing some demo work for various artists and singing at festivals. Her daughter, Katie Harford Hogue, has John Hartford Enterprises and has published an awesome book of John's fiddle tunes entitled, *John Hartford's Mammoth Collection of Fiddle Tunes, Volume 1*. It is one of the most beautiful coffee table books I have seen. John Hartford was not only a writer of songs and fiddle tunes, but he was also a very talented artist and calligrapher. At the time of his death, he had hundreds and hundreds of unpublished fiddle tunes and songs at his house in his own handwriting. Unfortunately, following his death, untold numbers of manuscripts and other valuable materials were destroyed by fire. Neighbors reported to the family of the burning going on each night. However, there was nothing that could be done about it, and it is unknown just what was destroyed. However, the family has rallied, and Katie has so wisely put together collections of those tunes, books, and CDs that are remaining. They are available on the John Hartford website.

Today, Betty and I are very good, life-long friends. Between the two of us (she is 84 and I am 88), we have a lot of history in the music business. We talk for hours about the people we knew, the

Barbara with Betty

things we did, where we went, and the music business, yesterday and today. Betty continues to help with the Hartford Festival, sing on demos, and enjoy life. Her daughter, Katie Hogue, is writing a book about her, and she is planning to record. She is very active in her church and with her family.

JOYCE JACKSON, *Personal Secretary and Assistant to Jim and Mary Reeves*

Joyce with Jim Reeeves

Joyce Gray Jackson may be small in stature, but she is one powerful lady. She can probably outwork all of us put together and, when she does a job, she does it correctly the first time. As Little Jimmy Dickens used to sing, "She's little, but she's loud."

Growing up in Kentucky, Joyce loved country music and cowboy movies. She dreamed of moving to Nashville and finding a job somewhere in country music as a secretary. She took all the required secretarial classes in high school—typing, shorthand, and bookkeeping. She made good grades in her classes, and her skills were excellent. After high school, Joyce worked a couple of different jobs for printing companies in Kentucky, saving money to move to Nashville. She left Kentucky on the Greyhound Bus at age 21 with $150 in her pocket and a determination to get a job. She wasn't planning to return to Kentucky any time soon.

Joyce arrived in Nashville on January 19, 1958, and found a place to live off West End Avenue. Living there made it easy to ride the bus down to Lower Broadway or to get to any offices downtown. The first few days Joyce was in Nashville, she spent most of her

The Women Behind the Sceness

time hanging out at Linebaugh's Restaurant, next door to the Ernest Tubb Record Shop on Broadway. Linebaugh's was a hangout for musicians and people in the music business for many, many years. The Merchant's Hotel was on the upper floors. It was an economical place for people associated with the music business to live. A bonus was the restaurant food was good and cheap.

Joyce had been in Nashville about nine days when, one day, while sitting alone at a table in Linebaugh's, Bob Holt, a promotion man for RCA Victor Records, came into the restaurant. He walked over to Joyce and asked if he could sit with her. Joyce didn't know Bob, but it was not unusual for a person (male or female) to sit with someone they didn't know. It happened all the time at Linebaugh's. You may not know them when they sat down, but, five minutes later it was like you knew them all your life. This particular incident was karma for Joyce. She and Bob struck up a conversation, and he asked her why she had moved to Nashville. She told him she was looking for a job. He then told her, "Herb Shucher, the manager for Jim Reeves, is looking for a girl." (Don't be offended ladies. The term, "girl" is the way they talked in the '50s.) Bob gave her Mr. Shucher's telephone number.

The next morning Joyce called Mr. Shucher's number, and Jim Reeves answered the phone. She didn't know it was Jim. Shucher wasn't available, and Jim asked Joyce to call back in about an hour. She called back promptly and had a good conversation with Herb Shucher. He asked Joyce if she was willing to come to Radio Station WSM, Studio C, in the National Life & Accident Building and meet Jim Reeves. She, of course, was more than willing to go.

At the time, Jim Reeves was hosting a radio show, *ABN Series*, in Studio C. Joyce was met and taken to the studio. This was the only time she ever saw Jim's show. After the show, Jim took her to the artists lounge located right outside the men's room. They sat down and had a great conversation. Jim asked if she could come to his office the next morning and meet with him and Herb Shucher.

The next morning, Joyce caught the bus and went to Jim's office located in the Primrose Center off Nolensville Road. She arrived about 9 a.m. on the 28th of January 1959 and was shown a seat behind Jim's desk. She sat there, and people were coming and going all morning, including Mary Reeves (Jim's wife), Leo Jackson (who would later become Joyce's husband and father of her child), and Jim Ed, Bonnie, and Maxine Brown, who were in town to record. Joyce was introduced to everyone. Around noon when things sort of slowed down, Jim called Herb into the office, and they sat down across from Joyce. Jim looked at Herb and said, "When do you want her to start?" Herb said, "Tomorrow." Joyce had a job. The first thing she did was rush out to a pay phone and call her mother. She told her, "I won't be coming home. I have a job."

Joyce started work the following day, January 29, 1959. She was assigned a desk facing Jim's desk. Joyce would be personal secretary to Jim and Mary Reeves, assist with secretarial duties for Jim's three publishing companies, and also help Herb Shucher. She was to provide assistance to whomever and whenever necessary, while still answering the phone, opening the mail, preparing correspondence, and filing copyrights. She was a quick learner and soon had all of her duties down pat.

Jim and Mary Reeves moved into their new home on Westchester Drive in Madison, Tennessee, later in 1959. Initially,

The Women Behind the Sceness

they had their office in the den of the new house, but they eventually moved it to the basement where they had a lot more room. The move meant Joyce had to transfer buses just to get to the intersection of Westchester Drive and Old Hickory Boulevard in Madison. There was no public transportation from Old Hickory Boulevard to the house on Westchester. So each morning, either Jim or Mary would pick Joyce up at the bus stop and return her there in the afternoon.

Joyce loved working for Jim and Mary. They soon all became like family, and Jim and Mary asked Joyce to stay at their house while they both went on a trip. They had her leave extra clothes, toiletries, make-up, etc., in an extra bedroom room and bath so she could stay there without notice. Whether you worked out of a house or in a downtown office, you had to be properly attired with your make-up on, heels (usually), and stockings. I dressed like this every day when I had my office at home. You never knew who would be dropping by the house.

Moving ahead, Jim was flying to Batesville, Arkansas to meet Mr. Griffith for a

Joyce on the stairs at Jim's new house.

The People and The Music—Country and Bluegrass that is!

business meeting. He had asked Hank Cochran, Ray Baker, and Leo Jackson to go with him. None of them could go. Dean Manuel walked into the office and Jim asked him if he would like to go, and he said, "Yes." Dean left to go get ready. Ray Baker was about to leave for his session, and Jim walked outside with him. They were standing next to Ray's car talking when Joyce called Jim inside. He had a phone call from Fred Bunyan at Berry Field about the plane Jim was flying to Batesville. Jim came inside and spoke to Fred. He confirmed everything for later that afternoon.

Following his phone conversation with Fred, Jim went outside and set out some plants Mary had gotten for Christmas. She had been trying to get him to plant them for a long time, and he picked that morning to do so. He was dripping with sweat when he came inside and told Joyce, "Thank God for air conditioning."

While they were laughing about the sweat, Mary called from Old Hickory Golf & Country Club. She played in a golf tournament that morning and lost. Jim told her, "I knew you were going to lose. You talked yourself out of winning this morning." Then they made plans to meet at Third National Bank in Madison to say goodbye and get money for the trip. When he finished the call, Jim went upstairs to take a shower and get ready to leave. Afterwards, he came back down to the office to let Joyce know he was on his way. Joyce said to him, "Be careful." He came back and said, "What did you say?" Joyce told him, "I said, 'Be careful.'" He laughed and said, "I always am." Those would be the last words Joyce ever heard him say.

The morning Jim's plane went missing, I had a call from Ruth Grammer, the wife of Grand Ole Opry star, Billy Grammer, and my partner in Gra-Mar Talent Agency. She told me Jim's plane was

The Women Behind the Sceness

Ruth and Billy Grammer

missing and asked me to meet her at Mary's. Joyce met us at the door. That was the first time I met Joyce. I was pregnant, and Joyce had just found out she was pregnant. We had a lot to talk about.

The house was running over with people coming and going. Ruth and I sort of positioned ourselves in the kitchen and started making sandwiches and doing whatever we could. Joyce was a dynamo. She was fielding phone calls from people all over the world, the governor of Tennessee, and I believe every singer and musician in Nashville and elsewhere around the world. She was tireless.

Mary was sedated and secluded in her bedroom most of the

The People and The Music—Country and Bluegrass that is!

Joyce year?

time. We were all in disbelief. This couldn't be happening again so soon after Patsy Cline, Hawkshaw Hawkins, Randy Hughes, and Cowboy Copas were killed in a plane crash. And, on the same day as their viewing, Jack Anglin, one half of the Grand Ole Opry team, Johnnie and Jack, was killed. The entire music community in Nashville was at a standstill. The search for Jim's plane went on for two days before it was found. Now, someone had to identify the bodies.

We knew Mary couldn't go. She asked Joyce to go in her place. Ray Baker and I went with Joyce. We were taken in the sheriff's car to the funeral home. They thought Dean's body was Jim's because of a wedding ring they found close to the body. Jim didn't wear a wedding ring, and Joyce knew what clothes he was wearing to fly. She identified him by the clothes. The scene is one I will never forget as long as I live. I can still describe down to the last detail the room and the bodies. But I will save everyone from that. It was not a pretty sight.

Following Jim's death, Mary took over the publishing companies and Jim's office. She immediately started sending out messages and thank you notes to all who had been so kind and thoughtful to her. Joyce was right there with her every step of the way. She stayed with Jim Reeves Enterprises for over 30 years, including the museum Mary started in 1969. The Jim Reeves Museum was located at the corner of Briley Parkway and Gallatin Road. A huge Home Depot Store is located in the very spot today. I never go to that store without thinking about Mary and Joyce. The last time I saw Mary was at the museum. And, Joyce? I didn't see Joyce again until 2020.

When interviewing her, Joyce said that Jim and Mary Reeves were both the best people she could have ever worked for. They became her family and she, in turn, theirs. She said Jim could be very comical, like the last day, she saw him. When he came back down the steps and laughingly said, "What did you say?"

Joyce married and divorced Leo Jackson while both were working for Jim Reeves. They had a daughter together, Joy Jackson, who is absolutely the "joy" of Joyce's life.

Put your hand on a *Who's Who* in country or bluegrass music, and Joyce Jackson has met them and had extended conversations. She is proud of all the relationships she has formed with people all over the world and feels herself extremely lucky to have had the opportunity of meeting those people while working for Jim Reeves. She is healthy and living a happy life in Madison, Tennessee with her daughter, son-in-law, and grandchildren. I am so lucky to have Joyce as a friend. When we get together for lunch, it is non-stop talking about the new, the bad, and the good times we have had over the last 64 years. That is a long time, and we have lots to talk about. The conversation never ends.

Mary Reeves remarried in 1969 to Terry Davis, a Baptist preacher. It wasn't too many years after she remarried when her health, and especially her mental status, started to decline. She

Joyce Jackson today

was placed in a nursing home until her death on November 11, 1999, at the age of 70 from Alzheimer's. She was a beautiful lady, and I am proud to call her my friend. She certainly didn't deserve the treatment she received after she remarried, or to suffer the way she did at the end of her life. Jim and Mary never had children, nor did she have any by her second husband. She is buried in "Mausoleum E" at Spring Hill Cemetery in Madison, a suburb of Nashville. If you are in the cemetery, drop by and put a rose on her tomb. She would love people remembering her with a rose.

Joyce has written a book about her life entitled, *My Memories of Jim Reeves…and Other Celebrities*. It is published by Nova Books in Nashville and available on Amazon, Barnes & Noble, and many other places. It is well-written and a most enjoyable read. I have an autographed copy, and it is treasured.

Today, Joyce Jackson continues to be active in her community and around town. She is 87 years old and still a dynamo. She is involved in her church, R.O.P.E., and other country music organizations. Joyce is always busy attending country music shows, television shows, or having lunch with all her old friends. At least, those of us who are still living. I hope we are all doing this at 100.

ELIZABETH (LIBBY) GRIGGS

Even though I didn't personally know the secretaries who worked in the offices on 16th and 17th Avenues South, I did appreciate how hard they worked and how dedicated they were. I started writing this book and reached out to Joyce Jackson (I knew Joyce). Through her, I met other ladies who worked on the Avenue when I was there. One of those was Libby Griggs.

Libby was born and grew up in Springfield, Tennessee, a small town about 25 miles from downtown Nashville. She graduated from Springfield High School and, like most of us in those days, went to work for Southern Bell (the predecessor of AT&T). Working at Southern Bell was the most boring job in the world. The only thing you did was face a switchboard, plug in, and say, "Number, please." Then, "thank you," and plug them into their call. There were 25 other women all sitting in a row saying and doing the same thing. Lily Tomlin was the switchboard operator on *Rowan & Martin's Comedy Show*. However, in the real world, we couldn't make funny faces and funny remarks. The supervisor standing over us would have been on us too quick to talk about it. I worked at Southern Bell exactly two months, and I quit. I told them, "I am not doing this the rest of my life." I was off to greener pastures.

The People and The Music—Country and Bluegrass that is!

Libby was sitting in a bar having a drink when this man came up to her and asked her, "Do you need a job?" She said, "No, I have a job." He said, "I know a man who is looking for a secretary and I think you would fit right in." He gave her John Kelly's name. Libby called John and made an appointment. When she went to see John, the first thing he asked her was "Do you know any country singers?" She said, "No, I don't know any country singers." He told her, "I want someone who doesn't know anything about the business and doesn't know any country artists because I want to teach them the way I want things done." She told John, "Well, I don't know a thing about it." John offered her $55 a week to start. That was $5 more than she was making at Southern Bell. Back in the day, when you were offered $5 more in pay, you changed jobs. She quit her job (much to her mother's chagrin) and went to work for John Kelly.

John Kelly's office was located downtown on Fourth Avenue North across the street from the Noel Hotel and next to the old Maxwell House Hotel. Libby worked for John Kelly about two years when they (he and his wife, Judy Lynn) decided to move back to Oklahoma. Around this same time, Hubert Long stopped by the office and said to Libby, "John is leaving. Will you come to work for me?" She told him, "I might. I will come and talk to you."

A couple of days later, Libby went to talk to Hubert. She liked Hubert and they agreed on a salary of $60 a week. Libby began working for Hubert at his offices in March, 1959. She was thrilled. Now, she was making $10 more a week than she had at Southern Bell.

A week after Libby began working for Hubert, he told her that he and the other employees were going on vacation, and she would be in charge. She told him, "You've got to be kidding." He said, "You know what to do. You will be fine." They all went on vacation, and she took charge.

Hubert could not have left his office in better hands. Libby, after working for John Kelly, knew what to do in a booking office. She ran the office smoothly while Hubert and the other agents were gone. When they returned, they all got back to business.

Hubert's office wasn't considered as large as Jim Denny's, but he was one of the power houses. In addition to Libby, Shorty Lavender worked there as a booking agent, and later, Dave Barton. He was representing many of the top artists around town and was heavily involved in forming the Country Music Association.

Libby said Hubert was a wonderful person to work for. She told me Hubert came into the office occasionally and said to everyone, "Let's close it down and everyone meet at my house." Everyone wrapped up whatever they were doing and headed to Hubert's house

View from backyard of Hubert's house.

The People and The Music—Country and Bluegrass that is!

on Moss Rose Drive in Inglewood, a suburb of Nashville. Hubert lived on the Cumberland River and Libby said by the time she got there, people were jumping in the river, floating on tubes, and playing in the water. Those days were always lots of fun and she missed them after she left. She worked for Hubert for the next nine years, leaving in November, 1968.

Ferlin Huskey was part of the Hubert Long Talent Agency's roster and Libby had known him for several years. Ferlin was a major artist, having had several No. 1 songs and appearing on all the national television network shows and in the movies. Ferlin's offices were in the same building as Hubert's located on 16th Avenue South when Ferlin stopped by Libby's desk and asked her to come to work for him as his personal secretary. After talking to Ferlin, she accepted the job. This would be a lateral move for Libby with no increase in pay, but she felt it would be a less hectic pace and she could still help Hubert if he needed it.

Ferlin was a good looking, down-to-earth, extremely talented man. He not only had hit records as "Ferlin" but also as "Simon Crum." Ferlin's first wife was Marvis Thompson-Husky. They were married for over 30 years and had several children together. Marvis and Ferlin worked together in movies and on the road. She was also a singer and a beautiful blonde. However, all good things must come to an end, and Marvis and Ferlin parted ways. After that, his personal life was not quite as successful as his professional life was, marrying three more times. Ferlin and Leona Williams were friends for over six years and remained so until his death.

Libby worked for Ferlin as his personal secretary from November 1968 to December 31, 2015. Libby said Ferlin went

The Women Behind the Sceness

on the road, he got paid and came back to the office. He would throw a bag full of cash, checks, and whatever else on the table. She would deposit the money and pay all his bills, including all of his household bills. She loved her job and stayed with Ferlin's company and the family even after he passed away from cardiac failure on March 17, 2011. As Libby puts it, "I stayed and taught the girls how to run the publishing company and handle everything else. Then, I gave it all up."

In talking to Libby about the difference in the way 16th and 17th Avenues South (Music Row n/k/a Music Block) are today as compared to when we were there she said, "You can't imagine the difference in the music business out there today. We (the secretaries, entertainers, booking agents) had more fun back in the day. Everyone liked everyone else. There was no back stabbing. If someone needed help, you helped them. If you needed help, they would help you. Everyone got along." Yesterday, it was a fun, thriving place of business with people on the street walking around, talking, laughing, and getting together. Today, with all the new buildings, condos and such, it looks sterile. Rarely have I seen a person on the street.

Libby's husband passed away on December 16, 1998. After her retirement from Ferlin Husky, she moved back to Springfield, Tennessee, about 25 miles north of Nashville, returning to the place where she was born and raised. At age 85, she is a still a beautiful lady, full of life, participates in the senior activities, and continues to join all of us oldies at the functions around Nashville. She is an absolute joy to be around. I wish I had met her before this interview and back in the day. I think we would have become life-long friends.

CORKY WILSON

You are probably thinking, "Is Corky a male or female?" Let me tell you, she is female and proud of it. Corky was a fixture on 16th Avenue South for many, many years. She worked for the best of them.

Coralee "Corky" Wilson was born in Warsaw, Missouri, but grew up in the suburbs of Kansas City, Missouri, with her mother, Irene, her stepfather, Ed White, and her half brother and sister, Larry and Janet.

From the earliest time she can remember, Corky has loved country music. As she grew up, whenever anyone from Nashville played near Kansas City, she and her friends attended the shows. In her mind, she was waiting for the time she had enough money to move to Nashville. Corky's early years were wonderful. She and her family listened to the Grand Ole Opry. If a country music act appeared anywhere around her hometown, Corky went to see them.

When Corky graduated from high school, her main objective was to move to Nashville and get a job as a secretary. She didn't care who she worked for, just as long as they had something to do with country music. She excelled in all her secretarial classes in high school but didn't like shorthand. (I can relate. I detested shorthand

and wouldn't take it again until I was in college.) But to reach her goal, Corky knew she would have to get a job and save some money to get to Nashville. She went to work for Commercial Credit in Kansas City, not knowing they would later open a Nashville office.

During the time Corky worked at Commercial Credit, she attended country music shows with her friends. She went to the Ozark Jubilee in Springfield, Missouri and John Ryan's Country Music Park in St. Louis. She made a point to meet some of the artists at every show. It was at one of these shows where she met Maxine Kirst. Maxine was the President of George Morgan's Fan Club. Maxine and Corky become good friends. She lived in St. Louis, and Corky stayed with her when she went to St. Louis.

In 1958, Corky learned Commercial had opened a small Nashville office. She asked for and received a transfer. At 22 years of age, Corky rode a Greyhound bus to Nashville. Unlike many others who traveled the same route to try and make their dreams come true, Corky had a job. She also had some acquaintances in the country music business.

Corky previously met Judy Lynn when Judy played for Lonzo and Oscar at shows in Missouri. Judy and Corky had stayed in touch and became good friends. Naturally, when she arrived in Nashville, she called Judy. Corky didn't drive and didn't own a car. Judy immediately came, picked her up, and helped her find an apartment on West End Avenue. The apartment they found was at 35th Avenue and West End Avenue. Commercial Credit was located at 19th and West End, so Corky would be able to walk to work. She could also walk over to 16th Avenue South, where most of the music offices were located.

Judy and Corky remained good friends, and Corky was a

The People and The Music—Country and Bluegrass that is!

frequent guest of Judy's for supper. One night when Judy was going to make corn on the cob, she got the corn ready and put it in the pot. As she was starting to run water in the pot, Corky asked her what she was doing. When Judy told her she was going to boil the corn, Corky said, "You should never start the corn in cold water, but get the water boiling hot and then add the corn." Judy never forgot this and told everyone, "Corky, taught me how to make corn on the cob."

Corky's goal was to work in the music industry. She met quite a few people while attending the country music shows in Missouri. Now, in Nashville, when she learned of a recording session or talked to someone who was getting ready to mail out records she went to the studio and asked if anyone needed help, she volunteered. This unpaid work was all done after her regular office hours at Commercial Credit, She also worked part-time writing letters to disc jockeys, stuffing records into envelopes, running errands, or whatever needed to be done. One of her jobs was to take things to Webb Pierce at his house, wait and bring work back to her house, do the work, and take it back to Webb.

One night Corky was backstage at the Grand Ole Opry when Lonzo and Oscar found out her real name was Coralee. Of course, they jumped on that right away and started singing, "She'll Be Coming Around The Mountain, Coralee." From that day forward every time they saw her, they burst into song.

Corky worked night and day for four years before she was finally offered a full-time job in the music business. Charlie Lamb, publisher of the *Music City Reporter*, asked her to come to work for him. Charlie's *Music City Reporter* was located in the Green Hills area of Nashville, which was a problem. Corky would have to take a bus from her apartment on West End Avenue to downtown Nashville and transfer to another bus to go to Green Hills. She accepted the job and gave her notice to Commercial Credit. Having previously worked part-time for people in the music business, she knew what to expect. Charlie was an easy-going guy. He had a great personality and was good at his job as publisher. Corky loved working for Charlie, but the difficulty of traveling back and forth, transferring buses every day finally got to her. About the same time, she was offered a full-time job with Ric Records. So, after one year with Charlie, she accepted the job with the record label.

Ric Records was located in the building at 801 16th Avenue South. The Glaser Brothers' multiple companies and Jo Walker, who had just opened a small office for the Country Music Association, were located on the second floor. Wil-Helm Agency, with its publishing company and talent agency, occupied the entire downstairs and owned the building.

Ric Records was a record label owned entirely by its stockholders. Lester Vanador was in charge of the office. Since Lester was out of the office most of the time, Corky would leave the door open so she could hear the phone ring and help Jo Walker if she needed a letter typed or something else done. Whenever she heard the phone ring, she would drop whatever she was doing and run to answer the phone. She also helped the Glasers if they needed extra help packing records, calling disc jockeys, writing letters to disc jockeys, or whatever they needed. She was the girl of all trades on the second floor. But when Lester Vanador starting cutting records, things changed. She was then busy with Ric Records and could no longer help Jo

Walker or the Glasers.

Corky loved Jo Walker, as did I. She was the sweetest and most wonderful lady around. The New York Office wouldn't let Jo pay Corky, so Jo went out and bought Corky a big bottle of nice bubble bath and gave her a one-year membership to the Country Music Association. This doesn't sound like much today, but believe me, in those years it was worth a lot. And it wasn't the size of the gift, but the thought that counted.

After they began cutting records, Ric Records relocated to the basement of the 801 building. Corky was extremely busy scheduling recording and demo sessions, taking the payments for the sessions, doing some bookkeeping work, packing and mailing out records to disc jockeys, writing letters to the disc jockeys, and making sure everything was mailed. Ric Records also recorded some pop artists, and Corky would have to do the same thing for them. Even though she was busy at the record company and felt like it was a pretty good job, the salary still wasn't enough to pay her bills. She continued to work for Webb Pierce running out to his house, picking up work, doing the work, and returning it to Webb. All of this without a car. Today, it would be impossible.

Labor Day Weekend, 1965, Corky was worn out. She had not had a vacation the entire time she had been in Nashville. She decided to quit her job, take a vacation, and go home to Kansas City, Missouri.

It turned out that taking a vacation was just what she needed. While she was home in Kansas City, the Wilburn Brothers played a show nearby. She had been the Missouri representative for the Wilburn Brothers Fan Club when she lived there. Corky took some of her friends to the show. She talked to Doyle and Teddy, and they offered her a job at Surefire Publishing.

Corky returned to Nashville and immediately started working at Surefire Publishing, their other two publishing companies, and their booking agency, Wil-Helm. Her office was located in the same building as her previous job at Ric Records. The only difference was she was downstairs with the Wilburns, who owned the building.

Corky's job was high-pressure. The Wilburns had three publishing companies, including Sure Fire. She was to obtain copyrights on the songs they published, write letters to disc jockeys letting them know about a new record whenever one of Sure Fire's songs was recorded, assist Smiley Wilson at Wil-Helm Talent Agency, answer fan mail, and in her spare time, do whatever else anyone needed done. She was one busy lady.

Corky and I were talking about her tasks at work, and she related to me how whenever she called Sonny Osborne, he would always answer the phone, "Yoh." The first few times she had to call him and he answered, she thought he didn't like her and that's why he was answering this way. Then, she found out he answered this way for everyone. Sure made her feel better.

She also did some copyrighting for Bill Monroe on a part-time basis. Bill would send her his songs taped. She would have to listen to them over and over to make sure she got the words correct. She then sent the words back to Bill so he could see if she had them right. If she did, he would call her and she would obtain the copyright for the song.

When she worked for Sure Fire, Wil-Helm Agency was booking some of the biggest entertainers of the time. Loretta Lynn,

The People and The Music—Country and Bluegrass that is!

The Osborne Brothers, The Wilburn Brothers, Connie Smith, and many others. She told me about typing 1,000 letters, and one part had to be in red so it would stand out. This was done on a manual typewriter. Every time you wanted red, you had to push down, put in red then reverse it when you wanted black. Can you imagine typing 1000 letters with carbon paper and shifting the ribbon every time you wanted to change color? Time consuming, and you had to be the best typist ever. I have been there and done that, so I know what time-consuming work it is.

Corky also told me how she wrote letters to the disc jockeys and let them know when an artist was going to appear in their area. She specifically talked about Connie Smith. If Connie was going to Pennsylvania, she would go through all her disc jockey cards (they were listed by name, address and phone number and then, by city and state), pull the names for the ones within a 200-mile radius of the show. Once she decided who she wanted to notify of the show, she wrote a letter and sent each of them a copy of Connie's latest single. Her job was to let the disc jockeys know Connie was going to be playing at such-and-such a venue on whatever date. I told her I did this same thing for Jimmy, but I kept my cards by state, city, and then by area. I didn't have time to go through every state looking for disc jockeys.

Corky stayed with the Wilburns and Sure Fire Publishing for three years. The Wilburns started Loretta Lynn Rodeos while she was at the firm. Corky loved the rodeos. She helped with the advertising, lining up the cowboys and others, promoting, and getting word to the local disc jockeys.

She was offered a job with Decca Records next door, making

more money, and with benefits. Polly Roper, Owen's secretary, called her and said Owen wanted her to come to work at Decca. There, she worked with Chris Doherty, who was a sales manager; Jack Brown, in promotions; Walter Haynes, a producer; Snuffy Miller, another producer; and Paul Lovelace, in promotions. Jack Parker, who she knew from Texas, came to work in sales. At Decca, she was a jack (Jill) of all trades. If someone needed something, she was the girl to go to. She stayed with Decca until 1979, when Decca became MCA/Universal and the Nashville staff was laid off.

Corky was one of those laid off at Decca. She drew her unemployment for several months when one day, unexpectedly, she received a call from Walter Haynes, who was then in Florida. Walter was working for a new record label in Nashville. The secretary was leaving and returning to Arizona because she was homesick. Walter asked Corky to pick up the key and told her they would talk when he returned to Nashville. She did.

Walter returned to Nashville, but he never got around to talking to Corky about making her an employee. Suddenly, out of the blue, he popped up and said, "When are you bringing your John Wayne pictures to put on the wall?" She asked him, "Why?" He said, "Because when your John Wayne pictures are on the wall, you are here. When they are not, you are gone." He wanted to make sure she was staying. She brought in her pictures and along with it, a picture of Bill Anderson that he had signed, "Next to John Wayne, I come first."

Corky was a fixture on 16th and 17th Avenues South. She was well-respected and known for her abilities to do an excellent job. She was never without work. Today, Corky is retired and living in

The People and The Music—Country and Bluegrass that is!

Madison, Tennessee. She is as cute as she can be and has a mind like a steel trap. I could talk about Corky and with her for days. I think she is a lady worth remembering. She helped so many artists get their start by sending out records to disc jockeys, answering fan mail, running errands, and most of the time she worked for free. Now, you know a little bit about this fine lady. Remember her. She was definitely a force in the '60s on Music Row.

CHAPTER 3:

Singers, Songwriters, and More

DONNA DARLENE and SHOT JACKSON

I decided to include Donna Darlene and Shot Jackson simply because I always loved Donna. Donna was a terrific lady. She was extremely talented, quiet, and a humble person. Shot, on the other hand, was partners with Buddy Emmons (world-famous steel guitar player) in Sho-Bud Guitars, and he was a gregarious kind of fellow and a good businessman whom I dearly loved.

Donna Darlene appeared on the WWVA Jamboree for many years before moving to Nashville. I met Donna Darlene the first night Jimmy Martin appeared on the WWVA Jamboree. It had been six years since I had a girlfriend, but I knew, after meeting her, she and I would be friends forever. The last friend I had was Jean Armstrong in Nashville. I didn't know anything about Donna, except she was a member of the Jamboree and I would be working with her in my new job at Gene Johnson's office. She had a beautiful smile and an easy way with people. I had a good feeling about her.

When Donna walked on stage that night, I saw a beautiful, blonde, petite lady, who could belt out a song like no other. The audience took to her immediately. She had an easy style that was reminiscent of the old-time singers. She was a lady singing her heart out in her little cowgirl outfit or her blue dress and boots.

Donna and I liked each other immediately. It wasn't long before we were telling each other our secrets. She told me about her marriage to Buddy Spicher, and I told her my secrets. When I met her, she and Buddy had either just divorced, or they were in the process of divorcing, I don't remember which. At the time, I only knew Buddy from playing on the Jamboree.

Donna Darlene and Buddy Spicher played in a band with Buddy's brother, Bobby, in Pennsylvania. They were around 14 when they first met. Touring Pennsylvania together, they soon fell in love and married very young. Buddy and Donna had one child, a daughter, Suzette Spicher, now Johnson. Buddy Spicher was a gifted fiddle player from Pennsylvania. He was also a member of the WWVA Jamboree. Buddy moved to Nashville around 1957 or 1958 at the urging of Audrey Williams. He subsequently became one of the most requested session musicians and was inducted into the Country Music Hall of Fame. I knew Buddy and always liked him and thought of

Singers, Songwriters, and More

him as not only an excellent musician, but a really nice guy. To my knowledge, Buddy is still living in retirement.

Back to Donna, she started dating Doug Kershaw shortly after we became friends. Rusty and Doug Kershaw were also members of the WWVA Jamboree and primarily played Cajun music. A little history—Donna and I were sitting with Doug at the piano in the studios of WWVA the first time he played and sang, "Louisiana Man." I told him then it was a hit, and what a hit it was.

Jimmy and I moved to Nashville in early 1963. Not too long after that Donna and Doug moved to Nashville. They didn't date very long before they got married. When they moved to Nashville, Rusty and Doug Kershaw's "Louisiana Man" was in the charts everywhere. It was a mega hit.

Donna and Doug had two boys, Doug, Jr. and Victor. Rusty and Doug were heavily booked all over the country. Donna was going on the road with them, singing on the shows. She needed a babysitter while she was on the road and my mother, Willowdeen Farmer Gibson, became their babysitter. Mother loved Dougie (his nickname) and Victor. She looked forward to having them around. They were like twins, and she would keep them for weeks at the time. When Donna and Doug divorced, mother missed the boys and asked about them all the time. She also missed seeing Donna and Doug. My son, Mike Morgan, remembers the boys and those days when they were with mother.

In Nashville, our lives took separate turns. Donna and Doug were on the road, I was booking shows, and Jimmy was on the road. I didn't see Donna for a while and, when I did, she told me that she and Doug had divorced. Of course, I already knew this from Mother.

The People and The Music—Country and Bluegrass that is!

Shot Jackson

About that time, Shot "Harold" Jackson came into the picture. Shot was a terrific person and entertainer. I first met Shot when he was appearing on the Grand Ole Opry as a Dobro player with Johnnie Wright and Jack Anglin and the Tennessee Mountain Boys. Kitty Wells was married to Johnnie Wright, and Shot played Dobro on some of her albums, as well.

The next time I actually saw Donna Darlene was at Shot Jackson's workshop. Donna called me and gave me the address. She asked me to meet her there. At the time, it was located in Madison underneath the overpass. It was in a garage-type building and Shot had a beautiful parrot he kept in a cage in the shop. I don't remember the name of the street or the parrot's name, but I do remember the location. Donna was madly in love with Shot and he with her. They made a good couple and moved into a two-bedroom apartment in Donelson. My sister, Betty Gibson Taylor, moved in with them and helped share the rent.

Shot liked to cook, and I will never forget my sister coming home from work one afternoon and Shot was ready to make scrambled eggs. He asked Betty if she would like to have some. She told him, "Absolutely, I am starving." Shot made the eggs and Shot, Don-

Singers, Songwriters, and More

na, and Betty all sat down to eat. After finishing her dinner, Betty said to Shot, "Those eggs were delicious. What did you do to them?" Shot casually said, "They are brains and eggs." Betty thought she was going to be sick. She told Shot, "Please don't ever cook eggs for me again." I laughed at that story until I cried and never forgot it. Of course, Shot was laughing his butt off. He knew how Betty was going to react before he told her they were brains and eggs.

I saw Shot Jackson often but only saw Donna occasionally after they married and moved out of Donelson. By now, Shot had moved his guitar shop to downtown Nashville on Broadway and teamed up with Buddy Emmons to form Sho-Bud Guitar. I had known Buddy since our days at Casey Clark's Barndance in Detroit. From time to time, I would drop by Sho-Bud to say hello. One of those times was when I lost my hair due to nerves and stress. I wore a wig to cover my bald head, and when I took the wig off to show Shot, I thought he was going to faint. He was livid because I was going through all the stress.

Buddy Emmons
The Bud in Sho-Bud

Shot suffered a major stroke in August, 1983, just two months after selling his beloved Sho-Bud Guitar. He suffered a second stroke in 1990 which totally incapacitated him. He passed away on January 24, 1991, at the young age of 70.

In Nashville, Donna performed on the Armed Forces Show hosted by Jim Reeves called Country Music Time. She also appeared with an all-girl band in Las Vegas. She recorded on Arc Records, Rural Rhythm, Kapp, Admiral, and several other labels. Her records can still be heard on YouTube. At one point in time, Donna was managed

Singers, Songwriters, and More

J.D. Crowe, Donna Darlene and Jimmy Martin

by Buster Doss and also by Shot Jackson. Donna and Shot toured the country together. Knowing them, they were loving every mile of the road they went down and every appearance they made. They were two very good people, playing the music they loved, together.

    I never thought Donna pursued her dream or got the recognition she deserved as an entertainer. She was such a good person and certainly not one to push herself. I admired that about her. She didn't like to promote herself and, in the music business, you have to promote yourself. I thought she deserved to be on the Opry and out on the road singing. In Wheeling, I booked Donna on a few of Jimmy Martin's shows. In Nashville, I never booked her. It wasn't because of her talent; she was a very talented lady. Now, I wonder why we didn't use her on some more of Jimmy Martin's shows. We

The People and The Music—Country and Bluegrass that is!

were always looking for a girl singer. Part of it is, I think, because a person doesn't look at what is right there under their nose. Or, in this case, think about who is right there. In my case, Donna.

The last time I saw Donna Darlene was at the Gulf Gas Station on the corner of Old Hickory Boulevard and Gallatin Road in Madison (a suburb on the north edge of Nashville). I was in Nashville from Fort Lauderdale, Florida, and had been to see Jerry Johnson, Wilma Leigh, and Peggy Gayle Leary. When I left their house, I stopped for gas, got out of my car, and the lady in front got out of her car and we both yelled each other's names at the same time. I went over and we hugged each other and talked for a few minutes.

You know you think of good intentions, but I just never get around to following through. That's the way I was. Every time I came to Nashville, I had intentions of going to see Shot and Donna. But once I got here, I was pulled from one person to the other and never got around to it. Then, when it's too late, you beat yourself up because you didn't take the time to go. It was the same way with Kitty Wells and Johnnie Wright. They asked my son, Ray Martin, to tell me to come see them when I was in Nashville. I never did, and now I am sorry I didn't. Another example of procrastinating is when Louise and Earl Scruggs and I sat together at Jimmy Martin's wake. It was the first time I had seen Louise in many years. We talked and talked. Louise gave me her new phone number (I didn't have it) and begged me to come see her when I returned to Nashville. She passed away before I could go. Regrets!

Donna Darlene Jackson suffered a stroke following open heart surgery that eventually caused her death. She was only 79 years old when she passed away on June 24, 2017. She is survived by her four

Singers, Songwriters, and More

Victor Kershaw and Suzette Spicher
Doug Kershaw Jr., Shotsie Jackson and Donna Darlene

children, Suzette Spicher, Victor Kershaw, Douglas Kershaw, Jr., and Shotsie Jackson West, many grandchildren and great grandchildren. She was a terrific lady and a gentle soul. I am so happy to have known and been friends with Donna and Shot Jackson: two caring, talented people doing what they loved.

Photographs are courtesy of Shotsie Jackson

JIM RUSHING, the SONG CRAFTER

Jim Rushing

I met Jim Rushing through my friend Dave Barton. One day Dave called me and asked me if I knew Jim and I said, "No." He proceeded to tell me about Jim, the songs he had written, and his experience in the music business. Dave told me I needed to include him in this book. He called Jim to see if it was OK to give me his telephone, and I called him.

After speaking to Jim on the phone, I drove to Columbia, Tennessee, to meet with him at his home. Meeting him was a most interesting and pleasant experience. He is a fascinating conversationalist. I could easily see how he could be a terrific writer.

Jim was born and grew up in Lubbock, Texas. His mother had dreams of him becoming a concert pianist. Jim was only four years old when he started piano lessons. He played classical piano or, as he tells it, "played at" the piano until he was 17 years old. Then Jerry Lee Lewis came on the scene, and that shut down the classical piano. I did notice he has a beautiful piano sitting in his living room. Must still tinker??? I didn't ask.

Jim was, in his words, "kicked out of high school." In 1959 he joined the service and was in Special Forces. His last years in service were spent in Vietnam, and he was discharged in October 1962. Jim returned to Texas, where he attended Texas Tech University. By the time he graduated, Jim had married and had one child born in 1965.

While in Vietnam, he developed a consuming interest for all things Oriental, Asian, and Chinese. Jim wanted to know everything he could about China and the subject of China. His professors at Texas State helped nourish his interest. One of his professors mentioned to Jim he thought the world's attention was going to be on China for the next 150 years, and he should think about that.

Upon graduation from Tech, Jim went to the University of Washington and studied the equivalent of five years of Chinese. He initially wanted to work for the CIA. But, after seeing the way the U.S. conducted policy in China, together with the CIA, he changed his mind. He decided to do something else.

While in high school, Jim began fooling around with songwriting. Then when he was shipped overseas, he started playing around with writing songs again. At the University of Washington, the songwriting idea struck him pretty hard. He began to think of it more as a profession rather than something to play around with.

The last issue of *Look* magazine hit the stands. The stories were about songwriters in Nashville. Kris Kristofferson was featured on the cover. The inside contained stories about Mickey Newberry, Chris Gantry, and others. Jim read the magazine cover-to-cover and said to himself, "Man, I want to go to Nashville and write songs."

In early 1971, Jim and his wife began talking about moving to Nashville so he could write songs and be involved in the music business. This meant taking leave of everything he had been doing since 1963 to become a China Specialist. He was taking a course

The People and The Music—Country and Bluegrass that is!

entitled, "Chinese Regional Studies," a study of the political systems and ideologies of all the countries that surrounded China. When Mao took over China in 1949, he had a big job to do. Then in 1964, China entered the nuclear club. It is fascinating to listen to Jim talk about China. I could listen all day. His interest turned to songwriting when he began planning a move to Nashville to start a new career as a songwriter.

Jim landed in Nashville in September 1971, he thought he wasn't equipped to do anything but "chase" his dream. He wanted to start from the ground up and didn't want any financial obligations to anyone. He vowed to do any kind of odd job he could accomplish to make whatever small amounts of money he could to sustain him while he wrote songs. When he arrived, the first business contact he met was Hubert Long.

At that time Hubert Long International included 13 publishing companies. Hubert told Jim, "We are always looking for writing talent." Jim said, "I am a songwriter, if I am worthy of the name." Hubert then said, "Young man, Can I help you? What do you do?" Jim repeated what he had previously said. Hubert said, "Well, come in here." Flossie and all of Hubert's publishing employees were in the office, and Audie Ashworth was running the company. When Jim and Hubert got to the publishing company office Hubert took Jim to Audie's office and said, "Audie, this man is a writer. I want you to listen to his songs. I want you to be candid with him and tell him what he can do and what he cannot do, and what he should and should not do." Then, Hubert left him with Audie. Jim said, "That was my introduction to Nashville."

It worked out pretty much like the article he read in *Life* magazine. Nashville was looking for talent, he was in Nashville in a publisher's office, and they were going to listen and critique his songs. Jim played four songs for Audie, and he liked three of them. Then Audie said, "Don't go out and sign with any publishing company." Audie didn't sign Jim to a publishing contract at that time, but they did give him a key to the building and a key to the offices. Hubert had songwriting rooms set up, and he could go there anytime day or night and write.

Isom and Flossie were both key in Hubert's publishing companies and other businesses, and Jim made friends with them. Hubert had another building that butted up to the CBS building. Isom was always doing something around the building—painting, fixing something, etc. Jim began picking up odd jobs with Isom around Hubert's building to help make ends meet. He was also doing some picking at Mr. D's on West End Avenue--something to make a little money. He didn't want to be financially tied to anyone. He had his nose to the grindstone, and he was focusing on music.

The odd jobs didn't last but a day or two at the time. Then he was right back to picking his guitar and writing songs day and night until another odd job came along. It was all about the music and not being financially obligated. He didn't own a car, and he was walking everywhere. His feelings were: "Stay with your nose to the grindstone and focus on music." That was what he lived by and the little he made, he lived on. He was determined to make music his career and not get into debt.

The Exit Inn on Elliston Place, a pizza place in Hillsboro Village, Frankenstein's on West End, and the Pickin' Parlor on Broadway were open. These became pivotal points in all that was going on

The People and The Music—Country and Bluegrass that is!

in the music industry at the time. Everyone imaginable would show up at the Exit Inn. People like Linda Ronstadt, Emmy Lou Harris… you never knew who would be there. They became his places to go, and all were walkable from 16th Avenue South. The goals were to listen to the music, meet people, play some tunes, and hopefully get a song recorded or at least make a connection.

Jim wanted to know Frances Preston at BMI (Broadcast Music Inc.) and he did. He was a BMI writer from 1972 to 1983, and then he went to ASCAP. Ben Kaye, head of Polygram Records, appeared on the scene. It was Ben's belief that four or five of the songwriters, including Jim, should go to ASCAP (Artists, Songwriters, Composers and Publishers). He thought the artists would be paid more by ASCAP than BMI. When the group left BMI, Frances was livid. She wasn't mad at the songwriters, but at the leaders of this organization that had precipitated the move. Looking back, Jim believes BMI would have been the better paying of the two agencies. But as Jim said, "That's neither here nor there, now."

Jim never signed with Hubert's publishing companies. They put a contract in front of him once, but there was no money involved and he did not sign. He still had the keys to the place. As Jim puts it, he was writing and just getting his feet wet in the business. One of the secretaries, Mary Rutlin, was friendly to Jim. Every time Jim wrote a verse or line on a song, he would go out to Mary and say, "Let me play you this." Mary listened and she was really into what Jim was doing. Her sister, Marie Rutlin, was publisher of *Record World*. (*Record World* along with *Cashbox* and *Billboard*, were the leading trade magazines in the United States.) Mary and Marie were playing a significant role in Jim's life.

Singers, Songwriters, and More

Some of Hubert's demos were cut at Bradley's Barn. He was also using other places around town. Jim knew Hubert had several significant writers signed to his publishing companies like Marijohn Wilkins, Kris Kristofferson, and others. Marijohn became a friend to Jim and talked to him about writing. Jim had much respect for Marijohn, and if he wanted anyone talking to him about writing, it was Marijohn. She was a terrific hit song writer, having written songs like, "Long Black Veil" and many others recorded by Stonewall Jackson, Debbie Reynolds, Webb Pierce, Lefty Frizzel, Carl Perkins, and Johnny Cash. After talking to Marijohn, Jim decided to leave Hubert's and go down the street.

Jim was still living at 1209 16th Avenue South, four houses beyond Edgehill on the right. This was right where he wanted to be and right where the business of music was happening. Jim lived there for 23 months, and he walked everywhere he went. He walked to Hubert's offices, to his part-time jobs, to the venues where he could listen to the music, to talk to other songwriters, sing his songs, and hopefully, get noticed. This is the way it was done in the '60s and '70s. Jim was thankful that he had a room with a view of the street where No. 1 hits were written and recorded, and stars were made.

In 1973, Hubert had passed and Mary, who was formerly the receptionist and secretary at Hubert's publishing company, had gone to work for Jack Music. This was at 1246 16th Avenue South. The office was located in an old house, and they built a brick façade in the front connecting two houses. Cowboy Jack Clements relocated his "Jack Music" to this location. Jack Music International (JMI), his record label, occupied one side, and Cowboy's publishing company occupied the other side.

The People and The Music—Country and Bluegrass that is!

By the fall of 1973 Jim was working for Jack Clements, and he was right where he wanted to be. Don Williams was breaking and his mentor, Jack Clements, was a gregarious man who drew talented people to him like a magnet. Jack introduced him to Bob McDill, who had 31 number one hits, including "Rednecks, White Socks, and Blue Ribbon Beer" and "Louisiana Saturday Night." He auditioned for Bob, and Bob liked him a lot. Jim had a great relationship with Cowboy, and Cowboy took him under his wing.

Jim's luck changed in 1974 when Jeanne Pruitt recorded, "You Don't Need to Move a Mountain," written by Jim and Wayne Holyfield. It would later be included in her album, *Jeanne Pruitt 1974*. The song stayed around for several years, and in 1975 Jeanne's version was covered by Philomena Begley, and again in 1978 by Tracey Nelson. It was the beginning of a good year for Jim.

Over the next few years, Jim continued to have success in getting his songs recorded. He and Bobby David teamed up to write his first No. 1 hit, recorded by Charlie Pride, "Hope You're Feeling Me (Like I'm Feeling You)." Jim described this as "hitting all the trades." I asked what this meant, and he said, "*Billboard, Record World,* and *Cashbox*." Even though I was associated with all three magazines in the '60s, I had never heard them referred to as "trades"—as in "trade publications."

During his career, Jim had several No. 1, No. 4, and No. 5 hits. The list of people who recorded and those who covered his songs is long, covering every genre of music. Debbie Boone, "I'd Even Let You Go," also covered by Paul Anka and Charlie Rich; Don Williams, "Lovin' Understandin' Man," covered by Telly Savalas. Remember Kojak? That was Telly Savalas. My mind's eye cannot picture him as a singer. Then there was Garth Brooks, Ricky Skaggs, Martina McBridge, The Seldom Scene, Charlie Rich, The Earl Scruggs Review, The Nitty Gritty Dirt Band, The Lewis Family, Kathy Mattea, Gene Watson, and the list goes on and on of people who have recorded songs written by Jim Rushing. Once his first song was recorded, he felt like he had gained the recognition of his peers as being a good songwriter.

Jim believes songs written today are of a different genre from the ones written in his day and time. If he were writing today, he thinks his songs would be overlooked. The country genre today is so very different. Even closely involved, he would need to be writing with someone who is up to writing today's lyrics.

Jim continued his run of success well into the early 1990s. His songs were being recorded by both bluegrass and country artists. He has been nominated twice for the Songwriters Hall of Fame. When talking to him about his songwriting, he refers to himself as being a "song crafter"—a very fitting title for a man who is hugely successful in the field he chose as his second career.

In September, 2001, 30 years to the day after he moved to Nashville, Jim laid down his pen and paper and retired. His boys are grown and have careers of their own. He lives a busy, quiet life at his beautiful home in Columbia, Tennessee, with his wife. It doesn't get any better than that. Jim is a mesmerizing conversationalist so if you ever have the opportunity to meet him, do so. You will be happy you did.

The People and The Music—Country and Bluegrass that is!

"NOTHING SURE LOOKS GOOD ON YOU"

Written by: Jim Rushing
Recording by: Gene Watson and several others

You found your greener pastures in a mansion on the hill,
With a flashy foreign car to drive and lots of time to kill.
Now my mind keeps on remembering the days of me and you.
But when we were down to nothin', nothin' sure looked good on you.

You said you needed simple things that I had plenty of,
And through the days of dark and rain we could always live on love.
With his style in life, he lured you and you could not refuse.
But when we were down to nothin', nothin' sure looked good on you.

When you honeymooned in Paris, it was carried on the news,
And I heard you laughed your cares away on a Caribbean cruise.
You were always one for dreamin'; now your dreams can all come true.
But when we were own to nothin', nothin' sure looked good on you.

You said you needed simple things that I had plenty of,
And through the days of dark and rain we could always live on love.
With his style in life, he lured you and you could not refuse.
But when we were down to nothin',
nothin' sure looked so good on you.

BOB AND BIRDIE LEE SMITH
and THE STATION INN

Bob Fowler, Ingrid Fowler, Birdie Lee Smith, Bob Smith
Jim Borenstein and Marty Lanham

The People and The Music—Country and Bluegrass that is!

My association with Birdie Lee Jones Smith goes back to the time when I was in the fourth grade and Birdie was in the sixth grade at Warner School. Warner School was (and is) located on the south side of Woodland Street in East Nashville. I will never forget meeting Birdie in the hallway and when she told me her name, I said, "Why did they name you Birdie?" She said, "I don't know." Our friendship would be forever, and I loved Birdie from that day until the day she died (and still do.)

Birdie and I didn't see each other for many years. I left Warner School and went to Memphis to stay with my dad. When I returned, my grandparents had moved to West Nashville. The next time I saw Birdie was at Bobby Green's Dusty Road Tavern after I left Jimmy Martin. I worked at the Metro Courthouse in Nashville and often stopped at the Dusty Road after work. I was sitting at the bar having a hotdog when I heard someone on the stage call the bass player, "Birdie." I thought, there aren't many people named, "Birdie." So, when the set ended and she was off stage, I went over to her and asked, "Did you go to Warner School?" She said, "Yes." I told her who I was, and it was like that day in the hallway at Warner School. We hugged, we talked, I met Bob, and we were back together. We remained close friends for the rest of our lives. She will always be, "my Birdie."

After that, I was at Bob and Birdie's house three or four times a week and would meet them at the Dusty Road after work. The Dusty Road was a tavern on Woodland Street. It was located on the south side of the street just after you cross the Woodland Street Bridge. The Dusty Road was a jamming place, and musicians gathered there to pick and sing. Bobby Green, an ex-prize fighter and a small man in stature, owned the place. He always had a cigarette in a cigarette holder hanging from his mouth. He was colorful, but he was a gentle soul. He had empathy for others. Many times, I didn't have money to buy a hot dog and a Coke. He would let me run a tab until I got paid. Metro only paid once a month, and it was extremely difficult to make ends meet. The little money I made sometimes didn't last a month.

Birdie had recently learned to play the bass. Bob was on guitar; Jim Borenstein played the mandolin, guitar, and banjo; and Eldon Burgess played fiddle. Sometimes, Onie Barr played banjo. Roland White was a regular there. Roland White, his wife, Arlene, and daughter lived in an apartment attached to Bob and Birdie's house on Maplewood Lane. Whenever he came to the Dusty Road, he would get up and play mandolin. Wayne Johnson would always get up and sing if he was there. Wayne was a terrific singer. One of his best songs was the Tina Turner classic, "Proud Mary." Other people would come and go and sit in with the group, including Harold Young on mandolin and so many others. It was always fun. A mural was painted behind the stage of the band of Bob, Birdie, Jim Bornstein, Eldon Burgess, and Harold Young.

If Bob Smith was on the stage when I walked in, he would immediately make the next song a Jimmy Martin song. He never stopped doing this, whether it was in a club, on a show, or at his house, even after I married Chuck Stephens. Fortunately, Chuck was one of the good guys and he would laugh it off.

The Dusty Road Tavern was sort of like Tootsie's on Woodland Street. It was dusty, absent of decorations, and had poor lighting. The hot dogs and camaraderie were the best. It was a neighborhood bar. Everyone knew each other, and Bobby Green knew everything that was going on. My parking lot for Metro was across the street, so I walked the Woodland Street Bridge twice a day rain or shine, snowing or freezing to the Metro Courthouse where I worked. Right in the center of the bridge is where I took off the rings Jimmy gave me and threw them in the river. I was mad but the minute I let them go, I thought, "What a dumb fool." I could have sold or pawned them for good money. And, believe me, I desperately needed money back then. I wonder if anyone caught a big fish that had a set of rings in it when they cleaned the fish. Wouldn't that be something!

On January 8, 1971, I married Charles (Chuck) Stephens. Chuck and I worked together at Metro (Metropolitan Government of Nashville and Davidson County). We dated for about a month when he asked me to marry him. That month had been spent introducing him to everyone at the Dusty Road. Even though Chuck was not a musician or singer, he was well liked by all. He was one of the good guys. When we decided to get married, Roy and Roberta Bounds went with us to Springfield and witnessed our wedding. Bob and Birdie were working that day and couldn't go. Bob and Birdie, Roy and Roberta, Chuck, and I met up after the wedding at the New Orleans Restaurant located on 8th Avenue North between West End Avenue and Church Street. None of us had ever eaten there. It was considered upscale in that era. Dinner was incredible. I still have the champagne bottle. After dinner, we all proceeded to the Dusty Road. Bob and Birdie and Roy Bounds all got on stage and acknowledged our wedding. Of course, Bob had to sing a Jimmy Martin song for me. He never let up with that. By the way, my marriage lasted 42 wonderful years, and Chuck died in my arms of a massive heart attack. Remember, we only dated for one month.

Singers, Songwriters, and More

Barbara and Chuck Stephens at the Abel Ball at Mar-a-Largo, Palm Beach, Florida

As with all good things, time changes everything. Metro decided to build a Metro Juvenile/Justice Building in the block where Dusty Road was located. But before they did that, Bobby Green died and his wife, Evelyn, took over. When she had to vacate the building, she moved around the corner where the Titans Stadium is located now. It was never the same after Bobby died, and the new location was unsafe.

The People and The Music—Country and Bluegrass that is!

The original location of the Station Inn

Around that same time in 1974, Bob and Birdie, Jim Bornstein, Bob and Ingrid Herman Fowler, and Marty and Charmaine Lanham decided to start their own bluegrass music club. They obtained a building next to Centennial Park on 27th Avenue just off West End. They did a little cleanup and remodeling and opened The Station Inn. Bob and Birdie's son-in-law (Elaine's husband), Larry Ruth, managed the place, and Elaine and her cousin, Paula Jamison, were the waitresses. Bob and Birdie, Jim Borenstein, Ingrid Herman Fowler, and Marty Lanham were the original band. Other musicians would get up and play whenever they came into the club.

Chuck and I were living in Madison when they opened. I had a new granddaughter, Michelle Sunshine Martin, Timmy's daughter. Michelle was about six months old and living with us. She adored Birdie and Bob and would jump up and down and wave her arms

Singers, Songwriters, and More

whenever she saw Birdie. I was coloring my hair the day Birdie called (I will never forget it) and told me the club was opening. I told her Chuck and I would come out on Friday. I then called Mother to see if she could watch Michelle for me.

Friday evening rolled around, and I was ready to leave as soon as Chuck got home from work. We arrived at the Station Inn, and the first person I saw sitting at the bar was Jimmy Martin. I said hello and Jimmy immediately looked at me and said, "Now, she is a redhead." That was the color I was changing to when Birdie called, a dark auburn/red. I remember fluffing my hair and saying, "Do you like it?" I couldn't let that opportunity pass. I then walked on by him and sat at a table. Fortunately, he didn't rag on me like he usually did when I ran into him. Later on I was told by Bob, "I love Barbara" was written on the wall of the men's room. I never saw it. Bob liked to tease me, and I sort of chalked it up to that. Chuck never mentioned it, and he did go to the men's room there.

From that night forward, I was at the Station Inn at least once a week until we moved back to Florida. But I was also at Bob and Birdie's house a couple of times a week, and sometimes more. Whenever I walked into the house, Bob was always laying on the sofa. He had constant back problems. This was a man who walked on the back of his shoes. He sort of slid his feet into his Dollar Store shoes but never all the way. I always laughed about that and told him, "Do you think if you bought some good walking shoes, your back pain would be better?" He never gave me an answer but picked up his guitar and started singing a Jimmy Martin tune. I think it was his way of telling me, "Mind your own business."

Bob (Red) Smith was a person that would, in one way or an-

The People and The Music—Country and Bluegrass that is!

Birdie and Bob Smith

other, let you know if you wronged him. While operating the Station Inn, there was a Metro Policeman that went by the name of "Moose" who patrolled the area. Moose, for reasons unknown, didn't really care for Bob. He did like Birdie. One night, Moose came in and walked around with his partner, who was very young, eyeing the customers. A lot of customers were kids from Vanderbilt who loved the music. Moose spotted these two young boys and went directly to their table and carded them. One of them was underage. At the time, Bob was on stage singing. At the end of the song, Moose walked over to Bob, told him he was serving alcoholic beverages to a minor, and arrested him. He took Bob out of the restaurant in handcuffs. Birdie told Moose she was going with them. Moose wouldn't let her go in the squad car. She got in her car and immediately drove to the jail.

While waiting for information at the jail, Birdie called her old high school friend, Gale Robinson, who was now a judge, and told him what had happened. Gale or someone made the charges go away. The next time Bob saw Moose come into the Station Inn, Bob was on stage and he immediately went into the old song, "Shackles and Chains." Moose didn't acknowledge the song, but we know he knew Bob was singing it to him. It was Bob's way of saying, "Arresting me didn't affect me."

Michelle Sunshine Martin-age 3 singing for Uncle Bob Smith

Moose's young partner later told Bob he couldn't stand working with Moose and was very happy when he was transferred.

Bob and Birdie continued to operate the Station Inn and moved it from its Centennial Park location to its present day location. Gradually, the original owners dropped out. In the new location, the original stage was located on the left hand side of the restaurant where you go to the ladies room. I don't know when it was moved to its present day location. I do know the stage was in its original place when my daughter graduated high school in 1983. She met me there that night.

In 1976, Chuck and I moved to Florida to be near his mother who had been diagnosed with Lymphoma. Every time I returned to

The People and The Music—Country and Bluegrass that is!

Nashville, I went to the Station Inn. I never stopped keeping up with Birdie. She and Bob would camp out in the winter at Placida on the west coast of Florida. Michelle, Chuck, and I drove over several times each winter and camped out for the weekend. Michelle was only three or four. She loved her Uncle Bob and Aunt Birdie. She would beg Bob, "Please Uncle Bob, can I go on the boat? Or, "Can I have an oyster or shrimp?" Or, "Can we go shrimping? Please, Uncle Bob." It was the cutest thing, and of course Bob always let her do or have whatever she was begging for. But Birdie would look at her and say, "Now, Michelle...," in only Birdie's drawn out fashion.

During the next five or six years, Bob and Birdie spent the winter camping out in their yellow van, equipped with a full-size bed, in Placida, Florida. Chuck and I were living in Plantation, Florida. They came over and spent weekends with us, or we took Michelle and camped out with them.

Chuck, Michelle, and I started our camping days by sleeping on a pallet in the back of our station wagon. Over the years, we graduated to a tent, and then rented a camper. The last time we went, we rented a large motorhome. My friend, Jill Hulin, my son, Buddy, his friend, Brian Currie, Michelle, Chuck, and I were on the trip. It was memorable. I had the flu on the way over and stayed in bed for the next day. Buddy, Brian, and Jill started playing quarters. This was the first time I had ever heard of the game. Shortly thereafter, Bob and Birdie bought their home in Englewood, Florida. We were no longer camping out, but going to their house to spend the weekend or they were coming to our house.

We continued to visit back and forth and talk on the phone. If there was a special occasion or a big show they were playing, we hopped in the car and went in Englewood. They were still playing music around the area. They had a good band and were well received locally. We were always going back and forth to each other's houses.

My husband, Chuck, Bob, and Birdie were all Krispy Kreme Donut-aholics (I don't think this is a word, but it fits.) One time when Bob and Birdie were in Fort Lauderdale, we all went to the beach to eat. Heading home from the beach, we passed a Krispy Kreme on Federal Highway. I was driving and they yelled, "Make a U-turn! Go back to Krispy Kreme." Scared the you-know-what out of me when they yelled. I did as I was told, and they bought three dozen donuts. The three of them ate almost two dozen in the less than six mile drive to our house. This was after having a big dinner at the beach. I did not eat any because I could care less about a donut. I teased them about eating so many. I told them, "If you have a diabetic attack, I am calling 911. I am doing nothing to help you all." I never forgot that, nor did I let them forget.

I think about "My Birdie" almost every day. Sometimes, I hear her saying in that way only she did, "Now, B a b a r a", dragging out the word, "Barbara." That's the way she would say it when she wanted me to think about something, or she didn't approve of something I said or did. I think about the night Birdie, Sue Toney, and I were drinking "sweet wine from Germantown, Tennessee (bootleg) and got drunker than skunks. Sue was sicker than a dog. She spent most of the night hanging her head over the commode while Birdie and I just kept drinking the sweet stuff and eating oysters and shrimp from the Barbie (bar-be-que). The next morning, Sue couldn't move, and Birdie and I weren't moving too fast. We never got sick to our stomachs, but we certainly didn't want any noise. Whenever Michelle

The People and The Music—Country and Bluegrass that is!

would wander over, Birdie would say, "Not now, Michelle." That went on most of the day. We laughed for years about that.

Bob passed away in 2004. Two years later, I was taking a couple of my granddaughters, Michelle Martin and Hollie Morgan, my daughter, Lisa, my daughters-in-law, Elisa Martin and Susan Martin, to Paris. None of my other grandchildren or daughters-in-law could go because of work. I invited Birdie to go with us. It took some arm-twisting, but she finally decided to go.

In Paris, Birdie, Hollie, and I shared a room and Michelle, Susan, Lisa, and Elisa shared a room. We had the smokers and non-smokers. But Hollie, being young and a non-smoker, was in for heckling from Birdie and me. We ragged her to death. She would say, "my husband," and Birdie and I would pounce on that right away with, "Does your husband have a name, Hollie?" She would look at us and say, "yes." We would then ask her to call him by name. Things like this we teased her about, and Birdie and I were getting the biggest kick out of it. Hollie was a trouper; she never got mad at us.

The group of us went to all the tourist attractions including Versailles and the castles. It was THE most wonderful time, ever. A couple of times some of the group went their own way, especially Hollie, but, ALL of us getting together at dinner was a must. We had fantastic dinners at various restaurants with great conversations and comradeship.

Michelle, Birdie, and I were on the upper deck of the hop on, hop off bus riding around, touring Paris, when Birdie informed us she had to go pee. She told us she had to go really bad. So we got off the bus at the Arc de Triomphe. We went down into the Arc thinking there would be a public toilet in the area where they sold tickets to the Arc. Wrong, no toilet. It was on the second floor. Birdie couldn't wait to take the elevator, so we took the stairs. On the way up the stairs, she was afraid of peeing her pants. So, she squatted on the steps and peed. Water was running down the steps. I was already at the second floor door guarding it.

Birdie Lee Smith holding her grandbaby.

Michelle was with Birdie and saying, "Aunt Birdie, you are desecrating a national monument. I am not going to jail for you." Then I said, "I will get you both out." By that time Birdie had finished, and she and Michelle took off up the steps to the second floor. We told everyone what Birdie had done. We took the elevator back down and bypassed the stairwell. We still laugh about "Birdie peeing on the steps" every time the Arc de Triomphe is mentioned. What a trip! Some good, some bad, but isn't that the way with every trip?

I also think about the wonderful Christmas trip we took. Elaine (Bob and Birdie's daughter) and Birdie, Chuck, and I went on a Christmas cruise down the Danube River in Europe. We landed in Prague and spent three days. Prague is a beautiful city, and the four

The People and The Music—Country and Bluegrass that is!

of us went to church on Christmas Eve. It was the oldest, coldest church service I had ever attended. We were huddling together trying to keep warm, and we were wearing our heaviest winter clothes, coats, scarves, and gloves. Prior to going to church, the entire cruise group had dinner in a basement restaurant. The evening was unforgettable. Not because the dinner was delicious, but because we were running down the streets trying to keep up with the leader and keep warm. The Christmas dinner was very interesting. It consisted of what I called turkey roulades with very little turkey. The stuffing was inside the roulade. The warm hot wine toddy was delicious, and we all had several glasses. Birdie and I were even drinking other people's drinks when they weren't going to drink theirs. Then we went to church. It was a good thing we had all that good warm wine in us, or we would have had icicles coming out our nose in the church.

The following day, we all caught the tour bus and traveled to Vienna where we boarded our riverboat. The next week was spent on the boat traveling down the Danube from Vienna to Bratislava, Slovakia, to Budapest in the Czech Republic. We even had dinner on the Ferris wheel in Vienna. Every stop on the cruise was wonderful, but COLD.

I would be remiss if I didn't tell you about Bratislava in Slovakia. It is a spectacular old town. The night we docked there, it had snowed and there was a good 18 to 24 inches of snow on the ground. The boat tied up about a mile from town, and the only way to get there was to walk. Birdie, Elaine, I, and several other women from the cruise trudged through the snow and ice to the town. It was well worth it. The city was beautiful, all decorated up for Christmas. The main hotel was wrapped up like a big Christmas package with ribbons and bows. There is a metal guy coming out of a hole in the street, and even he (not real) was decorated. We walked (and froze) all over town before heading back to the boat, through all the snow and ice. A lot of hot toddies were drunk that night.

My husband, Chuck, passed away on February 28, 2012, of a massive heart attack. He was in his eighth year of Alzheimer's, as well. I thought it was strange when Birdie called me and said she wouldn't be able to attend the funeral. She had plans with other people and they couldn't be changed. I didn't think too much about it, but knowing how much she liked Chuck, it just seemed rather odd.

Throughout 2012 and 2013, I would call periodically and tell Birdie I wanted to come over and spend the weekend. She had one excuse after the other as to why it wasn't a good time. I thought Birdie was mad at me, so I sat down and wrote her a letter asking what I had done to her. She immediately called me when she received the letter and told me, "I am not mad at you. I just have so much going on. We will get together soon." I didn't think too much about it and never knew it, but she was sick at the time battling cancer. She didn't want me to know. She also never told her daughter, Elaine. We found out when she was in the hospital for the final time.

I also found out many years later that she had some heart problems and surgery during the time she wouldn't let me come over. If I had known, I would have been knocking on her door.

The morning of March 13, 2014, I received a call from Elaine, Birdie's daughter. She had just arrived in Englewood and Birdie was in the hospital. She had suffered a stroke. I told her, "I am leaving now. I will see you in about three hours. Tell her I am on my way." Before I could get out of my driveway, Elaine called and told me Birdie had just passed away. My heart was broken; my Birdie was

The People and The Music—Country and Bluegrass that is!

gone. I cried my eyes out, sitting in my car in the driveway. I am crying as I write, just remembering that day.

A memorial service was held for Birdie a few weeks later. Michelle, Reagan, and I went over for the ceremony. Both Michelle and I got up and spoke about some of the good times and the years we had with my Birdie. Elaine gave me some of her ashes to put with Bob's under the carpet on the stage at the Station Inn. I have not asked J.T. Gray about doing that because I don't want to give them up. Birdie's ashes are in my glove compartment, and they go where I go. I know she would like that.

Bob and Birdie Smith, their daughter, Elaine and her husband, Brian Denney, my husband, Chuck, my family, and I all had a great relationship throughout the years. Enjoyable times always with Art Malmin, Mike Day, Julie Cotton, and so many others. Never a cross word amongst us and so, so many good times whether in Nashville, Fort Lauderdale, Florida, Placida or Englewood, Florida, or in Europe or Paris. Fun times: listening to music, going to concerts, eating, drinking, fishing, shrimping, eating lots of seafood, and talking, You name it, we did it. And, through it all, Bob never stopped singing Jimmy Martin songs to me.

Bob and Birdie Smith were instrumental in helping a lot of musicians in the field of bluegrass. They should be remembered not just by those of us who are left on this earth, but by future generations. They loved the music and the musicians. They should be in the Hall of Fame along with Marty and Charmaine Lanham, Ingrid Herman Fowler, Bob Fowler, and Jim Bornstein, as founders of the Station Inn and mentors to so many bluegrass musicians.

Personally, I will love them forever.

Singers, Songwriters, and More

Elaine and Brian Denny

MERLE KILGORE

Many times, I have heard people describe a man or a woman as being, "larger than life." Whenever I thought about whomever they were describing, it was difficult to envision that person being "larger than life." In fact, I often thought of the person being described as slightly pompous or self-involved, looking for attention. I was never able to wrap my mind around the phrase and actually associate it with a person.

Then, I met Merle Kilgore. He walked into a room and the room literally lit up. All eyes were on him, and he was the center of attention. He had a huge, infectious smile, and when he shook your hand, you knew he was happy to meet you. He was not pompous or self- involved. He was down-to-earth, a really good guy. In that moment, I knew I had found the person people had been describing as being "larger than life." It was Merle Kilgore. He was larger than life.

Merle was born in Oklahoma to Wyatt Kilgore and Gladys B. Clowers Kilgore on August 9, 1934. His mother, Gladys, was the sister of Clifton Clowers who lived on Wolverton Mountain. Gladys'

Singers, Songwriters, and More

son, Merle, would later write a smash hit about Clifton entitled, "Wolverton Mountain."

I remember meeting Merle Kilgore the first night I went with Jimmy to the Louisiana Hayride. When we were introduced, he shook my hand with a firmness I had not encountered from anyone. Yes, he was loud, but his smile told it all. It was from ear-to-ear and actually lit up the entire room. From that moment on, I considered Merle Kilgore to be my friend.

I didn't know anything about Merle being a songwriter, a disc jockey, or the fact he already had a hit song recorded by Webb Pierce entitled, "More and More." I thought I was pretty smart at the time, but I was just not into country or bluegrass music. I loved my rock n roll. Talk about singing, recording, writing, or playing music bored me. Regardless, it would not have made a difference to me whether he was famous or not, I just liked Merle Kilgore as a person.

After Jimmy joined the Louisiana Hayride, a group of us started going to Harry's Barbeque in Bossier City (across the river from Shreveport) after the show was over. The get-togethers were fantastic. The conversations were rarely about music, but were about everyday life and fun things. There may have been fleeting moments of conversation about music, but it was not the general topic. We were all young with young families. The kids were usually with us. We were just having a great time.

The usual group consisted of Margie and Shelby Singleton (Margie was a member of the Hayride), Merle and Dot Kilgore, their son, Steve, Jimmy Martin, our son, Timmy, and me. Sometimes, Carl and Kate Belew and their son, Bobby, would go. There were others who would show up from time to time like James O'Gwynn,

The People and The Music—Country and Bluegrass that is!

but he was never a regular. It all depended on who was in town and who could afford to go out to eat. These were fun evenings unless Jimmy got his feathers up about something and started a ruckus. That only happened a couple of times, and it was always because he had a woman waiting in the wings and he was anxious to get to wherever they were meeting.

If was during our times at the Hayride and Harry's Bar-be-que that my son, Jimmy (Timmy) Martin, Jr. formed a bond with Merle that would last throughout Merle's lifetime. Timmy was four years old and loved Merle. He called him, "Uncle Merle." Talk about Merle today to Timmy, and he will tell you a story about his "Uncle Merle." Most of those stories couldn't be printed for public knowledge. So if you run into Timmy, ask him to tell you some of the stories. Timmy is also lifelong friends with Hank, Jr. So continuing his friendship with Merle was easy. He saw Hank Jr.; he saw Uncle Merle.

Merle was super-talented. He was a terrific songwriter and had many, many hits under his belt including "Wolverton Mountain," "More and More," and "Ring of Fire." He co-wrote "Ring of Fire" with June Carter Cash. I recently saw Merle's son, Stephen, at the Troubadour Lounge on Opry Mills Drive in Nashville. He was the MC for the show. He talked about Merle writing "Ring of Fire" and said he got his inspiration from Preparation H and that was his "ring of fire." I laughed till I couldn't. I could see and hear Merle talking about hemorrhoids and the ring of fire.

Merle's songs were recorded by pop and country alike. Artists like Claude King, James O'Gwinn, Margie Singleton, Johnny Cash and June Carter Cash, Eddy Arnold, Johnny Horton, and even pop singer, Teresa Brewer. Ironically, one of his songs recorded by Margie

Singers, Songwriters, and More

Singleton was also recorded by Billie Jean Horton. Billie Jean was married to Johnny Horton, and before that to Hank Williams. Our little barbeque Saturday night group was well-represented, singing songs Merle had written. I don't know why Jimmy never recorded one of Merle's songs.

Merle was still working a D.J. spot while appearing on the Hayride. No one could make a living unless they also worked a daytime job. Jimmy didn't work a day job, but I did. Money wasn't an issue for us. Jimmy stayed home and kept Timmy, rehearsed, and was ready to leave when I got home. His nightly excursions continued in Shreveport. In fact, he sired a son while we were in Shreveport. This didn't come out until long after Jimmy had passed and my book was published.

After we left Shreveport and moved to the WWVA Jamboree, I didn't see Merle or Dot again until we moved to Nashville. By then, I was booking shows and Merle was playing with Johnnie and Jack and Kitty Wells.

Pushing ahead to when I opened my office on 16th Avenue South and became partners with Billy Grammer, Audrey Williams stopped by my office and told me Merle was going to be working with Hank, Jr. I was really happy about Merle going to work with Hank and Audrey. I thought I would get to see him more often. That didn't happen. I only saw Merle a couple of times after he went to work with Audrey. I think it was because we were all super busy. I was booking shows and Merle was playing shows with Hank, Jr. Our paths just didn't cross.

Things often go in circles. I left Jimmy Martin in September 1966 but continued to stay in touch with Vernon Derrick. Vernon and I were always friends. When he was working with Jimmy, he

The People and The Music—Country and Bluegrass that is!

drove from his home in Arab, Alabama, to our house. This was the place where everyone met up to go on the road. Vernon would always get to the house early. He and I talked and he ate dinner with us. A few times, Jimmy accused me of having an affair with Vernon Derrick. That was never true. We were friends and we remained friends for the rest of his life.

The next time I saw Merle was around 1982. I was married and we were living in Plantation (Fort Lauderdale), Florida. Out of the blue, I received a call from Vernon. He was working with Hank, Jr. and he told me someone wanted to speak to me, it was Merle. I was thrilled. We had a long talk. Merle invited me to the show that night at Sunrise Auditorium. He said I could bring Chuck. I told him I would be there. I called Chuck immediately and said, "We are going to see Hank, Jr. tonight. Merle and Vernon are both playing with him."

The minute I walked in backstage, Merle was right there to greet me, and he was smiling like a chimpanzee. I had Vernon on one side and Merle on the other. I was so happy to see my old friends. Every time Merle introduced me to someone he would say, "This is Barbara Martin. She is the best damn booking agent in Nashville." He meant it.

Over the next four years, Chuck and I traveled to see Vernon and Merle wherever they were playing in Florida. And any place we saw them, Merle would always introduce me to everyone as, "the best damn booking agent in Nashville."

After the 1980s, I became involved in many other things, including traveling the world. I did occasionally talk to Vernon, and I believe I saw Merle a few more times. Whenever I was in Alabama visiting my son, Mike, I always said I wanted to go see Vernon in Arab, Alabama. It was only a couple of hours by car, but I never did.

Singers, Songwriters, and More

Life got in the way.

Then, on February 6, 2005, that dazzling smile, heartfelt handshake, and enormous talent was silenced. Merle Kilgore had passed from this world. I cried like a baby, but that was only the beginning of the next several years.

Throughout 2005, 2006, and 2007, so many people I knew and loved died. Some of those were: Lightnin' Chance (79), a bass player on the Opry and someone I had been friends with since 1953; Vassar Clements (77), a longtime friend; Jimmy Martin (77); Merle Kilgore (70); Goldie Hill (77); Owen Bradley's brother, Charles Bradley (77)' Jerry Byrd (85); and Leslie Wilburn (79), brother of Teddy and Doyle. Good friends who all died too young, most of them still in their 70s. Also passing in 2005 was Sammie Smith of "Help Me Make It Through The Night" fame. She was only 61. It was a tough ten-year period of time.

Just remembering Merle and his infectious smile and the really nice guy he was, makes me smile. Reminiscing with Timmy brings joy to both of us. I will always remember this super-talented man who was a gentleman, a loyal friend, and was truly larger than life… Merle Kilgore.

I recently met Steve Kilgore and his beautiful wife, Silver, at the Troubadour Lounge on Opry Valley Drive. I knew Steve when he was a little boy in Shreveport, but he didn't know or remember me. I told him who I was, and we talked for a short while. He was the MC for the show, and he was awaiting his next turn at the mike. I was so happy that he was following in his father's footsteps. He talks about Merle on the show and sings a good song. Keep the Kilgore name active, Steve. Your dad would be proud.

LOUISA BRANSCOMB
Pioneer for Women and Songwriters

I met Louisa Branscomb at the SPGMA convention in January, 2018 where I was promoting my new book titled, *Don't Give Your Heart to a Rambler, My Life With Jimmy Martin, King of Bluegrass*. Someone invited me to join Louisa Branscomb and the alumni of the Woodsong Songwriters Retreats for cocktails. In addition to Louisa, were Patricia (Tricia Ann) Eaves, Nancy Posey, Katrina Kimbrough Brake, Lealaine Kimbrough Harris, and me. The girls were mostly musicians and songwriters, but in real life, worked other important jobs, as well. We were all different personalities with a common interest. The commonality was bluegrass music.

Sitting around the table in the bar of the Sheraton Hotel that day, we formed friendships that have lasted to this day. We have all attended Louisa's songwriter retreats and her 70th birthday party. I am the oldest of the bunch, with Louisa coming in second, but to look at us, you would never know it. The group accepts all ages, and we are like teenagers whenever we get together—talking non-stop, laughing like hyenas, writing songs, and being happy.

Louisa Branscomb is a force of nature and lives and breathes

Singers, Songwriters, and More

*Nancy Posey, Patricia Anne (Tricia) Eaves, Me,
Louis Branscomb, Francine Fitzgerald (standing)
Dawn Kinney, Katrina (Kat) Kimbrough Brake, Casey Lee Penn*

music. She has the energy of an Energizer Bunny. She is a mentor and started Screen Door Songwriters Alliance, a trust designed to teach school children and foster children songwriting as a means of expressing their views about the world and their lives. She also uses Screen Door as a tool for teaching adults music and songwriting. I have watched Louisa when she is involved with teaching someone, whether male, female, a child or a young adult. She is so patient with each person, showing them the good and not so good parts of their song, and how to improve it. The smiles, expressions, and nodding of their heads whenever Louisa is teaching is wonderful to see.

First and foremost, Louisa Branscomb is a passionate songwriter. She also loves playing her banjo, her guitar, singing and entertaining, riding her horses, her dog Idgy, and teaching. Speaking

The People and The Music—Country and Bluegrass that is!

70th Birthday Ride

of horses, I saw her ride her horse on her 70th birthday bareback and standing up. It was the most incredible, beautiful thing I had seen in a long time. She rode round and round the arena without holding on to anything. I understand she did this same thing on her 71st birthday at the Biltmore Estate where she boards her horses. I didn't get to see this, and I wish I had.

Being the diehard bluegrass musician and songwriter that Louisa is today, one would never think about her being born in upstate New York. Her father, Ben Branscomb, a young doctor in Nashville, caught tuberculosis from one of his patients. He became quite ill and was moving to upstate New York for treatment at a TB sanitarium. Her mother, Jane Moreland Branscomb, who was pregnant, planned

Singers, Songwriters, and More

Union Station, Nashville, Tennessee

to leave Nashville to join her husband in Saranac Lake, New York, close to the sanitarium.

Louisa's mother, Jane, five months pregnant with Louisa, left Nashville's Union Station for the long train trip to Saranac Lake, New York. This was Louisa's first train trip, and her love of trains for the rest of her life began before she was born.

Once the family was situated in New York, they found a small house only two doors down from the railroad tracks. Those same tracks brought tuberculosis patients to the sanitarium four times a day. Tuberculosis was a terrible disease running rampant in the United States, affecting the lungs. Iron lungs were used to treat the most severe patients. Many did not survive.

Louisa's father survived the treatment at the sanitarium and thrived. When he was released and ready to practice medicine

The People and The Music—Country and Bluegrass that is!

Louisa with statue of her Grandmother on Vanderbilt Campus

again, the family returned to Nashville. They would, once again, live in the cottage next to her grandparents' house on Vanderbilt campus.

Louisa's grandfather, Harvie Branscomb, was the chancellor of Vanderbilt University. He and his wife, Margaret, are interred in a vault on Vanderbilt campus. Louisa grew up in the cottage next door to her grandparents. She often worked in the garden alongside her grandmother. Her grandmother loved entertaining and gardening. She spent time with Louisa teaching her and tending to all the chrysanthemums and gladioli. She said the magnolia trees she and her grandmother planted on the Vanderbilt campus are still standing there today.

When Louisa was six years old, the family moved to Birmingham, Alabama. She had her beloved guitar, purchased for $18 from Sears, with her at all times. She began writing songs at age five, her first song being titled, "Ishy the Fishy." The song was about a bream her sister had caught while on a "learning how to fish" trip with their father. Louisa felt sorry for the fish.

After the family moved to Birmingham, Louisa and her guitar became regular passengers on the L&N from Birmingham to Nashville and back. Her mother would put her on the train, and she would travel to Union Station in Nashville to visit her grandparents. At the end of her visit, her grandmother would take her to Union Station, situate her on the train, and her mother would pick her up. It was not an unusual thing at the time for a child to travel alone. I was five years old when I started traveling from Memphis to Nashville to my grandparents. Times were safe for children traveling alone, and the conductors watched out for them.

Her grandmother, Margaret, was a force to be reckoned with much like Louisa is today. When she was seven years old, her grandmother decided to take Louisa and her sister, Betsy, to the Grand Ole Opry to learn how country music and Vanderbilt University went hand-in-hand, defining Nashville. Her grandmother had tickets for the first three seats on the second row on the left for the three of them. When Louisa saw Stringbean come on stage, she thought he was playing his banjo on stilts because he was so tall. She learned he was just tall. The picture never left her mind, and she wrote a song about it, "Grandma and Highway 65."

Growing up, country and bluegrass music were not the only genres of music in Louisa's life. Her mother and father always had a big stack of albums on the record player. Music ran the gamut with opera, folk, classical, and even flamenco. Her dad's mother, (Margaret), and her mom's father, Earl Moreland, sang amateur opera in college together at SMU (Southern Methodist University). Her maternal grandmother, Helen Moreland, sang folk songs to Louisa when she was a baby. Her Dad played classical music, boogie woogie, and blues on piano and harmonica. Her younger sisters, Betsy

The People and The Music—Country and Bluegrass that is!

and Melinda, both loved singing and were very musical. They both learned shape note singing. The entire family were all musical and loved music in every form.

Louisa went hunting with her dad in Demopolis, Alabama. They met up with other hunters and had jam sessions around the fire at night. She learned her first folk song, "Had a Dog and His Name Was Blue," around the campfire. At home, her dad let all of the kids sit on the piano bench with him and improvise. He gave Louisa professional lessons, but she had the piano teacher so frustrated playing an improvised version of Chopin or Beethoven the teacher would literally throw her hands up in the air. Louisa couldn't tolerate the formal lessons, but she continued. She was not your typical child. She just wanted to spend her days running wild in the woods, making up stories and songs. She was a shy child and liked being alone. She was in Heaven sitting at the back of the class, writing stories and songs.

The mid-1960s came to Birmingham, and so did racial unrest and civil rights violence. During this time, Louisa discovered the music going on in the dark streets near the steel mills and the blues bars where gaunt, African American men gathered to sing nightly. It was here in those streets of Birmingham and the blues bars that Louisa discovered the power of music.

Many of the musicians, listeners, and the men and women who worked to keep the steel mills and foundries going, had lung disease. Her dad, a physician specializing in lung diseases, made regular visits to see his patients who came from the mills. He would take Louisa along and after treating his patients, they enjoyed the music. She remembers her dad walking into a bar where a group of black men were jamming and they yelled, "Hey Doc, what are you gonna play, piano or harp?" Sometimes they also kidded him about her by saying, "That's a pretty lady you have with you, but isn't she a little young for you?" It was all in fun.

Louisa's first live performance and her first award for composing music was a far cry from those blues bars and backstreets of the steel mills. Her piano teacher entered her in a regional composing contest when she was 11. Her song, "Fantasy of the Trolls," won first place, earning her the honor of having her composition annotated and played by the symphony. She also earned the opportunity to perform her composition with the symphony at the Birmingham Civic Auditorium before an audience of several thousand people.

Frightening, scared, honored, excited. Yes, she had all those thoughts, but she could do it. After all, she was 11 years old. She remembers sitting on the piano bench facing the symphony and the conductor's back. He waved the wand ferociously, every so often turning towards Louisa and waving it. She thought she was doing something wrong but, toward the end of the piece, the conductor took over and finished the piece with a giant flourish of the orchestra in a sea of sound. She realized then and there she was a composer, she had a place in music, and music was her place in the world.

By the time Louisa finished college at age 21, she had 455 hand-typed songs she had written, and all were numbered. She feels like most of those songs were an exercise in "trial and error how to not write songs." That same year, she wrote "Steel Rails" while sitting on her couch at her home in Winston-Salem, North Carolina. She was meditating while suffering a broken heart after ending a relationship with her first love. It took her about 30 minutes to write the song. Louisa felt like the same steel rails that carried her mother and her unborn child, Louisa, from Union Station to New York, had found their way into another song. It brought her the comfort of letting go, moving on, and trusting the train with her destiny.

Louisa recorded "Steel Rails" in 1971 on a cassette demo. She gave a copy to Larry Lee, who was the bass player for Mel Tillis. She knew Larry from some of her country music friends in Virginia. Larry said he played it when the band was on the bus. Mel heard it and said, "I want to record this tomorrow." They turned the bus around, went back to Nashville, and recorded the song, but didn't release it at the time.

The following week, Mel invited Louisa to come to Nashville and to be there at 8 a.m. the next day. Living in North Carolina and naïve for her age of 22, she certainly didn't know much about the music business. In those days, there were very few women actively working in the field of music, and especially bluegrass music. Some of those women working in bluegrass were Wilma Lee Cooper, Jerry Johnson, and Gloria Belle (Flickinger). Bessie Mauldin was a predecessor, playing bass for Bill Monroe for many years.

Louisa arrived at Mel's office at Sawgrass Music the following morning at 8 a.m. sharp. Mel was already there. Pam, who was about 10 years old at the time, was with him. Louisa was surprised when Mel took her into his office, sat down in the chair, and put his feet up on the desk. He took some notes, sipped his coffee, and listened to her play one song after another of ones she had written. She was there for four hours, singing and playing her songs. He then told her, "You need to move to Nashville and write for Sawgrass. Nashville needs you. We've had Cindy Walker and Kitty Wells, and we need a woman writer like you to keep breaking new ground."

Singers, Songwriters, and More

Mel had chosen five of the 45 songs she had sung for him. He told her he had arranged for her to do a demo of the songs that afternoon. Louisa asked him in her naïve way, "Are you going to sing my songs?" Mel told her, "No, you are." That afternoon, she cut the four songs as a demo, including "Steel Rails." Appearing on that demo with her were Pig Robbins, Larry Lee, Jim Buchanan, and other musicians who worked the studio circuit.

When Louisa met with Mel, she had no experience in the music business, no one to guide or talk to her, and no one to talk to about what to do. She was wide-eyed and leaning on whatever anyone told her to be true. She trusted everyone. She thought songs she had written and published by a "publishing company" would reap rewards for her when they were recorded. She learned quickly that this was not true when she realized "Steel Rails" was being recorded by numerous people, but they were not getting the song through Sawgrass Music. All publishing royalties went to Mel Tillis personally and her friend Larry Lee who had partial publishing and introduced her to Mel Tillis.

Louisa tried to get the rights back, but Mel said, "You will have to pay for the session which was $5,000." She was 23 years old, didn't have $5,000, and was a full-time musician barely making a living. There are over 350 versions of "Steel Rails" on YouTube and countless recordings, but due to copywrite law in the 1970s, Louisa cannot get publishing back until she is in her mid-80's. In the meantime, while the song has been a major hit, she has received only small amounts in songwriter's royalties. The majority of the royalties went to the publisher.

Regardless of the wrench that was thrown into her life with

The People and The Music—Country and Bluegrass that is!

"Steel Rails," Louisa feels it was a pivotal, "time stands still" moment in her life. It validated her lifelong need to write songs, poems, and just put her feelings on paper and music. She learned this thing she had done all her life, like breathing, was not merely a natural survival tool, or even an "art," it is also something that drives an entire industry, a cog churning wheels that drives Nashville like a steady hum. She knew then, without songwriters, the music business couldn't or wouldn't function. However, she also knew that songwriters could be taken advantage of by some unscrupulous people.

In her 30s, Louisa began to think about giving back to others. She had performed for 20 years and had recorded three, mostly original, albums. She felt like it was time to give back and to educate those who wanted to be in the music business but knew nothing about it. She began to envision a more united songwriting community beginning with her genre, bluegrass music.

Louisa created Woodsong Mountain Retreats, which was later renamed and is currently known as "Lyric Mountain Retreats." She would hold the retreats at her beautiful farm home in White, Georgia. She had several guest cottages on the property to use for classrooms. Every retreat has been a whopping success, with many repeat students. She just completed her 33rd spring workshop with emerging talent as well as seasoned writers, Over the years, she has had over 700 people attend her retreats. She also holds several interim workshops during the year.

I have attended several of the retreats, including the spring retreat. They are always powerful and very organized, with terrific songwriters of all ages attending. Johnny and Jeanette Williams, both of whom are outstanding mentors as well, are generally there helping

Singers, Songwriters, and More

Johnny Williams, Louisa Branscomb, Jeanette Williams

guide the songwriters. Before the end of every retreat, everyone becomes like family. The spring dinner and banquet show on Saturday night was open to the public, and the room was filled to capacity. The performers/songwriters, young and old from all over the country, were incredible. I believe a couple of yet-to-be recorded hit songs came out of that group.

Louisa, the ever-forward thinking person she is, decided to pursue the idea of having a more organized songwriter community in bluegrass. She wanted to help organize a songwriter constituency that would assist bluegrass writers find and nurture each other to improve their art. She wanted to do this under the umbrella of the International Bluegrass Music Association (IBMA.)

The People and The Music—Country and Bluegrass that is!

One night as she was having dinner with some of her very talented songwriter friends at Demo's, during IBMA, they spearheaded the founding of the IBMA Songwriting Association. By the end of the year, they had 250 members signed up to be involved. Later, it was renamed the "IBMA Songwriting Committee." All its original activities such as the newsletter, song circles, and mentoring are still going on to this day. It has changed very little in almost 20 years. Louisa wrote the original criteria draft for the Songwriter Award for IBMA, and the award is now a regular part of the industry.

In 1980, Louisa realized that life on the road was not a glamour job. It was lonely without family and friends, and she saw very few women traveling as musicians. She wanted to be able to play and write music, but in her own way. She wanted more time with her daughter, Olivia. She returned to school and obtained her Ph.D. in Psychology. Since that time, she has been a full-time psychologist and a full-time musician. Currently, she prides herself as a songwriter, advocate, performer, mother, teacher and non-profit organizer.

Louisa feels that when all is said and done, the real lessons about the music business are not facts and numbers and spread sheets. They are the ones you can't put on paper. Here are a few of her ideas and I quote:

1. The song is a mirror, so if you are going to write one, be prepared.
2. It is an act of courage to write a song because it requires pulling back the curtains on the stage of the heart and seeing disarray of the furniture there.
3. The business of songwriting is relationships, and the main tool is empathy. The ongoing challenge is to relate authentically and

with empathy to first ourselves, and secondly to the invisible listener. Then, we depend on relations to the greater music community as a cog in the wheel of music.

4. Songwriting is not about oneself, except in the beginning. Songwriting and creative music making didn't start with her or even 1,000 years ago. It is something that has existed since ancient times to say or communicate something. To take part in this chain of humanity and this elemental way of conveying sound and image and word, is a great privilege.

5. Songwriting isn't "just" an art; it is an art that includes social responsibility. We have an opportunity to do good – and there are a hundred ways a song can do that. Songs of any style can make a difference for the greater good of the community and culture.

6. You never know when you have made or might make a difference. Your song might catch someone in a moment in time and carry them around the bend to a private destination that has everything to do with staying alive.

7. Comparisons are odious. Just write "you."

8. Rules for what makes a good song are a good place to start. But, in truth, it is more about knowing the practice intimately, so you know what your choices are at any given moment in writing the song, and the consequences of doing it this way or that way.

9. Learn both the art and business of songwriting. Find a mentor who feels like a good fit. Attend workshops and jams and songwriter events.

10. A song is bare bones with a little soul attached. Songs are around us and in us all, all the time. Learning to capture a song is a delicate art, and the rewards are never ending.

Louisa is concerned about where the industry is going now and if it can retain its soul. She has seen the commercialization of country music since she fell in love with Merle Haggard and Hank Snow. She feels music today is headed in the same direction, but the increased commercialization and emphasis on the business aspects of the trade are useful and good. However, she feels like the art at the center is a fragile thing. It needs things that seem like the "old days" – people gathering in living rooms or front porches singing, sharing, and nurturing the art of telling one's story in music or otherwise—working together for the sheer joy of creating, as opposed to manufacturing the "hit" song, and seeing each other as neighbors and friends rather than competitors.

The digital age has made the music business more complicated and made earning a living more complicated. It is easy to fall prey to living for the sound bite – the single release – the quick rise to the charts – then, on to the next song. It is irrelevant as to whether things are better or worse, but we all have to admit things are different.

Today, Louisa Branscomb feels so lucky to have a practice of regularly re-centering and mindfulness as a part of songwriting, because the value of living as a songwriter is expressed in many ways. She feels lucky to have experiences with magnificent talent such as Alison Krauss, Mel Tillis, Claire Lynch, John Denver, Dale Ann Bradley and many others recording her songs or co-writing her songs. She feels lucky for all her friends and the valuable stories about regular people who never take a stage, but accomplish and experience small miracles from the audiences.

Louisa credits her survival to songs and trains. The two are intricately woven together. Her heartbeat was just beginning when her pregnant mother left Union Station to join her father in New York. Those train tracks at Union Station that took her to and from her parents' home in Birmingham to her grandparents' house in Nashville are in her heart to this day. Those rows of magnolia trees she and her grandmother planted and are 100 feet tall now are living testaments to Louisa's love of Nashville.

As Louisa says, "I will take the train any day. Trains know where they are going. They take every bend; it's just the way it is. They are courageous in their power and in their giving. Even with all that iron and steel and fire, they accept. They surrender to the track, to what lies ahead, and they teach me to surrender to life and the next thing."

Louisa is one of the most iconic acoustic and country songwriters in country and bluegrass music. She has performed for over 50 years, while also blazing trails for songwriters and women performers in bluegrass and acoustic music as early as 1971. Her song, "Steel Rails" appeared on Alison Krauss' first Grammy-winning album and John Denver's last Grammy-winning album. It is said to be one of the longest running #1 hits and most played songs in the genre with over 350 video and album covers by other bands, and the 13th most influential song in the 75-year history of bluegrass music.

A short history of her notable awards and honors over the years includes:

The People and The Music—Country and Bluegrass that is!

- Being the first woman in bluegrass to front a band playing banjo while also writing a large part of the band's repertoire beginning in the early 1970's.
- Running one of the longest, continuously running songwriter retreat series for acoustic writers in the country, Lyric Mountain Retreat, originally known as Woodsong Retreat, since 1989.
- IBMA Distinguished Achievement Award 2017
- Song of the Year 1991 (SPBGMA) – "Steel Rails"
- Song of the Year 2014 – IBMA "Dear Sister," co-written with Claire Lynch
- Member of Atlanta Country Music Hall of Fame
- Member of Alabama Bluegrass Hall of Fame
- IBMA Recorded Event of the Year 2001
- IBMA Recorded Event of the Year 2006
- 7 nominations for Songwriter of the YEAR (SPGBMA, IBMA)
- 2 nominations for IBMA Mentor of the Year
- Over 30 top 10 chart hits, two Grammy cuts

Today, Louisa's passions are riding her John Deere tractor at her Lyric Mountain farm retreat, playing with her dog, Idgy, and riding her horse at the Biltmore Estate where she is boarded. She would much rather be doing all of these things than standing in the limelight. She is a down-to-earth, beautiful lady who has contributed so much to all of those she comes in contact with and to the millions of people who love her songs. Keep up the good work, Louisa. We look forward to your next hit.

Roll on, steel rails. Louisa is waiting at the end.

Singers, Songwriters, and More

Louisa and her horse, A Capella

GRANDMA AND HIGHWAY 65
Words and music by Louisa Branscomb

I guess that we are all wayfaring strangers
With our guitars and our country music dreams.
Well, I don't know too much about tomorrow.
But this guitar's filled with Nashville memories.

Grandma always met me at the station,
Waiting for the train that I would ride.
Now I'm longing for the music of the steel rails
As I'm rollin' in on highway 65.

She said country music raised the crime rate,
But she loved to hear me play that Sears guitar
And bought us front row tickets at the Ryman.
I guess she took me too close to the stars.

She said, "Don't walk in anybody's shadow,
And it was awfully cold on Music Row.
So, I set out with a guitar and a suitcase.
Grandma, I am finally coming home.

CHORUS
That L&N is somewhere rusting,
No silver rails to be my guide.
I guess that I will make it back to Nashville,
Thanks to Grandma and Highway 65.

Do you see those magnolias down on Broadway?
It was nearly 60 years ago
Grandma and me, two shovels and ice tea,
We planted every tree beside that road.

Now Grandma lies in those magnolia shadows,
Close enough to see how much they've grown.
She always loved to hear wayfarin' strangers.
Grandma, I am finally coming home.

CHORUS
That L&N is somewhere rusting,
No silver rails to be my guide.
I guess that I will make it back to Nashville,
Thanks to Grandma and Highway 65.

GRANT TURNER

For those of you who don't know, Grant Turner was a longtime host of the Grand Ole Opry. Grant was a gentleman, and I always thought of him as being quite a mystery.

Grant Turner was born in Texas, near Abilene, and was a journalism major in college. He worked for newspapers during the 1930s, but his love was broadcasting. Grant worked for radio stations in Texas during the 1930s and moved to Knoxville, Tennessee in 1942.

During the time he was working in Knoxville, he heard about a job opening at WSM, he immediately took a bus to Nashville to audition. It is well known that he was hired and started to work on D-Day, June 6, 1944. (D-Day is the day the Allies invaded Europe in World War II.) Grant was always proud of that. Can you imagine doing something like that in this day and time?

By the time I met Grant, he had been with the Grand Ole Opry for eight or nine years. He was the announcer for the Prince Albert portion of the Opry, a coveted position.

Jimmy Martin introduced me to Grant Turner the first time he took me to the Friday Night Frolics. My immediate thoughts were that Grant was old and why was Jimmy friends with this old man? This was in 1953 and Grant was in his early 40s. I was only 17 and Jimmy was 25.

Singers, Songwriters, and More

Once I got to know Grant, I understood why he and Jimmy were friends. They were both passionate about the music. Grant loved singing and tried his hand several times at recording. Looking at Grant, one would never think of him as a singer. I never heard any of his recordings, but I remember hearing that Grant had recorded with one of the Carter sisters.

I recall so many things about the times Jimmy and I would meet up with Grant. One was the first time we met him for lunch at the old Maxwell House Hotel. The Maxwell House was located on the northwest corner of 4th Avenue North and Church Street, directly across the street from the Noel Hotel. The Noel Hotel is still there today.

Grant was already seated in the magnificent restaurant in the hotel when Jimmy and I arrived. (We walked four blocks down Church Street from the Tulane Hotel.) We sat down, and I ordered a cup of coffee. I remember Grant saying to me, "That is Maxwell House Coffee. Do you know why they say, "good to the last drop?" I replied, "No." He said, "Teddy Roosevelt was President of the United States, and he came to Nashville. He stayed in this hotel and, after having their coffee he said, "This is good to the last drop." From that time on, Maxwell House Coffee used it as their slogan. I was thrilled to know that information and never forgot.

Grant then told us about the history of the Maxwell House Hotel and how tunnels were built under it running to the river. It was used by people living there to flee and get to the river in case of Indian attacks. He said the tunnels were also used during prohibition to store whiskey. I was fascinated. I thought he lived in the hotel, since he knew so much about it.

The People and The Music—Country and Bluegrass that is!

Several wrestlers lived in the hotel, and I remember Jimmy and I stopping by to have lunch with Grant and he introduced us to one of them who was a friend. I don't remember his full name, but I do know his first name was Billy and he had a Mohawk haircut. I thought he was a real Indian. I was dumb, or maybe I should say naïve, back then. If I wanted to see a "real" Indian, all I had to do was look at my mother or my grandmother to see one. I never thought of that at 17 years old. Back then, I just wanted Mother, Mama and Daddy Hollis to meet the wrestlers. They were avid fans.

Grant occasionally stopped by the Tulane Hotel to have lunch. There was a recording studio located in the Tulane, and Grant visited the studio before coming down to the restaurant. Occasionally, Bessie Mauldin would be there. Bessie lived in the hotel and played for Bill Monroe. I worked in the restaurant, and Jimmy also lived in the hotel. Grant, Bessie (when she was there), and I talked about the music business until Jimmy came downstairs. I hated to see Jimmy come into the restaurant because he was the world's worst tipper. I thought he might influence the other person with him when they tipped. Jimmy tipped in pennies under each plate, cup, saucer, or whatever. Fortunately, Grant was not like that.

I think Grant Turner and his fantastic voice paved the way for all other announcers on the Grand Ole Opry. He had a distinctive voice, whether he was speaking on the air or across the table to you. It was a very rich sounding voice, and he pronounced every word so that you could clearly understand what he was saying. Eddie Stubbs and Keith Bilbrey have that same voice.

Jimmy Martin and Grant Turner remained friends until he died. Grant occasionally stopped by our house in Hermitage if he had a day

Singers, Songwriters, and More

L to R: Bessie Lee Mauldin, Bill Monroe, Melissa Monroe (Bill's Daughter), Joe Stuart, Bill Keith, and Del McCoury, taken at Brown County Jamboree Barn, 1963. Photo by Jim Peva

off or was out our way. I never knew if Grant was married, nor did I ever meet a wife or girlfriend. I did find out later from his obituary that he was married. I knew Grant as a down-to-earth, very loyal person, and a dedicated husband (I am basing this on the fact I never saw him with a female nor ever heard anything derogatory about him in the over 50 years I knew him). I enjoyed talking to him because he always told me something interesting about history or some aspect of the music business, even though I wasn't involved at that time. I have always loved history and he was so well versed in the subject.

I have included Grant because he is another person who was so influential during the '40s, '50s, and '60s in promoting country and bluegrass music. He is one who should be remembered. And he was another very good person who died so very young. He was only 79.

CARL BELEW

Carl Belew was a farm boy raised in Oklahoma and Texas. Like so many others growing up, he started playing the guitar at a very early age. Carl had dreams of becoming a country music singer and would listen to the Grand Ole Opry and any radio station playing country music.

I met Carl Belew backstage at the Louisiana Hayride in 1958. He immediately introduced me to his wife, Kate, and his son, Bobby. Bobby was about six at that time, and my son Timmy was almost four. The first thing Kate did was give me their home address and invited Jimmy, Timmy, and me to come visit them. In those days, none of us had a home telephone. A telephone was a luxury. We either used the neighbor's or went to a pay phone if you wanted to call someone. You wanted to visit someone, drop by and you were always welcome at their home.

I liked Carl and Kate very much. They were very good, down-to-earth people. A week or so later, Jimmy, Timmy and I were riding around Shreveport and decided to visit them. They were living in a sparsely furnished, two-bedroom apartment in Shreveport. Kate stayed home with Bobby. I believe Carl was working side jobs as a pipefitter. One thing for sure, he had to work because the pay at the Hayride was only $32, and you can't support a family on that amount of money. Not even in those days.

Singers, Songwriters, and More

While we were visiting, Donnie Lytle (later known as Johnny Paycheck) and his buddy, Johnny Mathis (not THE Johnny Mathis but he is also a singer) showed up. They were good friends of Carl and Jimmy also knew them. They stayed around for a couple of hours and the guys were all laughing, talking and singing. This was the first time I met either of them. Kate and I just sat back and watched. Timmy and Bobby were off in another room playing. It was a fun-filled evening. We made sandwiches and iced tea for everyone and Kool Aide for the kids. We all had so much fun. We went back to visit Carl and Kate fairly often while we were all in Shreveport. Jimmy and I always stopped by the grocery and picked up bologna, bread, tomatoes, Kool Aide to take with us. Donnie and Johnny showed up regularly. They were always together. I often wonder what happened to Johnny after Donnie moved to Nashville and became famous.

Kate Belew

Visiting with Carl, Kate, and Bobby, you could tell they were a happy family. Carl and Kate had married when they were only 20 years of age. You could feel the love in the air when you were around them. Carl was a wonderful person. He was as honest as the day is long, very trustworthy. I always felt Carl was never fully appreciated for his talent as a songwriter or as a musician and singer despite the fact he had several records in the charts.

Before becoming a professional musician, Carl was a pipefitter. His father was also a pipefitter. With not much work for pipefitters in Salina, Oklahoma, both he and his father traveled around the

A flyer used by Decca Records to promote Carl and Jimmy.

country on various construction projects. Kate went with Carl. In fact, Carl's father was in Indiana working when Carl and Kate decided to get married there.

Carl's idol was Hank Williams, Sr. Carl had a physique like Hank, long and lanky. He was constantly singing around the house and wanted to become a professional. In the 1950s, he decided to pursue his music career. He found a job as a pipefitter in Riverside, California, and he and his family moved. Then, he heard about an amateur contest called "The Squeaking Beacon Show." He entered and he won! As luck would have it, he met Marvin Rainwater at the contest. This would lead the way to his path in the music business.

Marvin later introduced him to Bill McCall, the owner of Four Star Records and a publishing company. Bill was impressed with Carl's singing and songwriting and signed him to a contract. Once Carl signed his contract with Four Star, Patsy Cline, who was also on the Four Star label, recorded one of the songs he had written called, "I Can't Forget." Carl recorded a couple of rockabilly songs

Singers, Songwriters, and More

for Four Star, which led him to appear on two very popular radio shows, *Town Hall Party* and *The Cliffie Stone Show*. The appearances on these shows earned him enough recognition to propel him to other appearances in the area.

In early 1958, Carl moved to Shreveport and began appearing on the Louisiana Hayride. This is where I first met him. Jimmy and Carl seemed to like each other, and the kids enjoyed playing together even though Bobby was a couple of years older than Timmy. I definitely liked Kate. She was an extraordinary woman. Like her husband, she was a very down-to-earth and a solid-thinking person. We all became friends and spent time together while in Shreveport.

In February 1960, Jimmy was hired by Radio Station WWVA in Wheeling, West Virginia. We loaded up what little stuff we owned into a U-Haul trailer hooked up to the car and headed out to Wheeling—Paul Williams, Jimmy, Timmy, and me. Even though I was sad about leaving Shreveport, I had to do it. Unbeknownst to me, this move would change my life forever.

While we were moving to Wheeling, Carl, Kate, and Bobby were moving to Nashville. I lost touch with them and would not see Carl again until he dropped into my office one day on 16th Avenue South. I was very happy to see him. During the time I had my office on either 16th or 17th Avenue South, Carl would occasionally stop by when he was on the Avenue. I never saw Kate or Bobby again.

Nashville was a good move for Carl. He knew Shelby Singleton, who was an A&R man (Artists and Repertoire: a person sent out by the recording companies "in the day" to find new talent). Shelby's wife, Margie, was a star on the Louisiana Hayride. We were all good friends back then. Interestingly, Margie and I are friends on Facebook today, and we sometimes talk about the old days. Shelby was with Mercury Records at that time and doing quite well for himself in Nashville.

Carl signed a contract with Decca Records and cut a song he had written entitled, "Am I That Easy to Forget." Carl's recording reached No. 8 on the charts, and he was elated. His recording was covered by Skeeter Davis, Debbie Reynolds, Engelbert Humperdink, Jim Reeves, and many others. He then recorded "Too Much to Lose" for Decca, and it reached No. 8 on the charts. But his songwriting was gaining more popularity than his recordings. Owen Bradley, who was in charge of the Nashville office for Decca Records, recorded Johnnie and Jack's version of a song written by Carl entitled, "Stop the World and Let Me Off." At the same time, Andy Williams, who was very popular at that time in pop music, recorded "Lonely Street." Carl was on his way as a well-known songwriter.

Interestingly, in those days (and it probably still happens today), A&R men and artists negotiated deals with songwriters. The A&E guys or artists would receive a share of the songwriting credit if they got a song published, got it recorded, or recorded it themselves. This happened all the time. I have always heard that Carl sold a share of "Stop the World" for $100. It was hard times, and $100 was a lot of money. I do know that W.S. Stevenson's name is on several of Carl's hit songs as a co-writer. W.S. Stevenson was the pen name for Bill McCall (remember Four Star Records). Shelby Singleton's name is listed as co-writer on "Am I That Easy To Forget."

In 1966, after leaving Jimmy, I met a girl by the name of Sue Brewer. She invited me to a party at her house that night on 17th

Singers, Songwriters, and More

Avenue South, up the street from RCA Victor Studios. I went and had been sitting on the sofa for about 15 minutes when Carl Belew and Faron Young walked into the room. They saw me and came right over. Carl said, "What are you doing here, Barbara?" I told him, "Sue invited me to the party." Carl and Faron both said at almost the same time, "You don't belong here." And they promptly walked me out. The next day, Carl stopped by the office to make sure I was OK. I never did find out why they didn't want me there.

I don't remember the last time I saw Carl, but I am pretty sure it was about the same time I closed my office on 17th Avenue South in 1967. When I started writing this book, I wanted to include Carl simply because I knew what a very difficult time he and his family had in Shreveport and Nashville. I liked the Belew family very much. They were good, good people. I researched and found them in Salina, Oklahoma. Carl and Kate were both deceased. Their son, Bobby, was a minister at Lakeview Baptist Church in Salina.

Carl Belew passed away at the young age of 59 from cancer. He is buried at Ross Mayer Cemetery in Salina, as are his wife, Kate, who passed away at the age of 71, and their son, Bobby. Bobby was only 67 years of age when he passed in 2020. I called Bobby several times and he never returned my call. He died during the pandemic.

Carl, Kate, and Bobby Belew were a wonderful, God loving family, all of whom died too young. Carl was tremendously talented and should not be forgotten in the world of music. He deserves a place in the Songwriter's Hall of Fame, at the very least. A young God loving family gone in their prime.

Note: I looked through all of my pictures and didn't have any of the family. I tried to get some but didn't find anything.

WILMA LEE & STONEY COOPER, JERRY JOHNSON COLMUS, and PEGGY LEARY

The Leary Family: Jake and Lola. Leary, Jerry, Smiley Cooper as he was known then, Wilma Lee and Peggy Gayle

The beginning of my friendship with Jerry Johnson was in 1953 when she was appearing as a bass fiddle player for Roy Acuff on the Grand Ole Opry. At the time, she was married to Johnny Johnson who played guitar for Hank Snow. Even though I was only 17 years old, Jerry and I hit it off immediately. Of course, she didn't know until many years later that I was only 17 when we first met.

Jerry took me under her wing, and I would trail along with her. If Jimmy was waiting to play with Bill Monroe and Jerry was going to Mom's Place (aka Tootsie's), I went with her. We had so much fun.

Singers, Songwriters, and More

We laughed, talked about guys, and someone would have thought we were both teenagers, but Jerry was older and married. I also liked Johnny and thought he was a terrific guy. Jerry was beautiful, with her blonde hair and slim build. It wasn't long before she introduced me to Wilma Lee, her sister (really spelled, "Leigh") and Stoney Cooper, her husband. The three of us became pals quickly, (Wilma Lee, Jerry, and me.)

Jerry Johnson Columus and Peggy Leary

In March, 1954, Jimmy Martin left Bill Monroe and we headed to Middletown, Ohio. By then, I was pregnant with our son, Timmy. Leaving Nashville meant that I would not get to see my friends, Wilma Lee and Jerry. But on each trip back to Nashville, including when Timmy was born in August 1954, I would see Jerry and Wilma Lee. Nothing had changed. Jerry continued working the Grand Ole Opry with Roy Acuff and Johnny Johnson was with Hank Snow.

Wilma Lee & Stoney Cooper and the Clinch Mountain Clan joined the Grand Ole Opry in 1957. I was so proud for them. At the time, Jimmy and I were still in Detroit. He was with WJR, The Casey Clark Barndance, and CKLW-TV. I don't remember Wilma Lee

The People and The Music—Country and Bluegrass that is!

& Stoney appearing at The Barndance in Detroit or at the Louisiana Hayride when we were there. I only saw them whenever we went to Nashville.

My mother, Willowdeen Farmer Gibson, saw Wilma Lee and Jerry often. Mother and Wilma Lee loved each other. At one time, mother had a restaurant on Porter Road close to where Wilma Lee lived, and she and Jerry would stop by from time to time. Mother kept me informed about how and what they were doing.

When Jimmy and I moved to Wheeling, West Virginia in 1960 and I started working for Gene Johnson, I saw Wilma Lee & Stoney frequently. They were fan favorites of the audience at the WWVA Jamboree. Of course, they were originally from West Virginia. Wilma Lee and her two sisters, Jerry and Peggy, were all part of the Leary Family, a gospel group, known far and wide in the West Virginia area.

Wilma Lee, Stoney, Jimmy, and I had some great times together in Wheeling. We always went to the horse races when they were in town. We'd grab something to eat, and just sit and gab. Wilma Lee actually taught me about horse racing and betting after seeing me throw tickets away that were winners. She teased me about this forever.

After Jimmy and I moved to Nashville in 1962, I didn't see Wilma Lee, Jerry, or Peggy as often. I was very involved in the booking business and didn't have time for anything. If I wasn't on the road with Jimmy, I was working 12-hour days. I did talk to them on the phone every few weeks or so. By now, Wilma Lee & Stoney were thoroughly entrenched at the Grand Ole Opry and working the road frequently. She was playing bass with Bill Carlisle, Cousin Jody, and others at the Opry. Jerry and Johnny were divorced, and Peggy was

Singers, Songwriters, and More

singing in New Jersey. Everything had changed.

In September 1966, I left Jimmy Martin for the final time. After a couple of months living in Nashville, Jerry asked me to come and live with her. She would watch Lisa and Buddy while I worked. I was working in the Data Processing Department at the Metropolitan Government of Nashville and three nights a week as a bartender at the Holiday Inn on James Robertson Parkway. Jerry was still working the Opry with cousin Jody and Bill Carlisle.

Living with Jerry meant also living with Peggy, her sister. Peggy was a tiny little lady measuring all of 4'11" and didn't weigh a 100 pounds. But she was feisty, and she would tell a person off too quick to talk about it

She loved to fish, was a very good singer (worked some with Jimmy Martin), and she could do about anything. With me, Lisa, and Buddy living there, bedrooms were in short supply. Peggy decided she was going to add a do-it-yourself bedroom. And she did. She built it herself.

Jerry had a boyfriend that Peggy and I both despised. Between the two of us, we were on him every day. He would say something (he was a big liar), and Peggy and I would challenge him. We didn't let up! Wilma Lee came over every couple of days and she joined us in the harassing in her own inimitable style. Sarah Summey (Cousin Jody's wife--his real name was James Clemore Summey), was another partner in crime, and she did not like Dave at all. The four of us were unrelenting. It took us a while, but Jerry finally saw what he was doing and he was gone, never to return.

Then around 1990, my girlfriend, Jill Hulin, in Fort Lauderdale, invited my husband and me to a Christmas party. She wanted to introduce us to her new boyfriend. The minute I walked in, I saw Dave (I'm not going to use his last name). I couldn't believe it. He was Jill's new boyfriend. He saw me and tried to get out of my line of vision. I took Jill aside and told her what I knew about him and that I was going to confront him. When I did, he tried his best to deny he knew me. I told him, "You are still a lying thief." My husband was trying to get me to shut up, but I wouldn't. He was going to go out the door, and did. Once again, never to return. Jill was so happy that I confronted him, she made White Russians and we celebrated. I called Wilma Lee and Jerry and told them and how I confronted him. They got the biggest kick out of that.

Living in Florida meant I didn't see Wilma Lee and Jerry that often. But we were always in touch by phone. I would call them from work because I had an 800 number, and we could call each other free. I would go to the shows whenever they were playing close by, in Florida. Their houses were always the first places I visited in Nashville. So we continued to keep up over the years.

One of the funniest things happened was when Peggy drove her Checkers Taxicab to Fort Lauderdale. I have pictures of it parked in front of my house on 46th Avenue. Michelle (my granddaughter, whom I raised) was about four years old at the time. She was mesmerized by the taxi. She had never ridden in one and was jumping up and down to do so. Peggy put her in the backseat and just rode around the neighborhood. They stayed a week with me, and we took them everywhere.

My son, Ray Martin, played music on the cruise ship, The Carnival (Carnival only had one ship at that time). He had a band called, "The Martin Brothers." This was before COVID when a pas-

Singers, Songwriters, and More

senger or member of the crew could have guests onboard. Ray made all the arrangments for us to go onboard with Jerry and Peggy. On Saturday we took them down to the Port of Miami. Ray took us all on board and showed Jerry and Peggy the entire ship, with Michelle making every step with Aunt Jerry and Aunt Peggy.

We had lunch on board and enjoyed a wonderful day. They were thrilled and loved the ship. They had never been onboard a ship until then. I had never been on a ship or even thought about one, either, until we moved to Miami and Timmy and Ray started working on them. I have fabulous pictures from that time.

There were so many, many good times in both Nashville and Florida. When Wilma Lee, Jerry, Peggy, Sarah, and I were all together, it was nothing but laughter. It was the same when Jerry and I were together. We could always think of things to do.

Like the time, Jerry and I were working as waitresses at the Ramada Inn on James Robertson Parkway. We made good money, but the manager was a pure bitch. Neither of us liked her. Jerry waited on Charlie Pride and his wife. Charlie gave Jerry a $20 tip, which was unheard of. We were thrilled. The next day as we were getting ready to go to work, Jerry said, "Let's leave early and go out to the bar in West Nashville where Tommy Kozur is playing music." Tommy was a friend of ours from Harrisburg, Pennsylvania, and a terrific singer. Jerry got up to play music, and we were having the best time. I looked at my watch, pointed to the time, and said, "Time to go to work." She looked back at me and said, "Let's don't go." I said, "OK." She kept playing music and I kept enjoying it. We went back the next day and got our paychecks. So much for waitressing at the Ramada. We blew that gig!

The People and The Music—Country and Bluegrass that is!

Wilma Lee, Jerry Johnson, Sarah Summy, Me and Peggy Gayle

Every once in a while, Wilma Lee played a show with Jimmy Martin. She knew Lisa and Buddy (my children) traveled with Jimmy, and it gave me an opportunity to see them. They lived with Jimmy, and he wouldn't let me near either of them. I sneaked around, disguised myself, sat in front of the school, or did whatever I had to do to see my kids. It wasn't that I was a bad person. He just had political power, and in Tennessee that counts. So Wilma Lee called me, told me where the show was going to be, and I went. I disguised myself so neither Jimmy nor the kids knew me. I didn't want to cause trouble; I just wanted to see my kids. She and I got together and laughed like crazy after one of our "excursions" because I stood right next to Jimmy and he didn't know me as a blonde or redhead or whatever I was that day. I dressed like a bag lady, or sometimes a hippie. It was different each time. We had more fun on those excursions. But Jerry and I did the same thing to catch lying boyfriends.

In October 1979, Jerry called me and said that Peggy was dying. I cried all day and made plans to come to Nashville to see her before she passed. I flew up, spent two days at Jerry's house, and flew back to Fort Lauderdale. On October 24 Peggy passed, and once again I flew to Nashville for her funeral. Losing Peggy was horrible for Wilma Lee, Jerry, Sarah (Summey), and me.

After Peggy's funeral at Woodlawn on Thompson Lane, Jerry, Wilma Lee, Carol Lee and her family, and I went to Shoney's for lunch. The first person I saw when we walked in was Doyle Wilburn. He was sitting with a group of people (none of whom any of us knew), got up, and immediately came over, hugged me, and sat down with us and talked for a while. I thought Doyle looked so bad. He was clean, but unshaven and sort of ragged looking. When he returned to his table, it didn't enter my mind that this would be the last time I saw my friend alive. My heart ached for him. I don't know why

Following Peggy's funeral, I returned to Florida. Jerry started traveling some with Wilma Lee and I would see them occasionally in Florida, but more often in Nashville. Every time I came to Nashville, I spent a lot of my time with Jerry. Wilma Lee would come over. By now, Sarah Summey and Cousin Jody were divorced, and Sarah had a boyfriend who lived in Old Hickory. She spent quite a bit of time with him. Jerry and I would pop in to visit her at Bill's house when I was in Nashville. We liked to surprise her, so we didn't call. We just went.

The People and The Music—Country and Bluegrass that is!

The Music

In the 1930s, Wilma Lee, Jerry, Peggy, and their parents had a gospel group called "The Leary Family" in West Virginia. Wilma Lee was the first girl born, and she started singing with her parents when she was five years old. As Jerry and Peggy were born and became old enough, they, in turn, would join the group.

Stoney Cooper was a long, lanky, good-looking man who played the fiddle. One could easily compare him to Clark Gable. He had jet black hair and a mustache. He started working for the Leary Family in the late 1930s and by 1940, he and Wilma Lee married. Stoney came to my office in the Hawley Building starting around 1960. Whenever he was in Wheeling for the Jamboree, the girls at

Unknown, Howdy Foster, Jimmy Riddle, Unknown, Johnny Johnson, Jerry Johnson, Roy Acuff, Unknown, and Bashful Brother Oswald

Singers, Songwriters, and More

WWVA would swoon. We all thought he was the handsomest entertainer to appear at the Jamboree. And he was!

By early 1940, Stoney and Wilma Lee and Jerry were ready to leave the family group. Wilma Lee and Stoney would go out on their own, and Jerry would go to Nashville. Jerry played the bass and felt like she could get a job on the Grand Ole Opry.

Jerry was hired by Roy Acuff and played bass for him many years. She was the first female country singer to travel overseas for the U.S.O. after World War II. She would go on to travel to many other countries with Roy and the U.S.O. during the time she worked withim.

After leaving Roy Acuff, Jerry played bass for Bill Carlisle and Cousin Jody. She worked with each of them for many years. She was working with Cousin Jody when she retired from playing professional music in the early 1970s.

Peggy Gayle Leary, the youngest sister of Wilma Lee and Jerry, was a 4'11" ball of fire. She was extremely talented and cute as a button, and feisty as a banty rooster. She played guitar and sang her little head off. She played quite a few shows with Jimmy Martin. Peggy never earned as much recognition as her sisters, Wilma Lee and Jerry, but she was not a jealous or vindictive person the way some sisters are. She was herself no matter where she was or in whose company. The three sisters were very supportive of each other in anything they did.

The People and The Music—Country and Bluegrass that is!

The End of the Musical Dynasty

Peggy Gayle Leary was sickly for many years, suffering from Non-Hodgkins Lymphoma. She was the first of the Leary sisters to die, and her passing created a very big void in all of our lives. She had lived with Jerry for many years. I think the four of us (five if you count Sarah Summey) could not have been any closer if we were all sisters, calling each other often, and writing letters. When Peggy passed, Jerry and Wilma Lee became almost inseparable. Peggy was interred next to Stoney at Woodlawn Cemetery on Thompson Lane in Nashville.

After Peggy's death, I saw Wilma Lee and Jerry whenever Wilma Lee appeared in Florida or I was in Nashville. The last time I saw them was in West Palm Beach, Florida. This was sometime in the mid-1990s. It was a package show with Kitty Wells and Johnnie Wright, Little Jimmy Dickens, Freddy Hart, Jan Howard, Connie Smith, Jeanne Pruitt, and Wilma Lee. Jerry rode along with Wilma Lee in her camper and their dogs. Chuck (my husband) hung out with Wilma Lee and Jerry all day until the show ended that night. I was busy a lot of the time seeing my other friends on the tour, too. Connie was dating Marty Stuart, and she was on Cloud 9. I would talk to each of them, run back and see Jerry, Wilma Leigh, and Chuck, and then return to talk to someone else. This was all so much fun. This was the last time I saw Jerry, alive or dead. We kept in touch with each other by phone, and Mother often talked to Wilma Lee. If Mother moved or changed her phone number, Wilma Lee would call me and ask about her.

Things started getting strange after Peggy died. I never noticed it until one day Wilma Lee called me and said Jerry had passed away.

I asked her when she died and when and where was her funeral. She told me that Jerry had been laid to rest next to Stoney and Peggy at Woodlawn. I was upset that I didn't get to see her before she was buried. Wilma Lee told me that was what Jerry wanted. No notice and no funeral. This didn't make sense to me. Jerry and I had talked about having big funerals several times over the years. Nor did it make sense when I found out that Jerry's bass fiddle, the same one she had played with Roy Acuff, was sold and advertised as being her bass years after both Jerry and Wilma Lee had passed. Geraldine (Jerry) Leary Johnson Colmus passed away on October 10, 1998, not long after I had seen her in West Palm Beach.

I continued to keep in touch with Wilma Lee long after Jerry died. I saw her several times in Florida. I was a paralegal and Wilma Lee would call me whenever she had a legal question. One of those times was about property she purchased many years before in central Florida. She had questions concerning the property and wanted me to do some investigating. She sent me all the information, and I looked into it. The property had all kinds of rights-of-way on it, and I didn't think it was very valuable. I consulted with an attorney friend of mine who worked in real estate, and she agreed. I called and told her what I had found out and returned all the papers to her. I don't know what she ever did with the property.

The last time Mother and I went to see Wilma Lee, she lived at 100 Rustic Court in Donelson. I had spoken to Wilma Lee on the phone, and she wanted me to bring Mother to see her. Mother and I walked in, and Wilma Lee was sitting on the sofa. She had a plate of donuts and other sweets she was eating. I was appalled at the condition of the house. There were cats everywhere, and the stench was horrible. I never knew Wilma Lee to own a cat. She always owned and loved dogs. She often loaded her Cadillac up with dog food and distributed it herself to the animal shelters. Mother and I just looked at each other. The woman taking care of Wilma Lee never showed her face to us after letting us in the house. Wilma Lee offered us a donut, but neither of us took it. Wilma Lee was mentally sharp as a tack. She didn't appear to be in any distress. She was very happy that Mother and I were there. We stayed with her about two hours, laughing and talking and hugging. It would be the last time either of us would see her again. But, the first thing Mother and I said to each other when we got in the car was, "Let's go home and take a bath."

Where is Wilma Lee?

In writing this chapter about Wilma Lee, Jerry, and Peggy, a mystery arose. Wilma Lee suffered a stroke on stage at the Grand Ole Opry on February 24, 2001. The next morning when Wilma Lee woke up in ICU, Carol was there with Ed Gregory who had a Power of Attorney for Wilma Lee to sign. Jerry Strobel was also there and told Wilma Lee she did not have to sign the papers.

Immediately and, while still in the hospital, Wilma Lee began having problems with her only daughter, Carol Lee. In fact, she sent a letter to all the members of the Opry explaining what happened with her daughter. In case it is ever needed, I have a copy of that letter. It was definitely hand-written by Wilma Lee.

Sometime after that, a woman by the name of Margaret Akins was introduced to Wilma Lee by Billy Pack, her last banjo player. Margaret Akins became Wilma Lee's caretaker. Margaret Akins is supposedly an attorney. Why would an attorney be a caretaker for

Singers, Songwriters, and More

Margaret Akins and Wilma Lee Cooper

an invalid person, unless it is to inherit everything the patient owns? Margaret Akins opened the door for Mother and me when we visited Wilma Lee.

Years prior to her death, Wilma Lee purchased four cemetery plots at Woodlawn Cemetery on Thompson Lane in Nashville. She had intended for her two sisters, her husband, and herself to be buried there. Stoney Cooper, Peggy Gayle, and Jerry are all three buried in their plots. Wilma Lee Cooper's plot is vacant. The headstone is there, but the date of death is not. Woodlawn says there is not a body in the grave. If she died on September 13, 2011, as reported to the Grand Ole Opry in a phone call by Margaret Akins, where is she buried? And, if she really died, why hasn't her will been probated?

I called the Clerk of the Probate Court in both Cumberland County (Crossville, TN where she owns property), and the Davidson County Probate Clerk (where she also owns property), and her will has not been probated. The property at 100 Rustic Court is still in her name, is vacant, and Margaret Akins' name is now listed as a co-owner of the property.

Wilma Lee also owned property in Crossville, Tennessee. Following her death in 2011, the name of Michael Frazier was added as a person responsible for the payment of the taxes on the property which is located at 9548 Cherokee in Crossville, TN. His name stayed on the rolls from 2012 until 2014. However, in 2013 Wilma Lee's name disappeared from the tax rolls. The name(s) of the payor of the taxes for the property have been changed several times since that time. Now, suddenly, it is in the hands of the Bank of Putnam County to pay the taxes. How is this all being done when no will has been probated? Who is responsible for all the changes? Are they using a Power of Attorney (POA)? If so, this would be illegal since a POA ends when a person dies.

I also found out the bass fiddle belonging to Jerry Johnson Colmus, the one she played when she worked with Roy Acuff, was sold long after her death. And Wilma Lee's guitar was sold long after her death. There was also an auction in Gallatin to sell Wilma Lee's personal items. They advertised more would be coming, but that never happened. Who is doing all this and how do they have the authority? We know it is not Wilma Lee's family or Peggy Gayle's family. Jerry never had children, but I do know that she had all of her belongings willed to her nephew, Peggy Gayle's son, Bobby.

I met with Bruce McGuire, a long-time friend of Wilma Lee and Jerry, and he gave me an interesting case from the Court of Appeals of Tennessee, Middle Section, at Nashville and styled:

Singers, Songwriters, and More

Margaret AKINS vs. Joe EDMONDSON, et al, No M2004-01232-COA-R3-CV, decided on June 12, 2006, before Wilma Lee died.

This is a very interesting case since Margaret Akins is the very same person who was taking care of Wilma Leigh Cooper until her death. The subject case involves Josephine Notgrass, a school teacher, retired, widowed and with no children, but with lots of assets. Margaret Akins sued the accounting firm she had engaged for Mrs. Notgrass to render professional services, including tax services and estate planning.

Wilma Lee and Bruce McGuire

Mrs. Notgrass died, and Margaret Akins was unable to take possession and obtain a deed for a farm Mrs. Notgrass supposedly gave her. She sued to get her inheritance. The court decided against her.

To reiterate: This same thing happened to Wilma Leigh Cooper's property. Margaret Akins' name suddenly appeared as a joint owner of Wilma Lee's property located at 100 Rustic Court in Nashville. For the property she owned at 9548 Cherokee Court in Crossville, TN, the name of Michael Frazier was added as a person to pay the taxes in 2012. (Wilma Lee died in 2011.) Who was he and where did he come from? Both Michael's name and Wilma Lee's name were removed in 2014. In 2014, the payor was Edward Caples and Sandra J. Caples, Etux. How was all this renaming of the payor of taxes on her property accomplished?

Another question: How is Jerry Johnson Colmus' and Wilma Lee's property being sold without probating her will? If they are using a Power of Attorney, this would be illegal because it becomes null and void when a person dies. Whomever is accepting this POA (if that is the case), would be co-conspirators in the scam. Who is selling off their property and with what authority?

We also know that Jerry, Peggy, and Stoney are buried in their graves at Woodlawn Cemetery. Wilma Lee is not buried there. The only person who advised the Grand Ole Opry Wilma Lee had passed away was Margaret Akins. And, as of now, she is the only person that knows where Wilma Lee is buried, if she is buried.

I obtained a Verification of Death Facts from the Tennessee Department of Health, Bureau of Vital Records, saying she was cremated by the Littlebrook Cremation Company, in Maryville, TN. Why? Who authorized it? Why not put her body in the grave she had owned for years and where she wanted to be buried? Why the secrecy? It certainly wasn't because of the costs; she had plenty of money.

My final question is, "Where are her ashes?"

Regardless, Wilma Lee Cooper was a beautiful lady and…she was a lady. She didn't deserve the greed or the treatment she received at the end of her life. She deserves to be respected, honored, and remembered. I loved her dearly and miss her terribly. She was inducted into the IBMA Bluegrass Hall of Fame in 2023, and she deserves to be in the Country Music Hall of Fame, also. Wilma Lee Cooper was a lifelong pioneer of the music.

GINGER BOATWRIGHT

Let me introduce you to a lady who is a pioneer in the field of bluegrass and acoustic country music, Ginger Hammond Boatwright. She is not only a pioneer, but a lady who isn't or wasn't afraid to take chances.

Ginger Hammond was born into the field of bluegrass music. Her father, Hap Hammond, and her mother, Hilton Vice, had a radio show in Columbus, Mississippi. Their show was called "Bill and Kate." It ended when Hap joined the Navy and was sent to Guadalcanal. Her mother was known around the state as being a very fine singer. Naturally, Ginger learned to sing from her mother and sang on the radio with her when she was just a toddler.

Hap called his band "The Magic City Ramblers." They were well-known in Alabama. Her mother, who played bass in the band, wanted Ginger to be a concert pianist. Ginger's mother found a top notch piano teacher and sent her to Birmingham Southern College to take piano lessons. Ginger liked playing piano, but she desperately wanted to play guitar. She was in college before she finally chose to pick up the guitar and learn to play.

Ginger attended the University of Alabama at Birmingham, and it was there she met Grant Boatwright at one of his concerts. Grant noticed Ginger immediately in the audience and invited her onstage with him. Amazingly, that invitation led to a partnership with Grant. It wasn't long before they were married.

In 1969, Ginger was diagnosed with cervical cancer. The diagnosis was overwhelming for a 25-year-old. She was forced to quit the University of Alabama for treatment of the cancer. The doctors told her she had three weeks to live. Ginger's first thought was, "if I am going to die, I want to die playing music." She quit school and concentrated on her music and treatments. Fortunately today, after suffering not just one, but two bouts of cancer, she is cancer free and still playing music. The treatment or the music (or both) worked.

During the time she was recuperating, Ginger played music every day. She and Grant, her husband, talked about hiring a third person to round out their act. They decided to hire Dale Whitcomb, Ginger's cousin, to form a trio. They called themselves, "Red, White & Blue(grass)." GRC asked her to record as a single. Her answer could be heard from the rooftops, "Yes." In 1972, she released, "The Lovin's Over" on GRC while still a part of Red, White & Blue(grass). Everywhere they appeared, she was asked to sing it and always received an encore.

Ginger and Grant heard someone at Mulenbrink's Saloon at Underground Atlanta was looking for a band. They went to see the owner and were hired immediately. Mulenbrink's held 600 people. Ginger requested—and the request was granted—to put a fence up behind the stage. They packed 900 people in a night, so Ginger wanted a fence behind the stage. Ginger's daughter, Danae, was with her every night. She kept Danae backstage with the guitar cases during the show. Danae could play with her baby dolls in a safe area. Then somebody saw Danae backstage and called Child Welfare on

Singers, Songwriters, and More

Ginger. Child Welfare came in and talked to Danae. Following their conversation with the child, they told Ginger, "You are not doing anything wrong. This kid is having a ball."

Ginger met L.J. Leach, who would care for Danae. She introduced L.J. to Danae and Danae liked her. After introductions, Ginger told L.J. if Danae needed anything to get it for her. When Ginger went back on stage, Danae held her hand up and said to L.J., "I would like a Shirley Temple." Danae caught on quickly, and L.J. became one of Ginger's best friends.

Ginger and Grant Boatwright moved to Nashville from Atlanta after appearing at Mulenbrink's Saloon, Underground Atlanta for 18 months. They were tired. Their first record on GRC was hitting the charts, and they were Nashville bound to start a new chapter in their lives.

Red, White & Blue(grass) was popular with young and old folks alike. Their harmony was amazing. The critics liked the group and referred to them as "the most eclectic bluegrass singers of their time," "new grass," and "pretty far out for a bluegrass band." They saw it as, "old grass with a twist." The critics also called them "young bluegrass green horns" when their first album was released in 1972. This album featured Grant Boatwright on guitar, Ginger Boatwright, Dave Sebolt, and Dale Whitcomb.

Ginger and Grant started talking to Norman Blake about becoming a member of Red, White and Blue(grass). Norman recorded their second album, *Pickin Up*, with Ginger and Grant in 1972, and it was released the same year. The group was extremely successful outside the normal bluegrass circles, and they were nominated for a Grammy for their initial album. This same year, GRC asked Ginger to record as a solo artist. She did and released, *The Lovin's Over.*

The People and The Music—Country and Bluegrass that is!

Red, White and Blue(grass) were booked by an agency called Stone County, out of Denver. Keith Case was their agent. Lance LeRoy, who later became well-known in the bluegrass music circles and was inducted into the International Bluegrass Music Association Hall of Fame, worked with Keith. The two of them were keeping Red, White and Blue(grass) super busy, working 208 days a year on the road. Working so much and being gone from home was taking a toll on every member of the band, Ginger included.

Red, White and Blue(grass) decided they were leaving GRC despite their success on the label. They signed with Mercury and their next album, *Red, White & Blue(grass) & Company,* would be released on the Mercury label in 1977. By the time they went to Mercury, Dave Sebolt had left the group. Ginger added Ed Barnett on bass and Michael Barnett on drums. Following its release, dissention became a daily thing among the group. They finally disbanded in 1979. Each to go their own way.

By this time, it wasn't unusual for bluegrass bands to feature drums. My son, Timmy (Jimmy Martin, Jr.) started playing a snare drum with Jimmy when he was only six years old. I still have the red vest I made for him to wear on stage with his dad and many pictures of him wearing it. I made all the vests worn by the Sunny Mountain Boys.

In looking at the photos of Red, White and Blue(grass), I noticed that Ginger never had an instrument in her hands. She was usually photographed in the back or to the side of the band. When I asked her about it, she said the group, including Grant, didn't think she played guitar "good enough." The minute they told her that, she decided then and there she was going to start doing her own thing.

Singers, Songwriters, and More

Ginger is a progressive thinker, always thinking of ways to improve. The Pickin' Parlor came up for sale. She decided to become a part of it and financed the purchase of the Pickin' Parlor located on Second Avenue in Nashville. It was another place for musicians to gather and jam, like The Station Inn and The Dusty Road Tavern. Downtown, The Pickin Parlor was very popular with musicians and tourists alike. I asked Ginger why her name wasn't on the purchase, and she said, "I was a woman and the guys didn't think it would be good to have a woman as an owner. I became a silent partner because my money purchased it."

Regardless of whether her name was on the deed, she was an integral part of the establishment. Half of the Pickin Parlor was a store where instruments were bought, sold, and traded. Norman Blake was one of the first salesmen at the store. The other half of the Pickin Parlor was a food, drink, and jamming area. Ginger liked to go in and work the counter in the food area when she was in town and available. She jammed with the musicians, made sandwiches, and even invented a new type of sandwich. She found a fancy bread through Weight Watchers. She used the bread because it was good and different, buttered it on both sides like a grilled cheese sandwich, put a slice of Mozzarella Cheese on each side, spread a little pizza sauce over that and put four pepperoni slices on top of that. She grilled it, and the customers went crazy. She called her sandwich the "Grilled Chizza": a mini-pizza to be held in your hands and eaten, cheap, and also filling.

Red, White and Blue(grass) were becoming quite successful, so they decided to sell their part of Pickin Parlor to Randy Wood, the instrument maker, in 1980. He decided he didn't want a partner, silent or otherwise, and he reimbursed Ginger for her investment.

The People and The Music—Country and Bluegrass that is!

At or about the same time and after the breakup of Red, White & Blue(grass), Grant and Ginger were divorced and went their separate ways. Unlike most divorced couples, Grant and Ginger remained friends until Grant's death on January 17, 2013. At Grant's request, Ginger sang at his funeral.

Ginger decided to form an all-girl band known as the Bushwhackers. The Bushwhackers released one album in 1980 featuring Susie Monick on banjo, April Barrows on bass, Ingrid Herman Reese on fiddle and guitar, and Ginger on guitar. Despite the group's popularity on the college circuit and their record being a hit wherever they appeared, they broke up in 1981. Ginger decided it was time to concentrate on her music.

Ginger and a couple of partners re-purchased the Pickin' Parlor in 1980. They were still working with the Bushwackers at the time. Ginger and her partners hired Riders In The Sky to appear on Wednesday nights, Guy Clark on Thursday nights, and she and her band, Red, White and Blue appeared on weekends. A couple of times, she and the Bushwackers made an appearance.

In 1981, Ginger teamed up with Doug Dillard. Doug was well-known throughout country and bluegrass music. He was a master banjo player, and he and his brother, Rodney, teamed up to form a group called "The Dillards" when they were young. Before branching out on his own, The Dillards appeared on *The Andy Griffin Show*, the *Judy Garland* and *Tennessee Ernie Ford Shows*, and many other TV and Radio Shows around California.

Doug played banjo on Glen Campbell's hit recording of "Gentle On My Mind" in 1969. The song was written by John Hartford. Ginger had known John Hartford for many years before joining

Singers, Songwriters, and More

Ginger Boatwright and Doug Dillard

Doug and his band.

Ginger and Doug not only became full partners in music, but in real life. They were compatible both on and off the stage. Ginger had an accounting background, and it was decided that she would handle the money and do the books after they came up short two or three times. Doug could depend on her to keep the show running and the books straight. They recorded an album together in 1981 titled *Heartbreak Hotel*. The album was nominated for a Grammy, her second nomination.

When Doug launched the Doug Dillard Band in 1981, it was only natural Ginger became a part of that group. Watching some of the old TV appearances, Doug looks over at Ginger with pure love. In all the old shows I watched, every time he looked at Ginger, he had the same smitten look on his face. Unlike Red, White & Blue(grass), Doug wanted and liked having Ginger play guitar. He also had her fronting the shows.

One of Ginger's favorite memories with the Doug Dillard Band was a *Nashville Now* show on TNN. They had performed on the show several times previously. Ralph Emery was a person who like to pull pranks on people. This particular show Ralph had Billy Hunter, who was the audio engineer, turn off Ginger's microphone. Ginger noticed it and used Doug's mike for the show. Ralph came up to her after the show and said, "Those are nice shoes, Ginger." Ginger then said to Ralph, "Did you notice they are open toed, Ralph?" Ralph was completely flustered and didn't say anything else. Ginger then received a call from Cheryl White who said, "I can't believe you called Ralph "a toad." Ginger explained why. Cheryl told Ginger later she watched the show again just to make sure Ginger had called Ralph a toad.

The Doug Dillard Band was booked for a show in Alaska in 1984. This would be their first appearance in the state. Everyone in the band, including Ginger, loved Alaska. Doug didn't like it and just wanted to go home. They would not return to Alaska until the 1990s.

Ginger recorded *Fertile Ground* with the Doug Dillard Band backing her in 1991. It was released on Flying Fish Records. The album would become one of her biggest hits and was highly acclaimed. Ginger was also named as one of the 50 top female vocalists for her work on the Red White & Blue(grass) album of *Pickin' Up*, by *The Bluegrass Situation*.

Ginger and Doug began to have some disagreements at home. It was nothing to do with their music. They continued to love each other and loved to play together, but their personal relationship had come to an end. Ginger would continue to front Doug's show and handle the finances even though they were ending their personal relationship. She trusted Doug and he trusted her.

In 1991, Ginger recorded her first solo CD, *Fertile Ground*, with Doug Dillard backing her all the way. At the time this album was released, rumor had it from the reviews that Ginger "could be huge in the country market" like Loretta Lynn, Barbara Mandrell, or Tammy Wynette. But instead of focusing on the country market, she was totally immersed in the field of bluegrass music. She remained with Doug for 33 years, fronting his band and handling his finances, and was nominated for a Grammy Award with the Doug Dillard Band's *Heartbreak Hotel* album.

The Doug Dillard Band returned to play the Hunted Creek Festival in Alaska near Chugiak in 1991, 1992, and 1993. The Festival was a turning point in Ginger's life. It was there she met a man by the name of C.C. "Buck" Kuhn at the show in 1993. He was in the audience when she came on, fronting the show for Doug Dillard and the band. He saw Ginger, looked at his companion, and said, "I am going to marry that woman."

After meeting Buck, she told him she wanted to take the band salmon fishing. Buck was a bush pilot and owned several planes. He told her he would take them in his plane. Buck told them that three of them could go in the plane. The next day, Buck came to get them. Ginger said to Doug, "Come on, Douglas let's go." Buck then spoke up and said, "The plane only holds two people." Ginger thought, "Um, yesterday it held four people, today only two people. What's going on?" Ginger went with Buck. He took her flying, landed out in the bush on a sand bar, helped her cross the sand dunes because she was so sick, took her salmon fishing, and she caught a big Salmon King fish. She said she didn't want the fish, so walked out into the

The People and The Music—Country and Bluegrass that is!

water, got the fish swimming again, and let it go. Buck didn't want to let it go; he wanted to take it home, clean it, and eat it. But he let it go because that's what Ginger wanted.

All the time she and Buck were flying around, Ginger was suffering severe headaches. She didn't mention it to Buck, but she could barely hold her head up. She later found out that she had an undiagnosed brain tumor. When they got back to the plane and were buckled in, Buck said, "Can I ask you something?" Ginger said, "Shoot Luke." Buck then asked if he could kiss her. Ginger said she looked at him like, "What are you doing?" Then she told him, "Yes," and Buck gave her the sweetest little kiss.

Ginger returned home to Nashville. She told her daughter, Danae, about Buck and going flying and catching the salmon. She also told her about Buck and "the kiss." Danae looked at her and said, "Mama, you are twitterpated." Just in case you are not up-to-date on the young people's sayings, that means "swept off your feet by someone you quite fancy or a strong feeling of love." I had to look it up, too.

After talking to Danae (her daughter) about Buck, Ginger realized for the first time she was in love, and what love was all about. She knew that Buck loved her dearly and would put everything aside for her. She had never had anyone put her first. She never before experienced the feelings she felt for Buck. It was time to do something about those feelings. Ginger and Buck were married in 1994. She moved to Alaska but continued to go back and forth to Nashville to appear and go on the road with Doug Dillard, in what was now a purely platonic relationship.

Ginger said Buck was the sweetest man she ever met, and he played guitar. He owned a blasting company, was a game guide (a

Singers, Songwriters, and More

person who took groups of people out big game hunting on horseback), and a bush pilot. Just meeting him, you would think he was a cute, little old redneck. Once you got to know him, the man never let the grass grow under his feet. He told Ginger, "If I had to land my airplane on a landing strip or a tarmac, I would never fly again." He landed his plane on top of ridges, in the valleys of mountains, and if he could see a way to get his plan in safely, on sand bars, in the bush, anywhere he could land safely. He was the best bush pilot since John Grayfield. John was flying in bad weather and ran into a mountain and died. Buck only flew when he had clear weather. Ginger also describes Buck as an amazing man.

Once she was living and settled in Alaska, Ginger got involved with the music scene. Music was her life, and she couldn't give it up. She formed a band and began playing all over Alaska. When Betty Harford moved to Alaska, Ginger and Betty became singing partners. They were playing at the VFW, Denali, jam sessions, and anywhere someone wanted them. They played the State Fair every year. She even opened for Ricky Skaggs one year.

In 1998 Ginger was in Nashville with Mary O'Dan and Frank Solivan when she received a call about Buck. Buck was on a blasting job at the top of a mountain in Alaska. Another contractor who had a job on the same mountain came over to Buck and said, "When you finish what you are up here contracted for, I need you to come over. I need to move the corner of this building." The wind was blowing about 80 miles per hour. It was wet. Buck finished his job and went to get things ready for the TV building. In the back of his truck, he put the cap in the dynamite and was holding the leg wires in his right hand. They were shunted to protect them. The dynamite was in his left hand, laid open to the wind. He was 15 feet from the hole where he was going to put the dynamite, he heard a big smack, and it went off in his hand due to a faulty wiring on the cap.

The blast blew off his left hand, it shattered his ear drums, causing him to lose his hearing, and his abdomen was blown completely open. Ginger always fussed at him because he carried a complete office in the zippered section of his Liberty overall pockets. He had Meg lights, bits of wire, and a calculator, plus many other things. When the dynamite blew, the "office" saved his life. Buck was a very careful person when working and had never gotten his dynamite ready for the job before getting to the blow site. This was a first and last for him.

Ginger went to the airport and it was closed, but the doors were open. Her ticket was with Northwest and they were on strike. She went to the Delta counter, jumped over where you put luggage behind the counter and banged on the door until someone came to the door. The person told her, "We are closed." Ginger said, "I need to speak to a supervisor." The supervisor came out and Ginger told her, "I have to get a ticket. My husband been in a terrible accident and is not expected to live. I have to get home." The supervisor said, "We are not issuing tickets or accepting any cash." Ginger, being a tenacious person, told Delta's agent, "I have a credit card if you will just let me in and get a ticket on the next flight." Ginger got her round-trip ticket for $450, which was ridiculously low.

When Ginger arrived at the hospital and went to Buck's ICU room, there were 16 people in the room. When she walked in, they left. The doctor came in and said, "You must be Ginger." She said, "I am." He then said, "We have been trying to run all these people out, and they wouldn't leave until you got here."

Singers, Songwriters, and More

Buck was in the bed and looked like a big piece of hamburger meat. The doctors left Buck open for seven days before they closed him up. The doctors and technicians were pulling wires, fragments of every kind, and rocks out of him. The doctor told Ginger, "We are getting this blue stuff out of him." Ginger said, "He had on blue rubber gloves." Ginger had insisted he always wear rubber to keep from getting the residue on his hands after the job was done since he was always rubbing his forehead. Ginger walked over to Buck and put her hand on him. He opened his eyes and looked at her and said, "The Baby." He never called her anything but "The Baby." He was so happy she was there. Even with the excruciating pain he was experiencing, he lit up like a Christmas tree because his "Baby" was there. Two weeks later, Buck walked out of the hospital on his own.

Ginger went back to school and became an R.N. because her mother needed care. She wanted to be able to care for her mother through her final years and keep her out of a nursing home. She not only used those skills for her mother, but also for her brother, and Buck for many years after his accident and subsequent heart problems. For the rest of his life, she would remain Buck's wife, caretaker, partner in music, and partner in life.

Brian Bowers, a good friend of Ginger's, came to Alaska for about six weeks every summer. Brian played autoharp and he was at their house one day. Ginger had written a song about Buck playing the guitar, where she played the left hand and he played right. She intended to surprise Buck with the song on her next show. She had told Brian about the song and sang it to him. She called the song, "Heart and Soul." The chorus went, "You can still play music the way that you like. I'll play the left hand if you will play the right." Brian, without thinking, blurted

The People and The Music—Country and Bluegrass that is!

Buck and Ginger

out the words to the song in front of Buck. Buck looked at Ginger with a blank look on his face. Brian said, "Sing it for him." Ginger did and the next time she looked at Buck, he was crying. She just took the guitar off, hung it around Buck's neck, gave him the pick and started chording with her left hand. They did, "Have I told You Lately That I Love You." From that point on, Buck would say, "Let's sing." Ginger called their act, "The Dog and Pony Show."

Buck was diagnosed with Myelodysplastic Syndrome and later with Metastatic Pancreatic Cancer while they were visiting Ginger's childhood home in Alabama. Ginger took care of him while he was sick. He passed away in June, 2022 and buried in the family cemetery in Alabama.

Ginger is now 79 years old and as she tells it, "I am still walking." Not only is she still walking, she is a bundle of energy. She continues to write and play music, dividing her time between Alabama, where she maintains her family home, and Alaska. She is writing songs and hopes to record another album in the very near future. She is working on that now. Her songs with Red, White and Blue(grass), Doug Dillard, and from solo albums are all available on YouTube. Listen to them. Watch the videos.

JIMMY PAYNE

You probably think this is a book about Missourians who went to Nashville to become a "star." It didn't start out that way. In fact, in interviewing Betty Harford, I came to know several other people from Missouri who were active during my time on Music Row and decided to include them.

One of those people was Jimmy Payne. Jimmy just happens to be the uncle of Betty Harford, but he was more like a brother since they are almost the same age.

Jimmy Payne and his dog, Daisy

They grew up together and were singing partners from the time they could walk until Betty married John Hartford and Jimmy joined the Army.

Jimmy grew up on a farm in southwest Missouri. He was the youngest of 12 children in the family. Betty Harford's mother, Bertha Viola Payne, was one of his sisters. It was a difficult life for the family. His parents were sharecroppers. They never owned their own farm. The kids all worked and brought home their meager earnings to help support the family. It was the way things were done, and the parents were never questioned about taking the money. There wasn't a nickel left over at day's end. Pick cotton all day, earn fifty cents, give it to your daddy.

The People and The Music—Country and Bluegrass that is!

Jimmy was struggling in the tenth grade in high school when he decided he was going to quit. His father and uncle needed help on the farm, and he was old enough to drive a tractor. He understood his father was dead set against him ever becoming a musician. Knowingly, he helped on the farm daily doing his chores because of family loyalty. But Jimmy realized he could no longer postpone having a serious talk with his father. He didn't want to be a farmer or even continue working on the farm. He wanted to be a musician. When Jimmy finally sat down with his father and told him all the things that he had been thinking, his father said, "You will never be able to earn a living playing music." Jimmy thought about it later and knew his father was worried he was going to drag Betty into the music business and away from her job in St. Louis.

In the late '40s or early '50s, Jimmy's sister, Bertha, helped him order a guitar from Alden's, a catalog store like Sears Roebuck. His friend Jack Campbell, who owned a local furniture store, taught him to play it. He and Betty were already doing a Saturday morning music show on a local radio station and singing together at local churches. Basically, they sang any place they were invited. They just loved to sing and were not paid for either the radio show or singing. They might get something to eat if they were lucky.

Several of Jimmy's sisters had already moved to St. Louis to work. One time when he was visiting them, he walked past a music store on Jefferson Street. He saw a Silvertone electric guitar in the window. Jimmy loved the look of the guitar. He had to have it, and so he went into the store and tested it. He bought it for $50. That was a lot of money, and it had taken Jimmy a while to save up for it. When he took the guitar home, his father and uncle scrutinized it like it was a foreign matter and said, "Son, you can't plug this in." They were thinking he had to buy something else, costing even more money. Jimmy told them, "I can't plug it into a wall but, all I have to have is an amplifier." Jimmy's dad said, "An amplifier!" That was all he said. Jimmy told him that his friend, William Cook, who had also been teaching him on the guitar, had an amplifier. The subject was dropped because his dad knew he didn't have to buy anything else.

Around 1956, Jimmy finally moved to St. Louis. He was finished with farm life and never wanted to return. He was hired by a metal finishing shop that had a contract with McDonnell Douglas. His uncle also worked there. Jimmy sprayed metal parts and bits with a dry film or lubricant. In fact, he sprayed parts for Sputnik and other space shuttles of the day. It was a boring job, but it taught him to paint. He earned enough to buy his first car, an old Ford. He later used his painting skills to supplement his income while trying to break into the music field.

Jimmy soon tired of working at the distribution center. He decided to join the Army. He did his basic training at Fort Leonard Wood in Missouri, and he was transferred to Fort Lewis, Washington. The first night he arrived at Fort Lewis, he met Chuck Glaser at a service club. Chuck was putting a show together. As soon as Chuck introduced himself to Jimmy, he knew who he was and told him so. Chuck asked him to sing. Chuck liked his singing and told him, "I want you to play with me." He also said to him, "If you want to follow the music business when you get out of the Army, I will do everything I can to help you." Meeting Chuck Glaser was the night his life changed. Not only did he gain a friend for life, but Chuck was his catalyst into the field of music in Nashville.

The People and The Music—Country and Bluegrass that is!

Chuck, along with his brothers, Tompall and Jim, were already appearing on the Grand Ole Opry as a trio and backing up other entertainers. Jimmy and his dad listened to them on the Grand Ole Opry. The Glasers owned their own publishing company, thus becoming a God-send for Jimmy who was writing songs. Jimmy would later introduce the Glasers to John Hartford, who wrote a song they published, "Gentle On My Mind."

Jimmy was discharged from the Army in 1961. He returned to St. Louis and once again, began playing music with his future wife's brother, Bill Holmes. He soon met a man by the name of Bob Lyons, a record producer. Bob already had Ike & Tina Turner signed on Bobbin Records. Bob signed Jimmy to a contract with Lyco Records. As was common practice at the time, he leased him to Vee-Jay Records, a black-owned record label out of Indiana. At the time, Vee-Jay Records was the first American label to have the Beatles. Vee-Jay recorded Jimmy at the Quonset Hut, a recording studio in Nashville. (The Quonset Hut is still there.) His first and only record for Vee Jay Records was, "Why Can't We Love Each Other." Bill Justis produced the record, and the Anita Kerr Singers sang backup. The trip to Nashville was a blessing for Jimmy. He was able to meet people and see old friends in the music business.

Jimmy moved to Nashville in 1965. He lived with his niece, Betty and her husband John Hartford in a trailer park on Lebanon Road. In fact, the night John wrote "Gentle On My Mind," he babysat Jamie, Betty and John's son. He began writing for Glaser Brothers Publishing Company. John was already writing for the Glasers' publishing, and Betty was working in the office as an administrative assistant and singing on demos. By the mid-'60s, things began

Singers, Songwriters, and More

moving upward for Jimmy. He signed with Epic Records and appeared on the Grand Ole Opry as a guest. The first time he appeared at the Opry, he received two standing ovations.

The night Jimmy appeared on the Opry, he said that he was standing in the wings waiting to go on and he felt someone pinch him in the back. He turned around and it was Mr. Cooper from the Nashville Musicians Union. Mr. Cooper asked him, "Do you have a Union card?" Jimmy responded, "I do but I don't have it with me. You will have to wait to see it." Jimmy said he belonged to the Musicians Union in Illinois. I laughed and told him that was the way things worked *before* computers. The Union kept up with everything.

One of his biggest hits was a song he co-wrote with Jim Glaser entitled, "Woman, Woman." Jimmy told me he was at the Opry one night and Bill Anderson sang a song he was working on, "Ruby, Don't Take Your Love to Town". The entire time Bill was singing, Jimmy was thinking, "Woman, Don't Take Your Love to Town." A couple of days later, he went into the office and Jim was working on "Woman, Woman." He had four lines and Jimmy took those four lines and wrote a melody. They sat up all night and wrote two more verses. The four lines Jim had written became the last verse. At the

The People and The Music—Country and Bluegrass that is!

time, producers and singers wanted a bridge in the song. Jimmy and Jim attempted to write a bridge, wrote a couple of different bridges, didn't like them, tore them up and threw them away. A bridge was never used in the song. "Woman, Woman" was the first song he and Jim Glaser wrote together and their top hit.

"Woman, Woman" was recorded by Gary Puckett & The Union Gap on Columbia Records and released in 1967. It was their debut single and went to No. 3 on *Cash Box* charts and No. 4 on *Billboard* charts. It has subsequently been recorded by many various artists.

Jimmy went on to write numerous other hit songs including "And I'm Still Missing You" which was recorded by Dottie West as a single and by Dottie West and Jimmy Dean as a duet. Jimmy was a very successful songwriter. His songs were recorded by some of the greatest talent of the time, including Tompall & the Glaser Brothers, Jim Glaser, Bill Anderson, Tammy Wynette, Dottie West, Ray Price, Grandpa Jones, Jeanne Pruett, Charlie Pride, Gary Puckett & the Union Gap, Connie Smith, and Hank Snow.

I asked him what he thought of the atmosphere on 16th Avenue in those days. He replied, "It was like a college campus out there. Walking around, you would see Kris Kristofferson, Bill Anderson, Chet Atkins, Brenda Lee, Eddy Arnold, everyone." You could go in any of the offices, you didn't need an appointment. The windows were all open, and people were sitting in the windows. Few, if any, of the buildings had air conditioning. Jimmy said he was walking by Bill Anderson's office one day and Bill yelled out, "Jimmy, do you have any songs for me?" Jimmy replied, "I believe I do, Bill. He then gave Bill a song he had written titled, "I'm Still Missing You." When

Singers, Songwriters, and More

On stage at the Commodore in Nashville

Bill recorded the song, he asked Jimmy to leave the studio. Bill told Jimmy, "You can come back after I finish your song." Jimmy thinks the world of Bill Anderson, as do I. Jimmy Martin had a different opinion.

"Woman Woman" became the means to buy the first and only house he would ever own. The idea came the day Warner Mack called him and asked, "I am selling my house, are you interested in buying my house?" Jimmy went to BMI (Broadcast Music Inc.) and asked if he could get a $10,000 advance on his song. BMI gave him the advance, he went to Warner's house, and he bought it. He still lives there with his wife, Jo. They raised their daughter in this house.

The People and The Music—Country and Bluegrass that is!

At the time of this writing, Jimmy Payne was 86 years old, spry as can be and mentally, very sharp. He has written and recorded hundreds of songs by various artists. He continues to appear at songwriter venues around Nashville and in clubs. He rarely goes on the road anymore. As he told me, he has come to a "screeching half." That's Jimmy's sense of humor. If you have an opportunity to meet Jimmy or see him play, ask him to tell you some of his stories. I could fill up three books or more with his stories and laugh continuously while doing it. He remembers everything. Like I said, "mentally very sharp."

Earlier this year, Betty Harford and I went to the Commodore Lounge at the Holiday Inn Vanderbilt in Nashville to see Jimmy appearing on the Songwriters Night. We were sitting with two of Jimmy's friends, Gil Gilchrist (retired cartoonist of the comic strip, "Nancy and Sluggo") and Shawn Hunt. Both men said, "Jimmy is the finest person I have ever known. He is an honest person and will help anyone." I was very impressed, and I have found those things to be true. He is much admired by everyone who knows him.

Jimmy and I met at Bob Evans' restaurant on Music Valley Drive. I was going to interview him, but when I asked for a table in an area off by itself, they didn't have one. I went outside and waited on Jimmy to get there. When he did, I told him what had happened, and he got in my car. We went to Scoreboard, got a barbecue sandwich, and chatted for the next two hours. It was fantastic. I listened to Jimmy's stories and recorded him telling them. We then got back in my car, and I took him back to Bob Evans to get his car.

The following day, I learned that Jimmy had been taken to the hospital and diagnosed with COVID. However, the hospital where

Singers, Songwriters, and More

he was taken treated and released him.

A couple of days later, Jimmy's symptoms worsened. He was taken to the Hendersonville hospital where he was hospitalized for over a week. He was put on life support and was finally sent home with Hospice. However, being a fighter and a strong Missourian, he survived, came off Hospice and oxygen. Jimmy has returned to normal, the normal being for an 86 year old. He is driving, appearing at the Commodore Lounge and other venues around town again.

Since beginning this chapter, Jimmy has lost his beloved wife, Jo. She had been sick for a very long time. He continues to live at his home in Inglewood and to play and sing. With all that has happened, the prayer warriors remain out in force for this good and talented man. Go watch and listen to him on YouTube. Better yet, order one of his CDs.

Sadly, we lost our beloved Jimmy on May 15, 2023. Jimmy was well-loved by everyone who came in contact with him. He was a genuine, honorable, kind, sweet man. He was honest as the day is long, and when he told you something, you could take it to the bank. The greatest loves of his life were his wife, Jo, his daughter, Amanda, his music, his dogs, his family and friends. He will be missed by all of us. I will miss his phone calls saying, "I'm going to be at the Commodore on such and such a date." Those phone calls would sometimes last an hour because we would start talking about the old times and we would laugh and laugh and laugh. Songwriter nights at various venues were so special to him, especially the Commodore. Rest in peace Jimmy. I know you are singing to Jo in Heaven. Until we meet again!

WOMAN, WOMAN
By: Jim Glaser and Jimmy Payne

Woman
Woman
Have you got cheating on your mind?

Something's wrong between us
That your laughter cannot hide,
And you're afraid to let your eyes meet mine.
And lately when I love you,
I know you're not satisfied.

Woman
Woman
Have you got cheating on your mind?
On your mind

I've seen the way men look at you
When they think I don't see,
And it hurts to have them think that you're that kind.
But its knowing that you're looking back
That's really killing me,

Woman
Woman
Have you got cheating
on your mind?
On your mind?

A woman wears a certain look
When she is on the move,
And a man can always
tell what's on her mind.
I have to have to say it,
But that look's all over you

Woman, Woman,

Have you got cheating on your mind?
Woman, Woman,

Have you got cheating on your mind?
Oh woman,
Oh, ho, woman
Have you got cheating on your mind?
Oh

BILLY HUNTER

William Dale (Billy) Hunter is an audio engineer. He grew up in Tuscaloosa, Alabama, the son of a World War II radio man. His father, Eugene C. Hunter, flew in B26 Bombers during the war. When his father was discharged in 1946, he returned to Tuscaloosa and started a radio repair shop. He was also a University of Alabama student, and he located his shop just off campus. During those days, radios were prevalent like televisions, computers, and iPads are today. Eugene had been corresponding with his best friend's sister, Beverly, while he was in service. Beverly lived in Missouri and by the time Eugene was discharged and came back home, they were in love. They married and he moved her to Alabama. There they had three children, two sons, Billy and Eugene, and a daughter, Sheryl. Billy was named for his father's best friend, James William Edwards.

As a young boy, Billy worked with his father on Saturday. He swept floors, picked things up off the floor, dealt with customers, met his father's friends, and his father taught him how to repair radios. He enjoyed going to the shop and continued during high school and working. In the 1950s they started to work on television. His father eventually employed Billy on a part-time basis.

The Vietnam War was the focal point of the news. Billy decided in high school he didn't want to go to college at that time. Growing up, he loved hearing his Dad talk about his days in the service. Billy decided he wanted to get his time in the service finished as soon as he graduated. He started talking to his mother and father about it and convinced them to sign a waiver allowing him to join the Navy at 17.

Billy's friend and Jimmy Hankins, who lived in his neighborhood, worked on car and motorcycle projects together. Jimmy was going to the University of Alabama and enrolled in the Reserves, getting a head start on his service obligation. Jimmy would get decked out in his dress whites on Wednesdays. This impressed young Billy. Jimmy was Billy's mentor. Like his mentor, Billy joined the Navy Reserves while a senior in high school. The Reserves had a class for radio at the Northington campus in Tuscaloosa. He dressed in his uniform and went to radio class.

Upon graduation from high school, Billy received orders to go to the U.S. Navy Training Center in Port Deposit, Maryland, where he attended Radioman Communications Technician (CT) School. A security clearance was required for the class in order to enter the room. The first thing he learned was Morse Intercept. The manual

The People and The Music—Country and Bluegrass that is!

typewriter they used in class had the alphabet removed and replaced with Russian characters on the keyboard. You had to memorize the characters in Russian. Billy graduated from Radioman CT School and was sent to Germany. He said the "Shooting War" and the "Cold War" were going on at the same time. Billy spent the remaining years of his four years in the Navy in Bremerhoffan, Germany on the North Sea, monitoring the Russians and their mobile missile launchers and submarines. The Navy had a communications station in Bremerhoffan on an old German base.

Billy was on duty and remembers clearly the Six Day War starting. He was receiving messages from The Liberty, a Navy communications ship sitting, clearly marked, off the coast of Israel. Israel attacked, firing napalm and rockets at the ship. The Liberty was only lightly armed, loaded with sailors, and almost sunk. It was in international waters off Egypt's Gaza Strip. All attempts to radio for help were blocked by Israel. They were finally able to make contact with the U.S.S Saratoga. Twelve fighter planes and four tanker planes were dispatched to defend the Liberty. When word of their deployment reached Washington, Robert McNamara, who was Secretary of Defense, recalled the jets. The jets never reached the Liberty. The reason for the recall was never known.

Billy returned home from Germany after spending seven years in the Navy. He immediately went back to his Reserve Unit. One day, while speaking to the Officer in Charge, he told him that he would like to start attending the University of Alabama. Fortunately, the Officer in Charge was also Dean of Admissions to the University. Billy enrolled in Business School, but he didn't like business as a career. He quickly switched to a class for Broadcast. The introductory class consisted of working in the studio, working with cameras, sound and lighting, and producing short commercials. He said, "That fit me perfectly." The GI Bill was paying for Billy's books and tuition while going to school. He was working a part-time job, paying for living expenses.

A television studio operated by Alabama Public Television Network was located a couple of floors below his Broadcast studio. There were several other satellite studios around Alabama, including one in Birmingham, Huntsville, and Montgomery, as well as several others. He applied for a job at the TV studio and was hired part-time doing weekend playbacks on the Network. He continued to work there during the remainder of his school years until he received his degree in Broadcasting with a minor in photography.

By the time Billy finished school, videotapes were very expensive and not affordable. The alternative was 16 mm film. TV stations were operating that way, in order to afford to do remote work. Billy took a course in Birmingham learning studio sound, while still working for The Network. His goal was to be knowledgeable in all facets of the business.

Billy's close friend in Nashville, Ginger Boatwright, had a bluegrass band. He met her and her husband, Grant, through Ginger's brother, Jerry. He had seen them perform in Birmingham and other areas around Alabama and was quite impressed with the group. Ginger's husband, Grant, told Billy about a big bluegrass concert where he and Ginger were going to appear in Champaign, Illinois. Also appearing on the concert was John Hartford, New Grass Revival, Vassar Clements, and Red, White and Blue(grass). Grant asked Billy to come up and shoot (film) them for TV. Billy was thrilled. He

The People and The Music—Country and Bluegrass that is!

gathered the crew together and headed to Illinois.

It just so happened the week Billy took the crew to Illinois, Alabama Public Television was doing a show called, "The Bluegrass Block." They were taping different bluegrass shows in Birmingham. The shows Billy filmed in Illinois became a welcome addition to the bluegrass series.

Around this time, Ginger and Grant started talking to Billy about moving to Nashville. They felt he would be able to get a good job in Nashville with his experience and work ethic. Billy was concerned about moving, and Ginger told him she needed someone to babysit her teenage daughter when she and Grant were out of town. They would help him. Billy became very interested and began checking things out in Nashville. Billy was fascinated, just thinking about moving to Nashville. He quit his job and moved.

Billy previously worked for the very small Stagehands Union in Alabama. They primarily did projection work in the theaters. They didn't do any live work. After arriving in Nashville, he started pursuing work around town. He checked in with the International Alliance of Theatrical and Stage Employees, Local 46. The Union's contract dated back to the late '40s with the Grand Ole Opry. They did all the stage work at the Ryman Auditorium and had theatrical jobs as well as technical jobs.

By 1974, the Grand Ole Opry had moved its operation from the Ryman Auditorium to its new building on the banks of the Cumberland River. Billy toured the building with one of Ginger's friends who worked at Opryland Park. Opryland Park was constructed as an amusement park, together with the new Grand Ole Opry House. He was shown around the park, and the different stage shows were taking place live every day. He then took Billy over to the Opry House, and he walked around the stage to get acquainted with it. After that, they went to the back of the Opry House where Studio A, the Opry's TV studio was located.

Billy was walking around Studio A when he noticed Martha Grahame, from New York, was there. She had a TV series about ballet in America and was videotaping the series in the studio. His was curious when he saw Martha Graham as to "why would someone from New York come to Nashville to videotape her show?" He knew the people in Nashville were doing some good work, but he wondered about the difference between the work done in New York and Nashville.

After touring the park and seeing the work done by Union employees, Billy decided to let the International Alliance of Theatrical and Stage Employees Local 46 become his business agent. The Local put qualified people in different positions. It was providing members to work at Channel 4, the local WSM channel. Union members were working on the filming of package shows like Porter Waggoner, Dolly Parton, and shows that were done on location. Opryland Productions was also using IA (International Alliance of Theatrical and Stage Employees Local 46) to create a production team.

Billy's business agent told him that he didn't have any shows going at the time, but he could put him on the Grand Ole Opry stage and he could fill a position there. The Opry was a live radio show, and the stage hands' job moved the microphones around on stage. The announcer said, "And that was Porter Waggoner, and our next performer is Hank Snow." During the short time between the introduction and the performer walking on stage, Billy and the

The People and The Music—Country and Bluegrass that is!

crew's job was to lower the curtains containing the advertisement, walk out before the audience and move the microphones, get them in place for the next performer or performers if it was a group, and run spotlight duty. This avoided having to move audio boards, which was a cumbersome task. Those were the job responsibilities at the Grand Ole Opry.

Billy worked at the Grand Ole Opry for four years. Each person or group appearing on the show was different. Some of the entertainers are short, some are tall, bands, duos, and trios. He had to learn different band setups, such as a bluegrass band and how to mic a banjo and a fiddle. Where each musician was standing was important, and how they were going to work the microphone. Wilma Lee Cooper usually sang on Microphone 3. So, you walk out on stage and give her the microphone. The Grand Ole Opry was a radio show, and when an artist used the house band, you didn't have to strip (or take away) the microphones. One had to know all the microphone movements, their position on stage, and be ready. Nothing was written down -- no manual was available. Everything was done by memory and repeating the same job for the same performer(s).

It was not unusual for a performer such as Dottie West or someone else to be late showing up. Their name was then crossed out for that time period, and a new name inserted. It was your job to keep track and look constantly at the list, knowing what or who was next. Making quick decisions was part of your regular duty as a sound engineer.

Not too long ago, Billy was listening to one of his favorite morning shows titled "Coffee, Country and Cody." Frequently Bill Cody has live guest artists on the show and is broadcast over WSM

Singers, Songwriters, and More

from the Opryland Hotel Radio Room. Steve Wariner was on the show recently, and he mentioned that the first time he played the Opry, he was a musician with Dottie West. He told a story about being on their way to the Opry and said, "We were in the car driving there and they were announcing her on the radio." Then Bill Cody said, "You know she was always perpetually late." Dottie was the sweetest, kindest, most generous, and beautiful friend to all who knew her, including me. Like all of us, we have bad habits. Hers was being late, and unfortunately, it led to her death. Running late and headed to the Grand Ole Opry, she died in a car crash on the curve of the road leading alongside the Opryland Hotel to the Artists Entrance of the Grand Ole Opry.

When Billy was working the Grand Ole Opry, he was required to be there at least 30 minutes before show time. Anne Bunkman met Billy at the back door one evening and asked him to move some boxes out of her car and into the Opry. Billy asked her what all the papers and records were for. She replied, "Well, we are starting a new network. It's going to be called "The Nashville Network." This was early 1983.

A few days later, Billy asked his business manager, "What about this Nashville Network? He said, "Since you already know all the mike moves and the band moves from the Opry stage, we are going to put you on a live music show starting in mid-1983. Ralph Emery is going to be hosting a live show and will be called *Nashville Now*. Billy went from working weekends on the Grand Ole Opry to working, still as a Union employee, fulltime five nights a week at a live music show.

Leaving the Grand Ole Opry and joining the TNN Network,

The People and The Music—Country and Bluegrass that is!

Billy had his own studio where they did the show and the house band to keep up with. The show would book about three guest acts per night. Billy was responsible for coming in every afternoon around 2 p.m. First up, he checked the house band, making sure all the microphones and audio connections were working. He met the guests for the show to see what their audio needs were. He would get them set up, and then check to see if any musicians were being substituted for the house band or they had new members. If so, this meant he had to move microphones to accommodate the substitute or add microphones. The stage had to be ready for the TV cameras and everything ready for rehearsal by 5:30 p.m.

Whether it was Bill Monroe, the Osborne Brothers, or another bluegrass band was scheduled, they were usually the first to arrive at the studio. The bluegrass musicians were always very, very punctual and self-contained. Working on the Opry all those years, he knew how bluegrass musicians liked their microphones and the way they wanted to be staged. He learned how to put pick marks down on the floor. His "pick marks" were simply a piece of gray tape matching the floor with his microphone numbers on them. It was important to keep everything staged for the camera, so it could be repeated for the performance. The director would make his camera shots like Camera 1, 2, and 3, 4, or 5, who had close ups, where the camera was going to shoot from, so the staging for rehearsal didn't have to be duplicated for the show.

When Bill (or another bluegrass band) arrived in the house, Billy told the director "Bill Monroe is here, and they don't need the house band to rehearse." The studio was large, and the bluegrass bands didn't need to be on the house band stage near the audience.

Singers, Songwriters, and More

He always asked the director where he (the director) would like to set up the bluegrass band. Billy then set up the band, so they were ready for rehearsal and filming.

Billy kept extra microphones for the acts appearing on the show. They were pre-set and labeled for each of the acts in the wings. When the show started rolling, one act would finish and the next one came on stage during the commercials. Billy had to be ready to change out the audio, have the audio for the next act ready to go, make sure the lighting guys had the lights focused and ready to go, and be set up to strike an act while the announcer was doing the commercial. If someone like Martina McBride was appearing with the house band, he walked out and handed her a microphone, and then sat in front of the stage and waited for her to finish. Then he would take the microphone, and she would walk over to where Ralph Emery (the host) was sitting and had a conversation with him. Billy was already getting the next act on stage.

The TV show had bookers, and they would contact the booking agents for the various acts like Randy Travis, Steve Wariner, Garth Brooks, or Martina McBride. If the show couldn't get performers, they could get songwriters. The ones they booked came and sang their hit songs. If a full band was booked, they would send Billy their instrument list and their needs—a stage plot of where they were used to standing, and what microphones they needed. In the beginning of the show, they didn't get a lot of full bands because they had their own house band.

Many times, a performer brought someone to the show that accompanied him/her on vocal backups, bass, or both. When that occurred, Billy added a remote location for the bass player or a mic if

The People and The Music—Country and Bluegrass that is!

they wanted the bass player to be near them on stage.

Nashville Now had its own in-house band, and they were set up to play with any artist. It was required that an artist submit three songs they would sing on the show when they were booked.

The Nashville Now show was like a new beginning for Billy after leaving the Grand Ole Opry, which just had one bandstand. If they had a guest band, it was rather difficult to move inputs around. The piano was always stationery unless you had a guest who wanted it moved. One day Jerry Whitehurst, who played piano in the house band, told Billy, "That's OK. I will go in and play the piano where it is." The headliner was Leon Russell.

There were always compromises to be made when you were setting up a stage. For instance, you might have a left-handed drummer come in. Maybe he could play the toms and the cymbals where they were, but you had to have the Snare in a different position to accommodate his needs. Billy said, "I became adapted to seeing what was necessary for the television show." If a performer is used to having a guitar player or a bass player on one side or the other, he would put that into a mix in the monitors. Though he couldn't move the guitar player or the bass player, he could put a monitor mix off to the side where he/she was used to hearing it.

Billy remembers well the night Mickey Newberry was a guest on the show. Mickey was going to play one of Elvis Presley's songs that night called "The Trilogy." Mickey brought his acoustic guitar; it was a little pocket guitar. But this one had a mini-guitar rack. What he had done as a songwriter, he had hooked his guitar to the keyboard, and he could trigger the accompaniment while he was playing the strings. He convinced Billy that they could set it up and it would

Singers, Songwriters, and More

work well. Mickey brought all the connecting cables. The guitar was stereo with left and right output channels. The keyboard was also left and right stereo, so that was two more channels. And then there was Mickey's vocal mike. Altogether, Mickey was going to require five places on the audio board. Billy got everything set up, and it went fine during rehearsals and the filming.

The kicker came after Mickey finished his song and Ralph Emery told him to bring his guitar over to the interview area. Billy came rushing onstage and yelled to Ralph, "No. He can't bring things over there; you need to interview him here. His equipment can't be moved. It won't work where you are sitting." So, Ralph, being the good guy he was, came over and interviewed Mickey on the performer's stage.

Billy was the main audio engineer for the Television Studio C. But if times were busy, he knew friends from the Opry he could call for help if it wasn't a Friday or Saturday night. Wilburn Bates was one of his helpers at the Television Studio C who helped him take care of the guests at the home base (where the interviews were occurring.) A lot of those microphones were planted next to a chair. Some of them had to be adjusted to suit the situation. Then Wilburn Bates would step in.

When the *Nashville Now* show ended, the next show taking that time-frame slot on the schedule was *Crook and Chase* hosted by Lorianne and Charlie Chase. The entire studio was redone because now they had two hosts. They liked Jim Owens as a producer. Jim was one of the producers in Nashville doing package shows. These were shows Billy watched Saturdays when he was living in Alabama like *The Porter Waggoner Show*, the *Bill Anderson Show*, and *Nashville*

The People and The Music—Country and Bluegrass that is!

on the Road. These same producers were going to be providing a lot of content for the Nashville Network. Jim Owens was doing the *Crook and Chase Show* near Music Row. He moved their filming to the Trafco Building, previously owned by the Methodists, and which had once been a sound stage for Elvis Presley to rehearse for his sessions.

Jim took over the Trafco Building and remodeled it. He was doing several shows for TNN in this location. They moved the *Crook and Chase Show* to prime time. It was an hour and a half show. Crook and Chase wanted to remodel the studio once again to make it look more like their show. They ended up having a house band and a guest area. The old house band part of the stage sat in an area where there were doors. Crook and Chase wanted to get a hard reveal so when they announced, "Ladies and Gentlemen, here is Alabama," the doors opened and out came Alabama.

Bill Turner was the producer at the time. Billy knew he couldn't be in the back with the guests and up front with the house band and do interviews at the same time. Billy told Bill, "I can't be behind the hard wall and in front as well. I am going to need someone to help behind the wall with the tour bands." Bill Turner thought it over and asked him what he wanted done. Billy said, "Make me the audio coordinator." Bill told him, "Hire whomever you need to help." The house band was on the extreme right of the stage. Billy did his regular house band duties and set up the interview area. He hired a second person, Jackie Brooks, to work with the guest tour bands behind the hard wall.

It was easy, the way the stage had been set up before the renovation for *Crook and Chase*. Billy could just meet someone at the

Singers, Songwriters, and More

back door and find out what their needs were. The show went from having one stage to having three stages. He said, with the changes, they had two extra full tour bands coming in each night. The acts sent Billy their stage plots (the diagram showing where each member of the band would be standing), their instrument list, and the songs they were going to be doing. He would share this information with the director and then hand off the information to Jackie, who worked behind the hard wall. They needed this information to see whether they would be assigned to Stage B or Stage C. Stage A was always the house band. Stages B and C were behind the wall.

The Crook and Chase Show remained on TNN for 13 years, and Billy worked on every episode. Lorianne did a cooking show from the Opryland Hotel, and Billy worked with her. Crook and Chase decided they wanted to have an outside producer, and they put that up for bid. Dick Clark won the bid. Billy thought that was fabulous. He had never worked for Dick Clark and desperately wanted to have that on his resume.

Dick's son, Rac (Richard A. Clark), came to the area to produce a TV show, and Billy got ready to do the show. He learned that Tom Wopat, from Dukes of Hazzard, was going to be the first host of the show and he was elated. The show turned out to be three times as much responsibility as the other shows they were doing. The network executive's designers wanted to see what the building was like and how much room they had to do the show. A mistake was made, and the producers were given both the footprint of the studio and the plans for the Gaslight Theatre. The studio was attached to the Gaslight Theatre. The Gaslight Theatre was actually where the audience sat for the live show, but it also had a stage. Dick Clark's people included it as part of their studio, which was not originally going to be included. The network ended up spending over a million dollars to outfit the Gaslight Theatre stage so Dick Clark could have the show.

Billy said they found themselves during the month of December having to gut the Gaslight Theatre, all the HVAC, duct work, and completely put a whole new set of bleachers in for the audience. They also had to hang 80 audio boxes over the audience so the sound and music could be heard from every angle.

If you were sitting in the audience, the area covered about 160 degrees of view. The interview was done in the middle of the stage, and where the audience used to sit was where the guest band was. The house band would now be on the Gaslight Stage. Billy continued to work with the house band, and his crew continued to work with the guest bands.

The studio and the Gaslight Theatre were located on land that was Opryland Park. The TV show was being planned as Opryland Hotel was planning to get rid of the park and replace it with a shopping mall. The mall is there today.

When the park was open, the Opry played during park hours. They had an audience come in, and each act was allowed 15 minutes. Billy and his assistant went to the park early, worked on the stage, and set up the microphones. Whenever the Carlisles were appearing, Bill jumped around on stage. Bill told stories, and one of Billy's favorites was, "You people out there be on the lookout. There may be some pick pockets out there. When they come to me, I have a trap set for them. I have the bottoms of my pockets all cut out. A pick pocket gets in there and, "I getcha getcha getcha." Bill Carlisle would then say, "I met my wife that way."

Singers, Songwriters, and More

Billy has so many fond memories of the Opry and the artists. He remembers being a newcomer to the Opry and seeing so many people he watched on TV, who accepted him so readily. People like Little Jimmy Dickens and his funny stories, and Jean Shepherd and Benny Birchfield. He remembers Jean as being so down home and such a nice person. I told him she was what she was: a good, good person who always spoke her mind. Someone I loved and miss.

Billy had a motorcycle accident in 1988. He broke his left leg and arm and could not do his job. While in the hospital, Ralph Emery mentioned Billy's accident on the show. Then, Bill Turner called Billy after his release from the hospital and told him, "We are having a few problems in the studio, so if you could just come over and tell us what to do, I believe it will help." Billy went over to the studio and helped them. He said, "Just being back on the job even though I couldn't physically do anything, helped me to heal better and quicker." He thinks all the "Get Well" cards he received as a result of Ralph's announcement helped him mentally to heal.

Billy enjoyed his work in the radio and TV industry. At the time he started with the Grand Ole Opry, they didn't allow anyone to bring in amplifiers. You could attach to one that was already on stage. The amplifiers on stage were attached to the audio boards. The bands didn't rehearse. They could do so in their dressing rooms if they liked. Now-a-days, they allow the artists to come in and rehearse. Rehearsing makes it easier for the audio engineers and their digital equipment since they can hit "save," and the band's audio needs are saved. Things were much more simply done in the '80s when Billy started. Five stagehands were assigned to the Opry, but only two were assigned as audio people on the stage. Today, there are probably five to do the same job.

In the '80s, they would just put a general wash up for lights. A "wash" is generally a level of lights. The audience needed that to be able to see. Then, as the song played, they would add color or something like that; now, they are throwing graphics and everything into it. Things were so much simpler and straightforward before the digital world came into being. Billy said, "I still like the simpler stuff and the straightforward songs. You can touch someone's heart without all the external stuff."

Billy still loves the sweet, country music. He said, "That is what I enjoyed so much about the Opry. The camaraderie, the personal contacts, people having time to stand and have a conversation." When you walked in the back door of the Ryman Auditorium, music was everywhere. People were talking to each other, rehearsing in the hallways, in the dressing rooms, and talking at the same time. It was pandemonium and wonderful at the same time. Everyone's mind was focused on one thing, and that was MUSIC.

When Billy turned 70, he retired. People ask him, "Why did you retire? You are still active, and you have your health." Billy says, "That is true. This is the time I grow my spirit." Today, Billy is active in church, with his family, and very importantly, with his friends. He misses the Opry, and every now and then he goes to the Opry House just to see his friends. It's been a good life for a good man.

DOTTIE SWAN, THE 901 CLUB

Dorothy (Dottie) Maxine Henderson was originally from a little town in West Virginia called Hundred. She was born in 1916, which made her one year younger than my mother.

I met Dottie at the WWVA Jamboree in Wheeling, West Virginia. I liked her immediately, and we became friends. Dottie was much older than me, but, I never thought about age at that time in my life. My mother was born in 1915, so they were the same age. I just knew I liked her. I was also a mother's girl.

Dottie Swan and daughter, Dottie Lee Snow Tubb

Dottie began her radio career early in life. She came from a musical family, some of whom made a career in music. After graduation from high school, Dottie attended Eastern Nazarene College for a short while. But the music called, and she soon left school and joined Cowboy Loye and his Bluebonnet Troupe. Dottie moved with Loye to WMMN in Fairmont, West Virginia. This association was short-lived, and soon she struck out on her own.

In October 1937, Dottie formed her own band she called, "The Jubilee Boys." Dottie was the lead singer. The band stayed to-

The People and The Music—Country and Bluegrass that is!

Radio Dot & Smoky

gether for a short while and then began to part ways. Dottie brought in her brothers, Jack and Ted Henderson. Smoky Swan also joined the band. Dottie was truly a female leading the way for others, a pioneer, in the field of country music. Women were branded by others as being unfit when they ventured out and took on a profession. Women didn't go out and lead bands, sing in honky-tonks, and on the radio. But Dottie followed her passion, which was singing.

Dorothy Maxine Henderson and Louis W. Swan, who called themselves "Radio Dot and Smoky," married and traveled together for the next 18 years. They had one child together, a beautiful little girl they named Dorothea Louise Swan and called "Dottie Lou."

Singers, Songwriters, and More

Radio Dot and Smoky entertained on radio stations in Huntington, West Virginia; Charleston, South Carolina; Topeka, Kansas; and Shreveport, Louisiana. They operated a park in Huntington, West Virginia. Eventually settling in Nashville, they appeared on the Grand Ole Opry as guests as early as 1946 and became the opening act for Ernest Tubb on his road shows. In 1947, they appeared with Ernest Tubb in a motion picture titled, *Hollywood Barn Dance*. They became part of a show in Cleveland, Ohio, and in 1955, broke house records for the Circle Theatre Jamboree. They were known and billed as, "America's Ace Sweethearts."

Hank Snow joined the Grand Ole Opry on January 7, 1951. It was a memorable night at the Opry and also one for Radio Dot and Smoky. They appeared on the 7:30 p.m. show on the Grand Ole Opry hosted by Roy Acuff. They would sing, "Blue Eyes Crying In The Rain" and "Sleepy Rio Grande." They returned to the stage on the 10:30 p.m. portion to join in with Roy Acuff and everyone on stage singing, "Waiting For My Call to Glory." They appeared many times on the Grand Ole Opry on Ernest Tubb's and Roy Acuff's segments. They also appeared live at the Ernest Tubb Record Shop.

In all the years Dottie and Smoky sang together, appearing at various live shows throughout the country and on radio stations, they never recorded together until 1954. At that time, they recorded four songs for MGM as "Dot and Smoky." A couple of years later in 1956, they got a divorce. Smoky went back to his home in Pennsylvania, where he remained until his death in 1980 at the age of 73.

Following their divorce, Dottie moved to Wheeling, West Virginia. She hoped to become a regular on the WWVA Jamboree. I met her when I moved to Wheeling in 1960. I was working for Gene

The People and The Music—Country and Bluegrass that is!

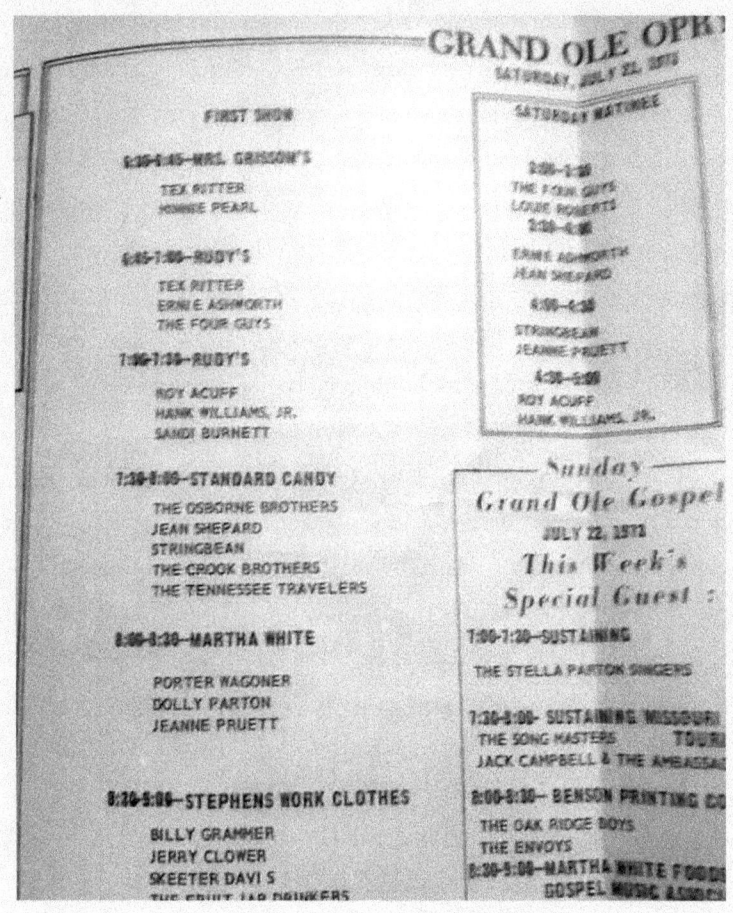

Johnson, the director and booking agent for the talent on the Jamboree. Dottie lived across the street in a hotel. It was easy for her to go to the studios at WWVA or come to our office. We became friends, much to Jimmy Martin's disapproval.

Jimmy Martin, our son Timmy, and I moved to Nashville in March 1963. I would continue to book talent for and on the Jamboree. After moving, I didn't see Dottie again until one day she walked into my office on 16th Avenue South. It was good to see her. She told me that she had also moved to Nashville, but we never discussed what she was doing. To tell the truth, I didn't have time to carry on long conversations and something like asking her what she was doing or where she was working seemed liked invasion of privacy.

The next thing I knew, I heard a new private club was opening on 16th Avenue South, near my office, and it was owned by Dottie Swan. I couldn't believe it.

Billy (Grammer) and I decided we would have lunch there one day if they served food. We never got around to going for lunch. One of us always had to stay in the office during the day.

However, it wasn't long before I did stop by the club. Little Dottie was tending bars and Dottie was busy. I forget who I was with, but I didn't stay too long. Then, one night, I went with Mooney and Loretta Lynn and my husband, Chuck. Again, I didn't stay long. But I heard from others that it was a great place to go, and they were always busy. Dottie ran the club until her death on December 1, 1972. She was a very young 56 years old when she passed. She is buried in Hendersonville, Tennessee.

Dottie was a true pioneer. She pursued her dream of singing and having her own band when other women were cleaning houses, having babies, and just being wives. Then, she opened a Club on 16th Avenue South. That took foresight. If the Country Music Association had a place for pioneers, Dottie should definitely be in it. She was not only a good entertainer and a pioneer, but a really good person.

Dottie's daughter, Dottie continues to live in the Nashville area. She was twice married—first to Jimmy Snow, son of Hank Snow, and later to Glenn Tubb, nephew of Ernest Tubb. Dottie and Glenn were both pastors in the Nashville area. Glenn passed away in 2021.

CHARMAINE LANHAM AND MARTY LANHAM

Charmaine Lanham and her husband, Marty, have been a fixture on the Nashville bluegrass music scene since the early 1970s. Before moving to Nashville, they were playing music in California with Ingrid Hermann Fowler (who was the daughter of famous musician, Woody Hermann), and her husband, Bob Fowler. Marty was a banjo player, Charmaine played guitar, Ingrid played fiddle, and Bob played guitar.

Charmaine, Marty, Ingrid, and Bob moved to Nashville from San Francisco, California. They were part of the bluegrass music scene in San Francisco. Marty is not only known for his banjo playing, but is also a well-known luthier. Charmaine loved photography and was honing her skills to become professional. All their professions would serve them well in Nashville.

As soon as the group of musicians landed in town, they were looking for a place to play music. In Nashville, the Dusty Road Tavern on Woodland Street was THE PLACE everyone went to play music and jam. It was extremely popular, and it didn't take the four California musicians long to find it. You walked in, introduced yourself to Bobby Green (the owner), and started jamming. From then on, you were a regular.

Dusty Road was a nondescript place from the outside, and even more so inside. As you walked in the front door, the stage was on the right hand side with a mural painted on the back wall of Eldon Burgess and his fiddle, Roy Bounds with the bass, Harold Young and his mandolin, and Bob (Red) Smith with his guitar, plus a bare concrete floor, tables, and chairs in front of the stage.

On the left hand side of the front door as you came in was a bar running the full length of the room. This bar is where you could get the best, melt-in-your mouth hot dogs in the world. Bobby only served beer and sodas at the Dusty Road. At the time, Nashville had an ordinance saying you couldn't serve beer and wine in the same place. Grocery stores couldn't sell wine because they sold beer. If you sold liquor, you had to serve food. Not just hot dogs. Even in the late '60s and early '70s, this law was antiquated.

Food and beer weren't the only things that attracting people to the Dusty Road. The main attractions to the Dusty Road were the camaraderie, the music, and Bobby Green. He was a very interesting,

The People and The Music—Country and Bluegrass that is!

take-no-prisoners type of person! Standing only about 5'4" tall and probably not weighing over 120 pounds, he always had a cigarette holder with the longest cigarette I had ever seen hanging out of his mouth. He could throw the biggest of the big out the door. A former prizefighter and strong as a mule, he took care of his people. He knew I didn't drink beer. However no one else knew it, so everyone bought me beer. He would sit a beer in front of me with the cap still on. When it started getting warm, he would put it back in the fridge. In turn, I never paid for a Coke at the Dusty Road. He always gave them to me. Quid pro quo. I think he had the best of the Quid.

It would only be natural for Charmaine, Marty, Ingrid, and Bob to find the Dusty Road. Once there, they could pull out their instruments and pick all night. And if they were not picking, they could be listening to other people. It was a good thing Bobby could care less if you didn't buy a beer or if you bought twenty. He was happy to have you at the Dusty Road.

It wasn't long after Charmaine and the group began going to the Dusty Road that Bobby Greene was diagnosed with lung cancer and passed away. The city decided that the location of the Dusty Road was the best spot for the new Juvenile Justice Center, and so the Dusty Road closed its doors forever. Evelyn Greene, Bobby's wife, moved the Dusty Road around the corner where Titan's Stadium sits today but it just didn't work out.

The group (and everyone else) needed a place to play music. Together, Marty Lanham, Ingrid Herman Fowler, her husband Bob, Bob Smith, and Jim Bornstein, decided to open their own place. Thus The Station Inn, the place for bluegrass music in Nashville, was born. They were all active in the Station Inn for many years.

Singers, Songwriters, and More

Marty Lanham and Wilma Lee Cooper

Charmaine and Marty are both super-talented. Marty is known for his banjo playing and also for playing electric bass. In addition to being a talented musician, he is also a sought-after luthier. Charmaine is a commercial photographer, a terrific writer and blogger, and she plays guitar. They were a couple waiting to be hired.

Marty began working for Wilma Lee and Stoney Cooper on the road and on the Opry playing banjo and electric bass. He worked a day job at Gruhn Guitars as a luthier. Gruhn Guitars was located

The People and The Music—Country and Bluegrass that is!

in the shadow of the Ryman on Fourth Avenue, so Marty could leave one job and literally run over to the next one.

Charmaine began her career as a photographer and writer in earnest. She went to the Grand Ole Opry and photographed any and everyone. I spent a day at her home, and she showed me several albums of photos she had taken all over Nashville of musicians from every genre of music. Her pictures are all excellent. I was also able to read all the notes she put together with the pictures in an album. I told her, "This is ready for a publisher."

Marty has a shop in front of their house where he works on musical instruments. I didn't get to see Marty the day I visited because he was working in the shop. The cars coming and going told me he was busy, so I didn't bother him.

Charmaine has thousands of photographs she has taken over the years. She has donated all her work to the Country Music Hall of Fame. Everyone will get to enjoy the old photos and her writing for years to come.

Marty and Charmaine live in Inglewood, a suburb of Nashville. Marty works in his shop, The Nashville Guitar Ship, five and sometimes six days a week, as a luthier. Charmaine just keeps taking photographs. They have one daughter and two absolutely beautiful grandchildren. Spending an afternoon with them is certainly a pleasure. They are super-talented, down-to-earth people who are lots of fun and love good music.

Ingrid Hermann Fowler Littlefield-Reese passed away in Nashville at the young age of 56.

James Henry (Jim) Borenstein passed away July 4, 2018 at 86 years of age.

JOHNNY AND JEANETTE WILLIAMS

I know this book is primarily about the business of music in Nashville as well as the people involved in the 1960s and the early '70s. However, for many years before the '60s and after the '70s, this business of music has attracted people to Nashville. It continues to do so, even to this day.

People come to record or to push their songs. The Nashville Sound is sought after. The artist puts on the label, "recorded at such-

The People and The Music—Country and Bluegrass that is!

and-such studio in Nashville," and it appears to the buyer they are part of the Nashville scene. When, in fact, they paid a hefty price to record here. Two of those people who made the trips to Nashville to record are Johnny and Jeanette Williams.

As Johnny would say, "We have been around bluegrass music as long as dirt." Johnny and Jeanette Williams are, one could safely say, diversified. They are terrific musicians; great singers; good, honest, hard-working people; and Johnny is an excellent songwriter and businessman. I forgot to mention, Jeanette writes incredible songs. The term, "salt-of-the earth" fits them to a tee.

Johnny began his musical career in high school where he was the leader of a Motown band. MOTOWN! That is a long way from bluegrass music. He and the group stayed together for about six months. Then, as kids do, they decided music wasn't for them. They all went their separate ways and never looked back.

The next time Johnny ventured out into the world of music, he was 37 years old. He started playing with a small bluegrass band out of Virginia called "Clearwater." He played shows with them all over the Virginia area, but his life was about to change. Jeanette joined the group.

With Jeanette's sweet voice and her ability to sing any part, the band was in high demand in the Virginia area. She was a big asset to the group. Not only did she sing like a bird, but she also played bass and was beautiful. She and Johnny started seeing each other when they were not on stage or rehearsing. It didn't take long until they fell in love and were married within two years.

Johnny and Jeanette have always lived in the Danville, Virginia area. That is the place where family is. There is a lot of bluegrass mu-

Singers, Songwriters, and More

sic in the area, as well. Carlton Haney produced the first bluegrass festival at Fincastle, Virginia. I booked Jimmy Martin and the Sunny Mountain Boys on that show. Don Reno and Red Smiley, The Stanley Brothers, and The Carter Family are from Virginia. Adopting a line or a thought from *The Sound of Music*, the hills of Virginia are alive with music – bluegrass music, that is."

After Johnny and Jeanette left Clearwater, they ventured out on their own. They began making regular visits to Nashville. They started recording with Bell Buckle Records, owned by Valerie Smith. It was during this time they met Tom T. and Dixie Hall. Tom T. and Miss Dixie (as Tom used to call his wife with much affection) were very active in the music publishing business, writing songs, and recording. They would all become friends and business associates. Valerie was (and is) not only active in the recording business, but touring and singing as well. By the way, she does a terrific show. If you can, go see her and tell her I sent you.

Except for a couple of months when they ventured out to try something new, Johnny has always been the booking agent for himself, Jeanette, and the band. They play approximately 40 to 50 days a year. The year has been steady for them. I asked Johnny how the world of booking acts today varies from when he first started. He said it is totally different and I agree. He remembers sitting up until midnight or beyond trying to book dates, making one phone call after the other looking for dates, and then rushing to get a contract finished and in the next morning's mail. But he persevered, and the band worked. Sometimes he was so tired the next day he couldn't hold his head up. He would get up in the morning, go to his regular job, and work all day. That night, he would do the same thing all

The People and The Music—Country and Bluegrass that is!

over again – try to book some shows. Booking and promoting was a never-ending job but well worth the time he put into it.

Johnny and Jeanette work regularly today. Jeanette is one of the top female vocalists in bluegrass music. Her first recording burst on the scene in 1994, *Cherry Blossoms In The Springtime*, and remained for nine months in the *Bluegrass Unlimited* National Album Chart. Since that time, Jeanette has received more than 10 SPBGMA (Society for the Preservation of Bluegrass Music in America) nominations for Female Vocalist of the Year. She won in 2009, 2012, and 2013. She also won two IBMA (International Bluegrass Music Association) awards (2006 and 2009) for Recorded Event of the Year with the *Daughters of Bluegrass*. My daughter, Lisa Martin, is also one of the featured singers on the *Daughters of Bluegrass* album. In fact, I believe she and Carol Lee Cooper are the only true daughters of bluegrass musicians on the album. Not only is Jeanette a fantastic singer and musician (she plays bass), she is an incredible songwriter, having won a 2007 Chris Austin Songwriting Contest at MerleFest and a 2008 IAMA (Intermountain Acoustic Music Association) Songwriting Contest.

Jeanette loves contemporary music (Bonnie Raitt, in particular). With her clear, soft, rangy voice, she released the flavored Raitt classic, "I Can't Make You Love Me." The song was written by Mike Reid and Allen Shamblin, who have each received rave reviews as writers. They both applauded Jeanette's version of the song and said, "Jeanette Williams is a wonderful artist. She is not trying to sell you anything. Her intent is pure; just the music, sung with an ethereally gorgeous voice deeply felt. She made this song her own. I love it." What a wonderful tribute!

The People and The Music—Country and Bluegrass that is!

In 2008, Jeanette recorded an album entitled, *Thank You For Caring*. The album was a huge success and featured songs written by Paul Williams, Tom T and Dixie Hall, Brandon Rickman, Laurie Lewis, and Marcia Harris. Also joining her on the CD was Tony Rice, Tim Stafford, Johnny Williams, and several other well-known entertainers. The biggest name guesting on the cut of "Thank You for Caring" was none other than the incredible George Jones. The song was written by Tom T. Hall and his lovely Miss Dixie. Dixie told Jeanette it came to them when they were at yard sales trying to find things to donate for the hurricane victims. The family where they had attended a yard sale was seeing them out when their small daughter put her hand in Dixie's and said, "Thank you for caring." And, thus, a song was born!

Recently, Johnny and Jeanette recorded another album which has been making the circle of top bluegrass hits. She recorded an album with Jay Shelton, and it is listed as Shelton & Williams. The album entitled, *So Much Time, So Much Love* is getting recognition in all the bluegrass and some country charts. It is a powerful duet. Prior to teaming up with Jay Shelton, Johnny and Jeanette released *30 Years Later*, a tribute album to their marriage.

One of Jeanette's favorite songs is one written by Johnny for her entitled, "Your Love Holds the Key." Johnny sings it as a solo to her, but they also sing it as a duet. The song is published by Grass Tank Music, which is owned by Johnny and Jeanette.

Johnny and Jeanette Williams are a tribute to bluegrass music. Hard working, very talented, and just awe-inspiring people. All of their materials are available on available on YouTube and Amazon. Take a listen.

YOUR LOVE HOLDS THE KEY
Words and Music by Johnny Williams

Do you remember the day we said hello?
I tried to pretend, tried not to let it show.
I tried to look the other way, but my eyes were stuck on you.
The feeling inside of me, I knew you were feeling the same way too.

Chorus:

Now my heart's on fire, with desire for you.
When we're far apart, I don't know what to do.
I believe in you, and you believe in me.
There's a lock around my heart, and your love holds the key.

So many times, I think of you when you're not around.
But the memories of your sweet kiss, they never let me down.
And knowing that you care for me still takes my breath away.
I will always love you, forever and a day.

Chorus

Bridge

What would I ever do without you?
No one could ever take your place.
But there's one thing certain my darlin'
My love for you time can't erase.

Chorus

THE NASHVILLE MUSICIANS UNION

Preparing to finalize my book, I reached out to Dave Pomeroy, who is the president of the Nashville Musicians Association, AFM Local 237 aka "The Union." wanted to know the way the Union keeps up with the shows being played in various cities and how the Union operates in today's market.

I learned from Dave a law passed sometime in the 1970s restricting the Union from forcing groups or individuals to file contracts in a city or town where they are appearing. This was both good and bad for the artists. In the 1960s, we had to file our contracts with whatever Union was in the area and pay a small fee. I was a Union booking agent, and all members of the band had to be Union working through my agency. My contracts were all written and filed with the Union.

However, enactment of the law in the '70s did not guarantee each member of the band and the artist would be paid for the show. The law created some inequities the Union would have dealt with, had they been involved when the law went into effect. For instance, when you sign a contract, it does not guarantee payment whether it is Union or not. But if the contract is for a Union member, there is an alternative.

There are some areas of the country that are still trying to enforce the rules to get traveling work dues from AFM members who are from another area doing a show in their jurisdiction. That is very difficult to do since the tight, restricted Union contracts that were around during the time I was booking shows no longer exist. Our contracts were all Union contracts. Some of the areas still trying to

Singers, Songwriters, and More

enforce this law are in Oklahoma and West Virginia.

Now-a-days, the Union has no guarantee everyone in a band is Union even if the leader does belong. Dave said some of the musicians who constantly work under AFM contracts refuse to pay the small dues to join the Union, but are quick to come into the office to pick up a check. They even refuse to pay the small collection fee requested by the Union for non-Union members. They just laugh

The People and The Music—Country and Bluegrass that is!

and smile, take their checks, and go away. Because of the right to work laws, the Union can do nothing about it. All the Union can do is ask; they cannot force the issue.

Dave said Nashville is the 25th largest city in the United States, but Local 257 is the 3rd largest U.S. Musician's Union, after New York and L.A. In many ways, Dave thinks Nashville's Union is outstripping New York and LA because they have gone from being the "hillbilly cousins" to being the ones who are asked, "How are you guys getting all that work covered down there?" This is because the musicians know they are protected by working under a contract. And if they get stuck and don't get paid, the Union can get them paid whether it is soon or 50 years from now.

Dave told me an interesting story about a 90 year old violin player who had been a member for 50 plus years. He came into the Union office to pick up a $1,500 check for a Patsy Cline record he played on in 1962. The fiddle player was a very happy camper. He was one happy, retired musician.

In terms of the touring part and the booking agency part, he said there used to be Union Booking Agents. I was one. The law concerning having to be a licensed booking agency changed sometime in the 1970s. However, as laws go, some are good and some are bad. In this instance, I do not believe it helped the booking agents or the musicians.

Dave definitely knows both sides of the spectrum since he moved here in 1977, knowing one person. He feels very blessed to do a lot of interesting things and know a lot of cool folks. He toured with Don Williams for a long time, slowly transitioned into studio work, and got more involved with the Union over the years. He replaced Harold Bradley as president of the Nashville Musicians Union in 2009. He said, "I love Nashville; it is a Union place."

Before we parted ways, I asked Dave about the Grand Ole Opry. He told me the Union presently has a solid contract with them. The contract has been renegotiated several times over the past 14 years. The Union has made healthy strides in getting the backup musicians paid for appearing on the Grand Ole Opry. The Union also, for the first time, negotiated a back end royalty for when the Opry syndicates The Opry broadcast and makes money from another network called Circle TV. Because of this agreement, the Union was able to distribute the first ever residuals from Circle TV in the amount of $189,000 to about 400 people. Dave thinks the current management of the Opry is more musician friendly than it has been in the past, and he is proud of their positive relationship. Currently, scale is just under $150 for one spot. Then if a song gets broadcast on Sirius XM, they get an extra $50 per spot. They also negotiated rehearsal time at $85 an hour under the contract. To think, when Jimmy was working for Bill Monroe, he was paid $15 a night. Of course, this amount of money went a long way in 1953. Now scale varies, but for a house band playing two, three, four times a night, they can make a very good annual income.

I believe belonging to the Union pays off whether it is the Musicians Union, the Steelworkers, or whatever. When I was working as a paralegal, I used to think, "If we only had an office worker's union, the employers would not able to pay workers pennies and gripe about giving them a raise." I have always loved the Unions, and after hearing Dave Pomeroy, I will always a Union advocate. Keep up the good work Dave!

RONNIE RENO

"A child of the music!" That is how Ronnie describes himself. And that is exactly what he is. Born on September 28, 1947, in Buffalo, Virginia, to Chole Robinson and Don Reno, he grew up learning to sing and play.

Ronnie's dad, the great Don Reno, was a major force in the bluegrass field of music, a legend, and a pioneer. Don began playing music when he was about 12 years old, as did his son, Ronnie. It seems "legends begat legends."

Don Reno would have two more two more sons, Dale and Don Wayne. Each of them was born with music in their heart and soul. They would follow in Ronnie's footsteps, joining their Dad's band when they were old enough.

The Reno household was full of music. Don had been on the road since he was a very young boy. He was innovative (as is his son, Ronnie), learning to play different songs on the banjo and other instruments including the guitar, drums, and bass. Playing other

Singers, Songwriters, and More

genres of music was equally as important to him.

Don Reno had an illustrious career playing with Bill Monroe, Arthur Smith, the Morris Brothers, and others. During the time he worked for Arthur Smith, he played banjo and guitar as well as bass, drums, or whatever the gig called for. Don thought he was a much better guitar player than a banjo player. He also learned to read and write music during that time, a skill he would use throughout his lifetime. However, it wasn't until he joined forces with Red Smiley that he became a household name.

Don Reno and Red Smiley had a partnership that would break records and become one of the longest, most successful partnerships in bluegrass music. They had television shows in the Virginia area lasting more than 10 years with sponsors such as Dr.

Don Reno & Red Smiley with Little Ronnie Reno Mack McGaha on fiddle

Pepper, Coca Cola, and Mountain Dew. They introduced "Little Ronnie Reno" on their television shows at 12 years of age. Ronnie became an instant hit with the television audience and would go on to play with his Dad and Red Smiley until he was 17. During that time, he learned to play a "mean" mandolin. He became a regular member of the cast. Unbeknown to him at the time, the show taught him how to put a good television show together, how to make it work, how to please the audience, and many other things he would not have learned without working all those years on the show. It also served him well when he did his own television show on The Americana Network, Blue Highways TV, and RFD TV.

Red Smiley was diagnosed with diabetes and was told by his doctors that he could no longer travel. In those days, they didn't have the choices diabetics have today. Regretfully, he and Don terminated their partnership and remained friends.

Red decided to stay in the Roanoke area since he had a TV show there that was doing very well. He was on the air five mornings a week. He could make a living for his family and take care of his health by staying put.

Ronnie was 17 years old when all these changes were happening. His mandolin skills were excellent. He had incredible forethought, and even at such an early age the business end of music was always on his mind. He was ready to step in and start touring with his dad. Before they did, he had to talk to his dad about expanding their territory and booking shows not just on the East Coast, but in other parts of the country as well. Reaching out further across the country meant more dates and recognition. After talking to his Dad,

Singers, Songwriters, and More

Don Reno, Red Smiley and Ronnie Reno

Don agreed they could venture out and play dates in other areas of the country. He liked Ronnie's ideas.

Ronnie toured with his Dad for a year or so until Don decided he wanted to team up with Bill Harrell. He had worked with Bill in Virginia in the '50s. He liked Bill's singing very much. Bill had a down-to-earth personality and would be easy to team up with. Ronnie liked Bill's singing and could understand Don wanting to go with Bill.

Once Bill and Don became partners, he moved the family to Riverdale, Maryland. The move was life changing for Ronnie because he met his future wife, Debby, a schoolteacher there. They actually met on a blind date, and it has been a wonderful union since that

The People and The Music—Country and Bluegrass that is!

time. They married in 1970, have two sons, each successful in his own right—just not in the music business. But both are incredible musicians, as Ronnie will quickly let you know, and they could be in the business of music. He is very proud of his boys and is equally as proud that he and Debby are still a loving couple over 50 years later. Bill and Don stayed together for about 10 years. Their partnership coincided with bluegrass music being rediscovered. The bluegrass music festivals were just beginning all over the country, and a new audience was born. Suddenly, the bluegrass bands were once again in demand.

In early 1967, Don and Ronnie made a trip to Nashville. By early 1968, Don had returned home, and Ronnie began performing with the Osborne Brothers. At the time, there were three in the band, Bob, Sonny, and Benny Birchfield. They needed a bass player and Ronnie said to himself, "I can play bass." He joined them and was the first person to play electric bass on their show. If I remember correctly, they were playing the Black Poodle Lounge in Printer's Alley and also working the Grand Ole Opry.

Ronnie loved to hear the Osborne Brothers sing, and he loved their harmonies. In his words, "I was fortunate to be with them," and he was able to record with them from 1968 to 1972. During this time, they were at their hottest with "Rocky Top." Ronnie loved everything the Osbornes were doing. He was thrilled Bobby and Sonny were venturing a little outside of the realm of bluegrass. He describes his time with Bobby and Sonny as one of the greatest times of his life. He was and remains a big Bobby and Sonny Osborne fan.

While working with Bob and Sonny, they began opening shows for Merle Haggard. When they were opening shows for the

Singers, Songwriters, and More

Bobby & Sonny Osborne, Dale Sledd & Ronnie Reno

Hag, he was at his peak. Bob and Sonny won "Vocal Group of the Year" in 1971, and Merle Haggard won six awards from Country Music Association at the same time. He took home just about everything there was to win at the Awards that year.

Following the Awards Show in 1971, The Osborne Brothers went to Reno, Nevada, where they spent the next two weeks opening the show for Merle Haggard at Harrah's Casino. Traveling the road, Ronnie and Merle got to know each other very well. They had serious talks about the music business; subjects like where they thought it was, where it was going, and how they could help take it there. He was already thinking about the business end of music even though

The People and The Music—Country and Bluegrass that is!

he was not involved other than as a side musician. His mind was ever-evolving, even at his young age.

Ronnie and Merle really liked and trusted each other. They became good friends and buddies. Merle decided to make some changes in his band, so he reached out to Ronnie. Ronnie, in turn, spoke to Bob and Sonny and told them he wanted to "do his own thing."

When Roy Nichols (Merle Haggard's guitar player) approached him about working for the Hag, he told him he would think about it. Roy went to Merle and told him to think about hiring Ronnie. Merle did and decided it was a good idea.

Merle approached him to talk about the job. Ronnie told Merle, "I really want to do my own thing." Merle said, "Ronnie, you help me, and I will help you. We will do this together." Ronnie thought that was a great idea. Right off the bat, he recorded Merle's 30th album with him. Merle had him sing a solo, one he had co-written entitled "Travelin'" on the album. Then Ronnie and Merle recorded a duet together.

Ronnie told Merle he would try the job for three months and see how it worked out. He told Merle, "I am not going to move to California." Merle told him, "I don't care where you live as long as you are there for the shows." Ronnie said, "I will be there for the shows." He stayed with Merle for eight years, all the while still living in Nashville and never missing a show.

Ronnie sang harmony with Merle Haggard and Bonnie Owens and recorded with them. Merle and Ronnie were friends before they became employer/employee, and they respected each other.

After Bonnie decided to quit touring, Merle was looking for another girl singer to replace her and sing the third part with them.

Singers, Songwriters, and More

Ronnie knew Leona Williams quite well. He thought she was a great artist and a fabulous singer. He and Merle were putting together a package together. Ronnie would open the show, the girl singer would then do her part, and Merle would come out last. They needed to get a singer.

Ronnie said to Merle, "Let's call Leona Williams and see if she would be interested. She would be a great asset to you. Not only can she sing harmony, but she is a great artist." So, Ronnie called Leona and the three of them started talking, and the next thing he knew, Merle had hired Leona. Leona was a beautiful woman and extremely talented. It didn't take long for Merle and Leona to get a romance going, and they were married. After Merle and Leona divorced in 1983, he re-hired Bonnie Owens to be the girl singer.

Ronnie told me an interesting story about the song, "Today, I Started Loving You Again" which was written by Merle and Bonnie. He said Merle and Bonnie were fussing with each other as they were walking through the airport. They made up and Merle said to Bonnie, "I just started loving you again today." Bonnie said to Merle, "No. Turn it around." Merle said, "What do you mean?" Bonnie said, say "Today, I Started Loving You Again." He then told her, "That right there got you half of that song." It was a monster hit. When Merle and Bonnie got a divorce he told Ronnie, "You know Bonnie owned half of "Today, I Started Loving You Again" and when we got a divorce, I gave her the other half. Now, she owns the entire thing."

Merle Haggard passed away on his 79th birthday. He had requested that the family get in touch with Ronnie to let him know and ask him to sing "Life's Railway to Heaven" at his funeral.

The People and The Music—Country and Bluegrass that is!

After working and enjoying playing with Merle for eight years, writing numerous songs, producing an album for him with Del McCoury records, and recording 10 albums with him, Ronnie never stopped thinking about doing his own thing. He finally quit Merle and went back with his Dad for a short time while he was trying to decide what he wanted to do next. He had a great resume, but how was he going to use it?

During the time he was playing with the Osbornes and Merle Haggard, his two younger brothers, Dale and Don Wayne, grew up to become terrific musicians. There was quite an age gap between Ronnie, Dale, and Don Wayne, but he was and still is the big brother. He never considered them half-brothers; they were just brothers with different mothers.

The brothers joined together and toured for three years with their father. Don became sick and passed away at the young age of 58. The three brothers regrouped and started touring as the Reno Brothers. In the meantime, Ronnie continued to have his own country band. The Reno Brothers were together as a group for 17 years before disbanding and venturing out in separate directions.

Don Wayne and Dale, even though much younger, were much like their older brother in thinking outside the box. They went with a group called, "Hayseed Dixie." The two younger brothers wanted to expand their style, and expand they did. Hayseed Dixie was a rock 'n roll band with a banjo and mandolin. They became hugely popular in Europe. They were affiliated with Hayseed Dixie for 10 years before retiring and coming back to the States.

While the brothers were playing rock 'n roll, Ronnie was digging his heels into the music scene in Nashville. He formed the

Singers, Songwriters, and More

The Reno Brothers: Don Wayne on banjo, Ronnie on guitar, Dale on Mandolin and John Palmer on bass

Ronnie Reno Band in 2001 and continued to tour with the same band until 2019. As Ronnie would say, "That's when this old road dog retired after spending over six decades (that's 60 years) on the road." The band consisting of Ronnie Reno, Mike Scott on banjo, Steve Day on fiddle, John Maberry on mandolin, and Heath Van Winkle on bass. All are fantastic musicians, professionals, and terrific men. It is easy to understand why they stayed together. Quite a feat in itself!

The People and The Music—Country and Bluegrass that is!

Mike Scott with me

Ronnie has never been one to stand still while he is doing something and not think of a dozen more things he could be accomplishing at the same time. "Never sit still if you don't have to," should be his motto.

He had an idea brewing in the back of his head since he was 12 years old and appearing on television in Virginia. The idea was for a television show of his own where he would have guests each week.

His friend, Stan Hitchcock, was one of the founders of Country Music Television. He and Stan were good friends. They started picking some together because CMT's storage didn't hold a lot of content. They liked to sit on the front porch and pick. They didn't just sit on the porch and pick, they picked and talked anywhere they could find.

One day they were picking and Stan said, "Ronnie, if I were

ever to produce a show, would you do a bluegrass show for me?" Ronnie replied with a big smile on his face, "Sure. I will be glad to do one." The Americana Network was started, and Ronnie's show was the first one on the agenda. Having watched his show many, many times, I know he always had a great lineup of guests, and the format was good. I used to record it when I lived in Florida. The show ran for 12 years. It was extremely popular, and at the time he retired the show on RFD TV, it was in 60 million homes nightly.

Ronnie's philosophy, both as an entertainer and as a businessman, has always been the more he can do himself, the more profit he will see in the end. If you are an entertainer and you have to pay someone to produce your record, cut your record, distribute it, and market it, then you have already eaten up your profits.

Toward the end of his life, Merle Haggard got in touch with Ronnie and wanted him to produce an album with him that he was cutting for Del McCoury. Ronnie was very happy to be included and worked with Merle, Del and his crew to create Merle's 61st album titled, *The Bluegrass Sessions*. The album was cut live in the studio, and featured guests were Alison Krauss, Marty Stuart, and Dobro virtuoso Rob Ickes. It was released on October 2, 2007 by McCoury Music and Hag Records. Merle wrote many of the songs featured on the album.

In 2015, Ronnie produced an album, *Merle & Mac*, featuring Merle Haggard and Mac Wiseman together, for Cracker Barrel. The album again featured Rob Ickes, as well as Carl Jackson on guitar, Aubrey Haynie on fiddle, Andy Leftwich on mandolin and fiddle, and Ben Isaacs on acoustic bass. Special guests included Marty Stuart, Vince Gill, Sonya Isaacs on high harmony, and Becky Isaacs with tenor harmony. This historical album couldn't have been cut at a better time. Mac was 90 years old during the recording of the album, and the following year on April 16, 2016, Merle Haggard passed away.

Throughout his career, Ronnie has produced, sang on, or distributed many top-selling records or videos for major artists including the video he distributed for Bobby Osborne, "I Can't Stop Loving You." The video was recorded in a couple of different places, including Bobby's home, and pieced together. It was released on OMS Records for social media and distributed by Ronnie Reno's company, Bluegrass Music TV.Com. Ronnie feels like distribution is one of the key areas in promoting your record successfully. As he tells it, "It is like the tree that fell in the forest. If no one is listening for it, no one knows it fell." You have to have the listeners. Fortunately, "I Can't Stop Loving You" has had the listeners. It gave Bobby the little push back into the spotlight he needed at the time.

During the time he was producing top records and albums for other entertainers, Ronnie also had his own TV show and was touring with his band. He believes that if you are going to be in the entertainment business, you better have four quarters to make the dollar. One little quarter of it is singing and playing. Then, there is the booking side, the publishing side, and the distribution. If you are not covering all of it yourself, then you are giving away everything you are working for. Ronnie has always abided by the rule that the more he could do himself, the more he could take home to his family.

He has always tried to help other entertainers be more self-sufficient along the way. For instance, when he was with the Osborne Brothers, he helped them start Rocky Top Music. He maintained a

Singers, Songwriters, and More

Ronnie Reno and his Dad, Don Reno

share in the company and when he left the Osbornes, he sold his half of Rocky Top back to them.

In 2019, Ronnie decided he was going to retire from the road. He couldn't rest; he felt like he could feel every bump in the road and tell you where he was at the time. This bump, that bump, up in Pennsylvania, it didn't matter. He could tell you where he was. He quit the road and came home to rest.

Since 2020, he has focused more on his production company and concentrating on the social media side of our industry including the digital side of the industry, whether it is streaming, downloading, or YouTube. He is involved with Sammy Passamano, who is third

The People and The Music—Country and Bluegrass that is!

generation in the music industry. He has a new venture with Country Road TV in Nashville.

Ronnie thanks God he survived 60 years on the road touring with his Dad (Don Reno and Red Smiley); his own band, The Reno Tradition; his brothers, The Reno Brothers; The Osborne Brothers; Merle Haggard; and others. He calls himself "a road dog." I love the name he gave himself, and it is quite suitable for a whole bunch of us who didn't have the luxurious buses to travel in, but instead, rode in a big old Buick, Oldsmobile, or Cadillac. We had the bass fiddle tied on top, and everything else was in the trunk unless you were lucky enough to have a small trailer to pull behind the car. I have spent many a day traveling in the middle front seat of the Mediterranean blue and cream-colored 1959 Cadillac. They called it "riding shotgun" back then, to keep the driver awake.

Ronnie Reno is someone I very much admire and respect. He is one of the most honest, intelligent, respectable, and caring individuals you could ever know. I could write about him all day. He has an infectious laugh. He and I sat and laughed and laughed and laughed while I was interviewing him. I have the tape, and I will cherish it forever. We would get so overtaken by laughter, we would forget where we were in his story. It was a fun time. Then again, I always have a fun time with Ronnie Reno, whether on the phone or in-person, and I have known him since he was just a kid.

Ronnie has accomplished more than your average person in his young life. He has been diligent since he began in the music business and worked very, very long hours and many days and nights on the road away from his family. Some of his achievements are:

Singers, Songwriters, and More

CD RELEASES

- *Lessons Learned* — Rural Rhythm Records
- *Front Porch Gospel* — Mandolin Records
- *In Concert* — Mandolin Records
- *Portfolio* — Mandolin Records
- *Three Part Harmony* — Pinecastle Records
- *Drawing From the Well* — Pinecastle Records
- *Swing West* — Pinecastle Records
- *Acoustic Celebration* — Pinecastle Records
- *Kentucky Gold* — Webco Records
- *For the First Time* — MCA Records

CAREER ACHIEVEMENTS

- Produced Merle Haggard and Mac Wiseman CD for Cracker Barrel
- Produced Merle Haggard's bluegrass CD, *The Bluegrass Sessions*, on McCoury Music
- Host/Producer of *Reno's Old Time Music* on Dish and Direct TV
- For RFD-TV Cable Network
- Songs recorded by Conway Twitty and Merle Haggard,
- "Boogie Grass Band," "Hero For A Day," "I've Got A Darlin'," "Union Station"
- Served on the IBMA Board of Directors (International Bluegrass Music Association
- Served on the Board of Directors for the Bluegrass Hall of Fame and Museum in Owensboro, Kentucky
- Served on the Board of Directors at Morehead State University
- Founder and Vice President of Entertainment at Blue Highways TV

The People and The Music—Country and Bluegrass that is!

AWARDS

- Blue Blaze Award – 2019
- Broadcaster of the Year Award by IBMA – 2015
- ROPE International Musician of the Year Award – 2013
- IBMA Distinguished Achievement Award – 2006
- Cable Fox Faxies award for "Cable Television Industry" – 2006
- BMI Award for Writer – "Boogie Grass Band"
- NAIRD Award for "Reno and Smiley" video
- Country Music Association (CMA) Vocal Group with The Osborne Brothers
- Academy of Country Music Award (ACM) with Merle Haggard

NETWORK TV APPEARANCES

- Host of *Reno's Old Time Music*
- *Austin City Limits*
- *Old Country Church* (BHTV)
- CMT Special (with Merle Haggard)

You can find out more about Ronnie Reno by going to RonnieReno.Com or his Facebook page. His records are available on YouTube, Amazon, and other channels.

He is and always has been a force to be dealt with in the music business. If you see him around Nashville, Hendersonville, or on the road, go up and say hello. You will think you're known him all your life after the conversation.

"BOOGIE GRASS BAND"
By: Ronnie Reno

There's a new kind of music going 'round.
It's known as the Boogie Grass sound.
So, grab your partner and swing her around,
And dance to the Boogie Grass sound.

I love to hear Bill sing about Kentucky,
And the Allman Brothers' "Ramblin' Man."
We put the music all together.
So, dance to the Boogie Grass Band.

Well, my daddy plays the banjo and saws a fiddle too.
He taught me how to sing and play for you.
I've got bluegrass in my soul and rhythm in my feet,
So, dance to the Boogie Grass beat.

I love to hear Bill sing about Kentucky,
And the Allman Brothers' "Ramblin' Man."
We put the music all together,
So dance to the Boogie Grass Band.

I love to hear Bill Sing about Kentucky,
And the Allman Brothers' "Ramblin' Man."
We put the music all together,
So, dance to the Boogie Grass Band
(yodel)

EPILOGUE

The Music Business Today

Sixty-nine years! Unbelievable. It has been that long since I took a job as a waitress at the Tulane Hotel in Nashville, met Jimmy Martin, and had an introduction to the field of country and bluegrass music. Time flies.

Here I am now so many years later, still thinking about business. Instead of moving at a fast pace, I am going much slower. I think of the new ways I have learned the music business is conducted today.

In my day, we filled our time typing letters using carbon paper to make any copies or sitting on the phone talking to our buyers or other agents and then typing the contracts in four parts without error (one copy for the Union, one for the buyer, one for the artist, and one for me (the booker). Then we ran the contracts and brochures to the post office to get them mailed quickly. A copy machine was unheard of. It would have been wonderful to have had one because using carbon paper to make copies of letters was very difficult. You had to be an accurate typist. A few errors, and it was starting all over again. Ugh!!

The People and The Music—Country and Bluegrass that is!

I knew about computers, but they were used by big businesses and not by the small offices. I worked at Washington Manufacturing during my senior year of high school and learned to use the old key punch machines. They had a mirror on the back, and you watched the card go through and punched the information in when the card reached the center. Once you learned to use this antiquated machine, the key punch machines used during the 1960s were a breeze to learn. This skill served me well. It was easy to get a job if you knew how to key punch, and I used it many times to feed us during the years I was with Jimmy Martin and after.

In speaking with people who are involved in the business of music today, nothing has been more surprising than the demands of the promoters. Videos of the artists are required, and some promoters want the artists to actually audition in person by Zoom. You can't blame the promoters since they are paying thousands of dollars to the musicians. They want to ensure they get a good quality act.

When I needed some information from the artists, I reached out to my beautiful banjo playing, songwriting, singer friend, Michelle Canning, on how the young or old artists go about getting themselves known today. Before we get into all of that, let me tell you a little bit about Michelle.

Michelle is from Massachusetts, and I first met her and her mother, Donna, at the Jenny Brook Festival. She was playing music and I was appearing in a workshop for my book, *Don't Give Your Heart to a Rambler*. It was Jimmy Martin Day at the festival. I fell in love with Michelle and Donna immediately. They were both so down to earth. Michelle was and is adorable. I try to see her play music and for lunch often. She works during the day at the Grand Ole Opry

The Music Business Today

Michelle Canning

and does backstage tours. She plays the banjo and guitar, sings and write songs, and has several new records out. She has appeared with her band at Loretta Lynn's Ranch several times.

I asked her what the first thing young artists do today to make themselves known. She told me they set up a website. It is an expensive proposition, not only in designing and setting up the site, but maintaining is also a problem. You either must know how to maintain it yourself (and still there are some hefty fees getting started), or you hire someone to do it all for you. In talking to Michelle, she maintains her webpage herself. She uses a service called Bandzoogle.com, and she pays $150 a month to get it managed online. It is a service used by musicians and songwriters.

Once the website is created, you set up a VPK. "VPK" was a foreign word to me, so Michelle explained it. That is an electronic press kit. It contains all your information: videos of your performances, a biography, your calendar, a bullet list of honors and awards, records that may have been in the top ten, clicks to download the information, contact information, etc. The VPK is then sent to promoters and buyers of entertainment. Everything is on the internet. No more getting all of this information in a package and rushing out to the post office and mailing it to the buyers. It's cheaper and easier than the way we used to do it, but not nearly as much fun as talking to the people directly.

I have discovered "Songwriter's Night" at various places around town. Some of those places are the Commodore Lounge at the Holiday Inn Vanderbilt (which is probably the largest), Twelve Keys Saloon in Hermitage, the VFW in Hendersonville, and the Maxwell House Hotel. Songwriter's night is generally on Wednesday. The songwriters do not get paid. Places like the Commodore Lounge do not pay the songwriters, even though they have a packed house. Their sets are 30 minutes each, and they normally feature four songwriters for each set, onstage at the same time. Each person has a turn and sings a couple of songs. Each artist sings about three songs per set. The Commodore does not allow tip jars, so the artist gets nothing. Regardless, it is one of the most popular venues in Nashville for songwriters and has been for the past 20 years.

Twelve Keys Saloon in Hermitage has a card on the table, and you can scan the card in, leave a tip for the performers, and at the end of the night the tips are divided among the performers. There are three performers per set, and each set does 30 minutes. When I was there, they had another set of three performers come on stage for 30 minutes after the first set. They alternated all evening. So, the

The Music Business Today

performers do get some compensation at Twelve Keys.

Hawkshaw Hawkins, Jr. is in charge of the music at the VFW in Hendersonville. I have been there just to see Hawk. It is also on Wednesday night and is a fun place to go.

I am sure there are many more places around town that I haven't heard of. I do know one is in Greenbriar. Just haven't gotten there yet.

I know a bluegrass music jam takes place at the American Legion Post #82 in Nashville every Wednesday night. It is very good, and I have been to this a few times. You can see and hear just about anyone at the American Legion. They also have shows from time to time featuring well-known artists. I have seen Bobby Osborne and Rocky Top Express and Missy Raines and her band there. The stage can be seen from all the tables. They also have a dance floor but, when Bobby Osborne appeared, the house was so packed, they had to use the dance floor to set up tables. Missy Raines also had a full house.

As far as live music is concerned, I asked another friend what the venues (like Bluegrass Festivals) were paying the artists today. He told me bluegrass artists were getting paid anywhere from $3,000 to $5,000 a day. The stars are paid $5,000 up to $10,000 or even $15,000. This is a lot of money, but in the 1960s people like Bill Monroe, Jimmy Martin, and the Osborne Brothers were paid $500 a day. They had to feed themselves because they didn't get catering written in their contract, plus pay their band, put gas in their car, pay 15% booking fees, and pay for a motel. That's why, sometimes, the band and I (when I went on the road) all stayed in one room. I have slept in many a bathtub. And, out of that $500, we still made a good living.

The People and The Music—Country and Bluegrass that is!

Country music artists are horses of a different color. (The horse saying was borrowed from my good friend, Eddie Stubbs.) They are being paid double and triple what the bluegrass artists are paid. However, they also have triple and quadruple the number of people attending the show. I remember I was told about an artist I knew who was making $50,000 for a private show. I couldn't believe it, so I asked around. Sure enough, it was true. This was a "private" show not even open to the public.

Johnny Williams

Johnny Williams told me that the side musicians for a bluegrass band were paid from $200 to $400 a day, and that had to come off the top. Country backup musicians are probably three to four times as much per day, or they are paid a salary. I know some of the bigger artists like Tim McGraw, Faith Hill, Garth Brooks, and others pay their band a salary. Also coming off the top is the booking agents' fee of anywhere from 20 to 25% of the contract fee. All in all, the promoters and the band leaders have a tough nut to crack. For the bandleader, management and publicity fees, buses, bus driver, maintenance of the bus, insurance, and sometimes, tractor/trailers, band fees or salaries, equipment, hotels, per diem (for bus drivers – for their meals), gasoline or diesel fuel, and other expenses that always come up when you are on the road. Promoters or talent buyers pay for the use of the venue (where the show is held), entertainers, publicity for the show, security, employees, and catering when it is required in the contract.

In addition to learning about the costs of putting on a show and the salaries paid to the performers, one of the most surprising things I learned along the way is how a disc jockey prepares his show for airing. In my day, the disc jockey always worked at the radio station. They would go in, pull their records, their commercials, etc. and be ready to sign on. Now, in speaking to my friend, Jeff Miller, I have learned things are very different.

Jeff Miller is an Alabama boy, he grew up in a musical family and went to school at Montevallo (same place my granddaughter and her husband, Rachel and Jesse Slayton went). Jeff majored in voice with a graduate degree in Musicology. His parents were gospel singers. Jeff worked in church music for 15 to 20 years following graduation from college. This dissipated after a while and he looked around trying to "scratch his

Jeff Miller

itch," as Jeff said. His itch was the music business, and he landed in the world of radio and podcasts.

Along the way, Jeff started a thing called, "Flash Point Arts Initiative." It was intended to be a forum and discussion for people to talk about the creative process of writing and creative areas, not just music. But while he was working on Flash Point, starting to write, he stumbled upon the new field of internet radio. He began listening to Worldwide Bluegrass with Gracie Muldoon-Davis in Ohio. He and Gracie started talking. Jeff was looking for a partnership with what she was doing, and what he was doing? She then asked Jeff, "Have you ever considered doing radio?" He had always been fascinated with radio, and he grew up with it. He loved the radio personalities. So, he said to Gracie, "I have never considered doing it myself, but let's talk about it." She began tutoring Jeff in the technology and how things work today. He found out things he needed to start doing internet radio were available in most households.

Jeff discovered he could set up a broadcast with today's technology and it could be heard all over the world easily. That was in 2016. Here it is 2022, and he has a show that is live once a week and re-broadcast eight more times a week on different internet platforms. He has a second show broadcast over the public radio station at the University of Alabama. It has been an exciting six years for Jeff, going from not knowing anything about internet radio to having a live show that is rebroadcast eight times a week and also broadcast on public radio.

We talked about the equipment he used for broadcasting from his house. He said he didn't have that much to buy. He already had a laptop he could use. Then he found a couple of older computers

*Becky Buller appearing on Jeff's radio program
With Jeff Haley, Becky's husband*

being phased out of a business. He picked them up fairly cheaply. With Gracie Muldoon Davis' help, he was able to use one of the older computers to broadcast to the internet. Using an app called Winamp allowed him to record and archive the shows and later to send the shows to a secondary format for broadcasting or re-broadcasting. It didn't require a big investment in those things. He did buy a microphone and a mixer so he could do interviews more efficiently. He said his setup is fairly simple. He has his computer, headphones, and microphones. He did purchase an external drive for the music catalog so he would have enough room to grow without relying on an old computer

The People and The Music—Country and Bluegrass that is!

We talked about the music catalog. When he gets a CD, he rips the songs from the disc and puts them in digital form so he can easily manipulate them during a broadcast. The wierd part about it is the studio for public broadcasting requires CDs for music files. He keeps the CDs and organizes and catalogs them for use on public broadcasting.

Physical CDs are phasing out in many ways. However, Jeff personally prefers a physical format and likes reading the liner notes, the artwork, and other notes on the physical CD. He likes tangible products. He has good reason, since he once had a hard drive failure, and everything had to be redone. That could happen to any of us.

We have come full circle in the music business. The recording industry is now releasing single records in place of albums. Sure, there are albums being released, but today's market calls for singles. The old style vinyl albums are being re-released and played. Wait, don't give them away yet. They are still in style, at least for a short time.

Today's world is evolving so fast. What will tomorrow's music world do? Who knows! It will be interesting to find out.

MY MEMORIES OF THREE OF THE GREATEST BANJO PLAYERS

Sonny Osborne, Bill Emerson, and J.D. Crowe

In just four short months, we lost three of the greatest banjo players and the finest gentlemen bluegrass music will ever know. I am not going to repeat all the accolades surrounding their banjo playing and their musical abilities. Everyone knows what great musicians they were. I am going to talk to you about the guys I knew, starting with the first banjo player I ever met. I wasn't a fan of banjo music and had never even seen a banjo.

I met Sonny Osborne when he was playing with Bill Monroe the summer of 1953. He was 16 years old, and I was 17. Sonny was never a tiny, petite person. He was always heavy and tall. The first day I saw him, L.E. White, Jimmy Martin, Jean Armstrong, and I were in Jimmy's room at the Tulane Hotel in Nashville. The hotel was not air conditioned, and Sonny was sitting in the open window. The window bordered the alleyway. They were all playing music.

The People and The Music—Country and Bluegrass that is!

Jimmy Martin and the Osborne Brothers with Casey Clark

I was not a fan of their music, and I guess Sonny could tell from my attitude and mannerisms. I definitely wasn't applauding them. So at every break he would make some snide remark to me, and I would counter back. This went on every time I saw Sonny for the rest of his life.

In 1954, Jimmy, Bob and Sonny Osborne decided to team up and bill themselves as "Jimmy Martin and The Osbornes." At the time, Jimmy was with WPFB, The Smoky Ward Show, in Middletown, Ohio and playing clubs in the area. J.D. Crowe was on a school break and playing banjo with Jimmy. He lived with Jimmy and me in an efficiency apartment with a living room/bedroom (J.D. slept on the couch, Jimmy and I in the bed), a small kitchen, and a path to the outhouse. Pat and Bobby Osborne lived in a trailer on Highway 25 in Middletown, and Sonny lived at home with his

My Memories Three of the Greatest Banjo Players

parents and Louise (his sister) in Dayton, Ohio.

We went back and forth to Mr. & Mrs. Osborne's house a couple of times a week. I loved going to their house. Bob & Sonny's sister, Louise, and I became friends. We were almost the same age. I remember vividly one time we were there when Sonny was sitting laid back in this recliner and Mrs. Osborne was going to make lunch. She asked Sonny if he wanted a sandwich. Sonny said, "Bring me one." I looked over at him and said, "Just get up and make it yourself. I did." He looked at me and said, "Go home." I said, "No." We were going at it and here comes Mrs. Osborne with Sonny's sandwich and she said, "Both of you kids be quiet." Sonny then stuck his tongue out at me when Mrs. Osborne left the room. We were both just teenagers being teenagers.

Jimmy had been in touch with Steve Shoals, who was the A&R man for RCA Victor Records. Steve told Jimmy to come down to Nashville and sign the contract. He would get them in the recording studio. In July 1954, Bob, Jimmy, and I took off for Nashville so they could sign with RCA. Sonny didn't go.

Bob and Jimmy wanted to try out Gordon Terry to play fiddle on the records they were going to record. We were all staying with my mother, and Jimmy, Bob, and Gordon would rehearse every day in the living room. Mother loved it. Her bird, Georgie, wanted to join in

Gordon Terry

The People and The Music—Country and Bluegrass that is!

and sing along. The first day, we all laughed. Later, Mother had to cover Georgie's cage to keep him quiet.

We stayed with Mother for a week with rehearsals every day. When we left, Jimmy wanted to go to the radio station in Mayfield, Kentucky to visit a DJ there. On the way, we heard Elvis Presley singing, "Blue Moon of Kentucky" for the first time. Bob and I were rocking to the song, but Jimmy said he didn't like it. Bob was driving, I was riding in the passenger seat and, as usual, Jimmy was sprawled in the back seat. He was literally a back seat driver! Jimmy became so negative about the song, He wanted us to turn the radio off. We wouldn't. That didn't sit well with Jimmy. I was very happy when we pulled into the radio station. The big surprise came later when Jimmy learned Elvis loved his music. Quickly, Jimmy loved Elvis and became friends with him. Jimmy and I received a Christmas card from Elvis every year.

*Timmy, age 6 months,
1203 Glover Street
Pictures back then were not good*

In August 1954, I returned to Nashville to have my son, Timmy. Pat, Bob's wife, went to Pikeville, Kentucky to her parents' home to have their son, Robbie. Sonny, Bob, and Jimmy found a place in Detroit, Michigan for all of us to live and moved us there. Jimmy and Bob had signed Jimmy Martin and the Osborne Brothers to appear on

My Memories Three of the Greatest Banjo Players

the Casey Clark Barn Dance at 12101 Mack Avenue. It was heard over 50,000 watt radio station WJR in Detroit. Soon, they would have records and a listening audience

The apartment they found at 1203 Glover Street was huge, but ugly. It had a large living room with bay windows, a couch, a couple of chairs, and tables. Timmy used to love to sit in his little chair and rock and look out the windows. Bob and Pat had the front bedroom (which didn't have a door), Jimmy and I had the middle bedroom (with the door), then, separating us from Sonny's room was the one bathroom for the entire apartment. No shower, just a claw foot tub. Sonny's room was on the back of the house next to the ugliest kitchen in the universe. It had royal blue and yellow cabinets. Sonny could get up, take a bath, eat, and leave out the back door, and we wouldn't know it. And he did that often.

I loved Sonny and Bob's parents and their sister, Louise. They always welcomed me when we visited them in Dayton. I was determined to do the same thing when they visited Bob and Sonny in Detroit. Louise and I went to see the movie, *Gone with the Wind* together while they were there. The movie theatre was located on Jefferson Street about two blocks from where we lived on Glover Street. It was the first movie I had seen since knowing Jimmy Martin. We had such a good time. We talked and laughed and just acted like young girls.

Suddenly, Bob and Pat were moving out. I didn't know why, but I knew they weren't going to be singing together anymore. Bob, Pat, and Robbie moved to an apartment at 1203 Fairview. It was a much better apartment, and after they vacated it, Jimmy and I would move in.

The People and The Music—Country and Bluegrass that is!

We continued to live in the apartment on Glover Street a few months after Jimmy and the Osbornes broke up. Sonny stayed with us. I think he felt that his room was private enough so he could come and go and never see Jimmy Martin. Occasionally, I was in the kitchen and saw Sonny coming out of his room. He was always in a hurry. I never asked him any questions about where he was going or where he went. But we talked a few minutes whenever I saw him before he headed out the backdoor. I never knew why they broke up, when their records were doing so well and everyone at the Barndance loved them. I never asked Jimmy. Bob, or Sonny.

After my book, *Don't Give Your Heart to a Rambler*, was released, I was backstage at the Grand Old Opry talking to Bob. I told him I had never asked Jimmy nor him why they broke up. Bob remembered the day very well, and he told me the following: "You remember when we were all helping decorate the Hall (meaning 12101 Mack Avenue) for New Year's Eve?" I said, "Yes." He said, "I was taking a break and sitting there when Jimmy came over to me and said, 'I have decided to go solo.' Bob told me he replied to Jimmy, 'Ok. We will separate in two weeks.'" And that was that! I didn't know all that was happening, and I was at the Hall that day.

There were several banjo players to come and go with Jimmy after the breakup with the Osbornes, until Crowe returned. By this time, we were living in the apartment on Fairview Bob and Pat had vacated. It was only a living room/bedroom and bath with a good size kitchen. It had a Murphy bed that folded up into the wall in the morning. Jimmy and I slept in the bed. Morning came, and we had a living room. Again, Crowe was sleeping on the sofa. Timmy was still in the baby bed, even though by now he was a toddler.

My Memories Three of the Greatest Banjo Players

Jimmy Martin and J. D. Crowe

The latter part of 1957, we moved to a two-bedroom apartment in a carriage house located behind a big mansion. It had a nice size living room, a good kitchen, and a bath. The main house rented rooms. That was convenient.

My son, James H. (Timmy) Martin, Jr., grew up with a banjo player or a mandolin player sleeping in the room with him—sometimes, both a mandolin player and a banjo player like Paul Williams and Crowe in Shreveport. Even though he was a little boy when

The People and The Music—Country and Bluegrass that is!

Crowe was living with us in Shreveport, he has a memory like me. He remembers everything. So he was the person I thought of when writing this.

Timmy was four years old when we lived in Shreveport. He shared a room with Crowe and Paul Williams and his dog. He remembers all the fun they had because Crowe and Paul constantly teased him. If they weren't teasing him, they were teasing his dog, and he couldn't stand that. They loved ragging him about the little girl, Patricia, who lived behind us. He and Patricia played together every day. Shaming him and singing, "Timmy is in love, yada, yada, yada." It was a vicious cycle that went on every day. They would tease Timmy and the dog, and Jimmy would get mad, yell and stomp around telling them to shut up. Then, all three, Timmy, Crowe, and Paul, would sit on the couch quiet, but laughing inside. It was all to get Jimmy mad.

Timmy remembers Crowe teaching him how to take a banjo apart, put it back together, re-string it, and put the head on it. He said once he got his drum, he knew how to do everything because Crowe had taught him that with the banjo.

He also remembers Crowe's old car he brought to Wheeling. Timmy said it had flames painted on the hood and how sad Crowe was when he had to sell it. He said the last time he saw Crowe was at IBMA. He walked up behind him and asked, "Can I carry your banjo?" Crowe never looked around and said, "I've got it." Timmy then asked him, "Do you know where I can buy a car that has flames painted on the hood?" Crowe looked around and said loudly, "Timmy!" They then talked about old times and the few times Timmy had played with the New South, picking and singing.

My Memories Three of the Greatest Banjo Players

Timmy credits Crowe and Paul for the way he is today....loving, honest, loves music and people, and a good person. Timmy loves Crowe and Paul as do I.

Crowe was always funny. We would laugh, and the more I laughed, the louder he sung or whatever he was doing. I had a good time when I was around Crowe. Jimmy was never funny; he was always serious. He only joked around when other people were there to see him, and then he wanted to be the "star" of the show.

Crowe was different. He was a kid. He liked rock 'n' roll music and, in particular, Little Richard, Fats Domino, and Chuck Berry. I loved rock 'n' roll but was not in love with bluegrass. I was a jitterbug girl. Crowe would go around the house singing lines from a Little Richard song or a Fats Domino song, and we would laugh and I jitterbugged by myself. We were both so young. I never thought of Jimmy having any influence on Crowe other than playing the banjo, and I was happy about that. They were such opposites in personality even back in the '50s and '60s. Crowe was level-headed, as my mother would say.

When Crowe left Wheeling, Paul Williams, Timmy, and I were all sad. Paul and Crowe had bonded like brothers. Paul continued living with us and sharing a room with Timmy, but Timmy and I felt like the fun had gone when Crowe left.

Following Crowe, Paul Craft came to play with Jimmy. Paul was from Memphis, Tennessee, where I was born and grew up. My family all still lived in Memphis, so we had things to talk about. Paul was a shy person. I never thought of him as being an entertainer, but he was highly intelligent.

The People and The Music—Country and Bluegrass that is!

Paul never lived with us. Instead, he rented the same room across the street and behind the school Crowe had rented. He could walk over to our house and rehearse with Jimmy. Don't ask me how we made the rehearsals work, but we did it. I was booking shows all day long in the living room where they gathered to rehearse. I was on the phone or typing or both. They were singing or playing, or Jimmy was instructing (he loved doing that). This was all going on in a 1,000 square foot house. Busy place.

And then, Bill Emerson arrived. I remember it almost to the day. I had Jimmy booked in Las Vegas, and they would be leaving in a few weeks. We were excited to have a banjo player again.

Bill and Yolanda, his wife, and two kids, Kelly and Bobby, rented an apartment about three blocks from our house in Martins Ferry, Ohio. The first time I saw Yolanda, I thought she was the most beautiful woman I had seen. She had jet black hair and was thin with beautiful skin. Together, she and Bill were a very handsome couple. He was very, very good looking. Bill had that air of sophistication about him, and he never lost it.

Timmy was so happy Bill had kids and he could play with them. Then Timmy found out they were just babies and he was in first grade. But whenever we walked around to their house, he would still play with them.

Bill never lived with us, but he was at the house every day. I liked Bill Emerson very much. He was intelligent, and I could sit and carry on a conversation with him. He had manners; I liked that. Bill became my friend and he remained so for the rest of his life.

During the time Bill played banjo for Jimmy Martin, I traveled quite often with the band. One memorable trip was to Key West and

My Memories Three of the Greatest Banjo Players

*Bill's son, Kelly Emerson, Bill Emerson, Me
At Bill's induction into the Bluegrass Music Hall of Fame*

Tampa, Florida. Hurricane David had just hit Florida. Back then, there was no internet and long distance calls were expensive. So we drove to the town and took our chances on finding a room. Not knowing Key West was a magnet for tourists. We found two rooms in a strip motel. The hurricane had soaked the motel and water stood about a foot high in the room. We had no choice since it was the only thing available. I was afraid to sleep—afraid a snake would be in the water, hiding somewhere. Regardless, we spent the night. The next day we found a room at the Quality Inn. It was one room: the band and Jimmy slept in the bed and on the floor. I slept in the bathtub. It was better than worrying about snakes.

When Bill left Jimmy around 1963, Doyle Lawson came to work with Jimmy. At the time, Doyle was playing banjo. He was married to Christine, and they had a small baby. Again, they shared the room with Timmy. Doyle didn't stay too long with Jimmy, but I liked him and Christine. Doyle and I have remained good friends all through these years. Jimmy had a couple of banjo players from around town before Bill Emerson returned.

Bill was still with Jimmy when I left him in September 1966. I remember hearing that Bill quit sometime shortly after that. He had been driving to and from the shows from his home near Washington.

I reconnected with Bill when he was with the U.S. Navy Band. They were coming to Fort Lauderdale, and I reached out to Bill. He responded very quickly and invited my husband and me to the show. We went to the show and took Bill out to dinner. I remained in contact with Bill for several years after, went to shows whenever he was in Florida, but then lost touch again.

In 2015, I started writing my book, *Don't Give Your Heart To A Rambler, My Life With Jimmy Martin, King of Bluegrass*. I again reached out to Bill, and he was right there. As was Lola, his wife. Bill was happy to talk to me about the years with Jimmy. He gave me his honest opinions. From that day on, I stayed in touch with Bill and Lola. I have wonderful hand-written notes from Bill and Lola that I cherish. One hangs in a frame with the envelope on my office wall.

I was with Bill, his sons, Kelly and Billy, and his adopted son, Mike, when he was inducted into the Bluegrass Hall of Fame at IBMA. His son, Bobby, was not able to attend. I am so proud a very deserving Bill Emerson was inducted into the Hall of Fame. It was also important for me to know I was there when it happened.

The last time I saw Bill and Lola was at the Bluegrass Hall of Fame in Owensboro, Kentucky. We were attending the premiere of the making of the film, *Bluegrass, Country Soul,* a film about the first

My Memories Three of the Greatest Banjo Players

Barbara, Bill and Lola Emerson

bluegrass festival in Fincastle, Virginia. Carlton Haney promoted the festival, and I booked Jimmy on it for three days. Albert Idhe, Ellen Pasternak, and Fred Bartenstein did a terrific job in producing the film. Bill and I found out we were both at the premiere when our names were called from the stage prior to presentation of the film. Once the film was over, I immediately started looking for Bill and Lola. We had a wonderful visit, hugged, made great pictures, laughed, and talked.

It seems like I have a habit (lately) of seeing people for the last time at a function. I saw Sonny at IBMA in Raleigh. Sonny was staying at the same hotel as I was, but I saw him roll on the stage in his wheelchair and it concerned me. I asked Bob Osborne's son, Boj (Bobby Osborne, Jr.), if Sonny was OK and he said he was. Back at the hotel, I saw Sonny and we talked. He told me he was having difficulty with his knees, and he was getting them replaced. We then laughed, talked and bantered back and forth about his knees. The next morning I saw him again, and we did the same thing. It was like old times, one trying to outdo the other with our jabs.

The last time I saw J. D. Crowe was during SPBGMA after my book was released. I was on my way out of the hotel meeting my granddaughter, Sarah Arnold Christopher, who was waiting in the car. Just as I started out of the hotel, Crowe was rushing into the hotel. He saw me, reached out, and grabbed my arm. I grabbed him, and we both smiled and said hello. Neither of us had time to stop and chat. Oh, how I wish we had. I never called him anything but Crowe from the time I first met him in March 1954. When I called him Crowe in place of J.D., it was with great affection.

I cherish the times I spent with all these gentlemen, Sonny Osborne, J. D. Crowe, Bill Emerson, and they are all gentlemen. Not because they were some of the greatest banjo players of all time; I care (cared) less about that. I liked them for the people they were. Good, kind, smart, funny men who just happened to be good at playing a banjo and the music they loved. I liked them for the joy they brought into my life and Timmy's life, and for the kindness, the music, and the happiness they bestowed on the world. But most of all, for their friendship whether I was young or old. I definitely needed it.

Who else do you know that can claim to have lived in the same house with all of these famous people, cooked for them, and washed their sheets, but me? The musicians who have lived or spent the night in the same house with Jimmy Martin and me could, and do, fill the halls of fame. Sonny Osborne, Bobby Osborne (known to me as

My Memories Three of the Greatest Banjo Players

Bob), J. D. Crowe (he will always be Crowe to me), Bill Emerson, Paul Williams, Paul Craft, Bill Yates, Vernon Derrick, Gordon Terry, Doyle Lawson, James (Hoppy) Hutchins, Earl Taylor, Johnny Dacus, Hylo Brown, Gloria Belle, Scotty Stoneman, and so many others.

Rest in peace to those who have gone ahead.
I will always have fond memories of you.
I love and miss you all.
Until I see you again.

—*Barbara*

Just Something Extra For Fun

In August, 2019, my good friend, Jacque Tuozzolo, and I took a land and sea cruise in Alaska. Our cruise departed from Vancouver, British Columbia. Jacque and I scheduled a day trip to Vancouver Island and took the ferry over to the island. On board, she went to pick up some snacks with a detour to the powder room. While Jacque was gone, I saw the cutest little house sitting on a point. I wrote a poem about it.

Little Gray House

The ship passed the little gray house by the sea
The curtains were open and the view was as clear as it could be
As She sat by the window in her rocking chair
Her chestnut color hair flowing as free as the air

A beautiful sight for all to see
Who was she waiting for so patiently
her lover, her daughter, maybe a son or even me
Whomever it was it would never be known
For The day was almost gone

As we rounded the bend,
The curtains closed and we could no longer see
The beautiful lady behind the door
Of the little gray house by the sea.

Recipes

IRELAND'S INN was located on Broadway where it curves and becomes 21st Avenue South in Nashville. Vanderbilt is located directly across the street. In 1963, Ireland's had the best Steak and Biscuits in town. Everyone went there to eat. I don't know anyone who ate anything there except the Steak and Biscuits.

Loretta Lynn, Mooney Lynn and I met the Wilburn Brothers there to discuss the new television show. We were all having the Steak and Biscuits.

Recipe compliments of Cathy Everette, a native Nashvillian. I have not tried it since I don't eat meat.

> **Ireland's Steak & Biscuits**
>
> Beef tenderloin sliced in 3/8" medallions
> Salt Pepper
> flour
>
> Marinade
> 1 TBSP Worchestershire
> ½ cup Olive oil - Extra Virgin
> dash Sugar
> 3 clove chopped garlic
>
> Mix marinade, place in plastic bag
> Add sliced steak and marinate over night
>
> Drain marinade and pat dry steak
> Salt & Pepper and dredge thru flour
> Use enough cooking oil to cover bottom of skillet
> Fry in batches
> Place steak in small biscuits.

Recipes

BARBARA'S BISCUIT RECIPE

- 2-1/2 cups Buttermilk – do not use skim milk
- 6 cups self-rising flour – I use Lily White Flour for all my baking
- ¼ cup butter melted. *
- ½ cup Crisco melted. *

You can use all Crisco or butter if you like. As long as you use ¾ cup.

1. Heat oven to 475
2. Mix the flour, buttermilk, butter and crisco in a bowl stirring gently together until blended. Do not overmix. I stir it with a spoon the way Jimmy Martin's aunt, Thelma Burchett Fields, taught me. You can also use a fork.
3. Pour mixture out on a floured cutting board and knead about 15 times adding a little flour until it is no longer sticky.
4. Pat or roll out to about ½ inch thick. Using a biscuit cutter or small glass, cut out and place on a well-greased baking sheet.
5. Bake about 8 to 10 minutes until the tops are golden brown. I like to brush the tops with a little melted butter when they come out of the oven.
6. Serve immediately while hot.

Recipes

BARBARA'S MARINADE

- 1/4 CUP Soy Sauce
- 3 tablespoons Honey
- 2 tablespoons Vinegar
- 1-1/2 tablespoons each: Garlic Powder and Ground Ginger
- 3/4 cup Salad Oil (like Wesson or Crisco Oil)
- 1 green onion, finely chopped.

1. Mix together and pour over meat.
2. Marinade for at least four hours.

We used this to marinate our London Broil (always ask for the first cut for London Broil) and we grilled it on the patio. Ray would do the grilling and he loved this Marinade. I bet he hasn't thought of it in years. But, actually, you could marinate any meat in it and it would be fantastic.

BARBARA'S HOLIDAY SUPREME SALAD

- 2 boxes Apricot Jello – if you can't find Apricot – use 1 box orange and 1 box peach jello

1. Dissolve in 1-1/2 cup boiling water.
2. After Jello has dissolved – add 2 cups cold water.
3. Pour into a square pan or one you plan on using to serve it. I always used one of my larger Corning Ware dishes to serve it. Let cool until it begins to thicken.

Recipes

4. Add 1 - #2 can crushed pineapple – drained and reserve the pineapple juice, 2 bananas diced and 1 cup small marshmallows. Let set till firm.

COOKED TOPPING

Combine

- 1/2 cup Pineapple juice
- 1/2 cup sugar
- 2 tablespoons all-purpose flour
- 1 egg slightly beaten

1. Cook together until thickened. Make sure you don't have any lumps. Stir in 1 – 3oz package cream cheese until it is well incorporated into the mixture. Cool.
2. While your cooked mixture is cooling, whip 1 box Dream Whip, according to directions on box, and fold into cooked mixture. Spread on top of Jello mixture and chill until firm.

DEDICATION

I am dedicating this to my former daughter-in-law, Heather Martin. She has been after me for 25 years for the recipe. She tried everything to duplicate it making trying to duplicate the recipe a lot of fun especially at Christmas. I always told her, "You are close but not close enough." I love you Heather. Now, you can make the real thing. The sad part, we won't get to play our game.

My mother-in-law, Mary Mooneyhan Stephens, gave me this recipe in 1971. I have never shared with anyone.

Recipes

BARBARA'S MEXICAN CORNBREAD

- 1 cup Dixie Lily Cornmeal
- 1/2 cup all-purpose flour
- 1/2 teaspoons baking soda
- 1 teaspoon salt
- 1/2 teaspoon sugar
- 1 cup cream style corn
- 1 medium onion finely chopped
- 2 or more chopped and seeded jalapeno peppers
- 1/4 lb shredded cheddar cheese
- 1/2 cup olive or vegetable oil
- 2 eggs slightly beaten
- 1 cup buttermilk

1. Preheat oven to 450°. Grease an 8 inch oven proof skillet, (I use cast iron for all my cornbread .).
2. In a mixing bowl combine dry ingredients. Stir in next four ingredients. Combine remaining ingredients and I had add to dry ingredients and stir only until dry ingredients are moistened, turn into skillet.
3. Bake 20 to 25 minutes or until lightly browned. Remove from oven and let's stand at least five minutes before cutting in pie shaped pieces makes 8 to 10 servings.

You may want to use Pam or some other spray on your skillet before you put the cornbread in.

My family likes this with beef stew. It is delicious with anything.

Recipes

BARBARA'S BEEF STEW

Medium size bowl: place the following
- 5 potatoes, peeled and quartered
- 5 carrots, peeled and sliced
- 3 onions, halved and cut into four parts
- 1 1/2 to 2 1/2 pound stew beef
- 1 1/2 tablespoons sugar
- 3 tablespoons tapioca
- 1 1/2 teaspoon salt
- 1/2 teaspoon pepper
- 1/2 cup of water plus 1/2 cup of a good red win or 1 cup water
- 1 28 ounce can of good tomatoes like Marzetti, squished to break up tomatoes

1. Preheat the oven to 275
2. Layer in the order the above.
3. Bake covered for 5 hours. Do not remove the lid while baking
4. For the larger bowl, place the following ingredients:

My family loves this stew. My son, Buddy, and my husband, Chuck, both used to ask me to make it so they could take it to work. Buddy even had a contest with one guy whose mom could make the best beef stew. I don't know if I won or not. He never told me.

Recipes

BARBARA'S BEST GINGERBREAD

When I make gingerbread, I'd like to grease and flour my pan first and set it aside so that it will be ready. I use an oblong baking pan, 11 x 8 x 4". This is the absolutely the best gingerbread that I have ever made or tasted. I use two bowls to make this.

Medium size bowl: place the following
- 1 cup Brer Rabbit Molasses
- 1/3 cup Wesson or Crisco oil
- 1/2 cup sugar
- 2 eggs beaten

Beat this mixture well until all the ingredients are combined.

For the larger bowl, place the following ingredients:
- 2 1/2 cups, all purpose, flour sifted
- 2 teaspoons cinnamon
- 1 level teaspoon ground ginger,
- 1/2 teaspoon ground cloves
- 1-1/2 teaspoons soda
- 1/2 teaspoon salt

1. Mix all the dry ingredients together thoroughly and then pour the liquid mixture from the other bowl into the larger bowl.

2. Add one cup of boiling hot water into this mixture and stir by hand to mix. This will look rather strange at this point.

3. Pour this mixture into your prepared, baking pan and place in a 350° oven and bake 45 minutes or until the cakes springs back when touched. if you like marshmallows on top of your

Recipes

gingerbread, it is a good idea to sprinkle the top good with mini marshmallows a few minutes before the cake is finished. This will give you a toasted marshmallow finish.

This cake is also very good served plain either warm or cold with ice cream or whipped cream.

Photo Memories

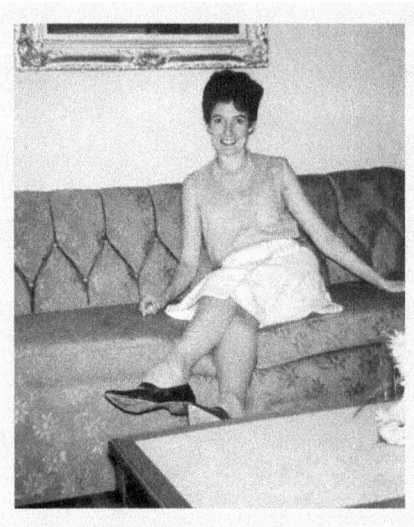

My sister, Betty Taylor, in m living room at 224 Jacksonian, September, 1963

Jimmy with our pale green Cadillac 1953

Me, Jimmy, Norma and Roy, June, 1954. I was pregnant with Timmy.

Left: Jimmy listening to his records. Right: Shotgun (played by Paul Williams) points out ot J. D. and Jimmy, The Joke's On You record could be improved.

Bob Osborne and Jimmy Martin

*Left: Jimmy Martin Jr., Hank Williams Jr., an Jimmy Martin.
Right: Roy Acuff and Ginger Boatwright*

Casey Clark Barndance, 1201 Mack Road, Detroit MI, 1954

Left: Bob Smith at the Dusty Road Tavern. Mural painted on the back wall of Bob Smith, Eldon Burgess, Roy Bounds and Harold Young. Right: Roland and Arlene White at the Dusty Road Tavern, 1971

Paul Kraft, Jimmy, and Paul Williams at Casey Clark's Barndance

Johnny Dacus, JD Crowe, Jimmy Martin in Detroit, MI, 1957

Me at 17 with Frances Preston at the Grand Ole Opry in 1953 watching a skit by Lonzo and Oscar. Filmed by Bob Grannis.

Show at the fairgrowns in West Palm Beach

Back row: J.D. Crowe, Earl Taylor, and Jimmy Martin with three fans.

Jimmy Jr. on stage with Paul Williams, Vernon Derrick, Jimmy and Bill Emerson

 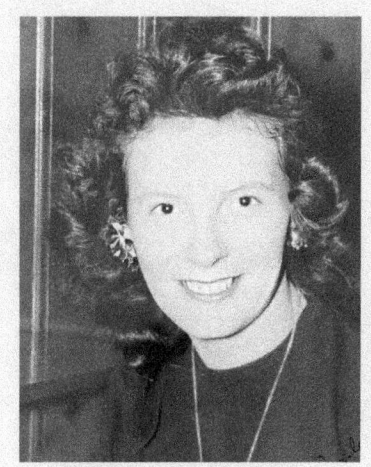

Left: Willie Samples played the last show I booked in September, 1967 in Guelph, Ontario, Canada with Hank Williams Jr. Right: My portrait in 1958, Detroit, Michigan

Sisters: Barbara, Betty, and Billie

Left: Barbara and Bill Emerson   Right: Barbara and Doyle Lawson

Barbara with Bobby Osborne backstage at the Grand Ole Opry, 2018.

Barbara with Ronnie Reno and Bob Osborne at the Bluegrass Hall of Fame.

Barbara with David Heath at WWVA Jamboree in Wheeling, West Virginia, April, 2023.

Barbara with granddaughters Sarah and Samanth, Lisa's daughters, and her great grandchildren, Cash Christopher and Braylynn Stralco at the Louvre in Paris in front of the painting of the Mona Lisa, October, 2023.

About the Author

BARBARA MARTIN-STEPHENS' life has come full circle. In 1953, she met Jimmy Martin, a sideman for Bill Monroe, on the Grand Ole Opry in Nashville, Tennessee. That was the beginning of her life in the music business and would become the catalyst for a career in the field of management and booking of country and bluegrass musicians over the next fourteen years.

She has been a pioneer for women as the first and only booking agent on Music Row, in Nashville, and for the WWVA Jamboree in Wheeling, West Virginia. Ms. Martin-Stephens was the talent agent at WWVA from 1961 to 1967. Her agency, the Barbara Martin Agency, was broadcast nightly over the Lee Moore Show on 50,000 watt radio station, WWVA, as the place to call for talent. Additionally, she booked Grand Ole Opry acts from Nashville for appearances on the Jamboree, fairs, fire carnivals, package shows, and clubs.

Her first book, "Don't Give Your Heart to A Rambler, My Life with Jimmy Martin, King of Bluegrass," was widely acclaimed. It was

The People and The Music—Country and Bluegrass that is!

a courageous, intimate read on her experiences as partner and business partner of the well-known but controversial musician, Jimmy Martin. More than a history and more than an exposé on early Bluegrass, the author's message reaches out to women and musicians everywhere on the difficulties that women have faced, and still face, whether as musicians, wives, mothers, or—indeed in any role in society. She commands a disarmingly honest comment on both the hardships and moments of joy and fulfillment that she felt with Martin, who struggled with alcoholism and anger reached the level of domestic violence. This culminated with Ms. Martin-Stephens barely escaping one morning with her life, with a pair of shoes on her feet borrowed from Gail Yates, with a child on each hand, and only the clothes she wore on her back. Her resilience, however, is the triumph of the book, as she had meantime become the first woman booking agent on the male-dominated Music Row scene, and subsequently time after time found ways to not only survive - from waitressing to high level paralegal work - but also to live life to the fullest. Barbara is a tell-it-like-it-is speaker who engages listeners with warmth and wisdom at the get go, and goes the extra mile to answer personal questions and give feedback to all those who have the fortune to hear her speak.

Barbara is currently 89 years old an is still actively involved in the music community. She makes her home in Goodlettsville, Tennessee, a suburb of Nashville.

A lady of "firsts": First female booking agent in Shreveport, Louisiana, Wheeling, West Virginia, and Nashville, Tennessee. First Female Kentucky Colonel on Music Row in Nashville, Tennessee, and one who could never take no for an answer, she is now working

About the Author

full-time in promoting her book. She has appeared at East Tennessee State University's School of Appalachian and Bluegrass Music Studies, where she participated in the classroom and for Question and Answer Sessions at the Reese Museum. Other appearances have included South Florida Bluegrass Festival, North Miami, Florida; Jenny Lind Bluegrass Festival, Turnbridge, Vermont; the Swamp Festival, Davie, Florida; the Sertoma Spring Bluegrass Festival in Brooksville, Florida; Friends of the Library Spring Luncheon, Plantation, Florida; for Friends of Helen B. Hoffman Library, Plantation, Florida; the IBMA where she participated in a Q&A sponsored by Ken Irwin and Marian Levy, Co-Founders of Rounder Records; a Facebook Live Q&A at SPGMA in Nashville, Tennessee sponsored by the Handsome Ladies; Leadership Bluegrass of the IBMA Presented Booking History: From the Hayride to Music Row with Katie Harford Hogue and can be seen on YouTube; and numerous radio and television appearances.

Index

*Locators in italics indicate photos

901 Club, 26, 263

A
Acuff, Roy, 72, *208,* 209, 261
Anderson, Bill, *63,* 64, 127, 235, 236–37
Andrews, Jack B., 26, 42, 53, 74, 75
Armstrong, Jean, 63–64
Arnold, Eddy, 70
Ashworth, Audie, 140–41
Atkins, Chet, 95, 102
Aud-Lee Attractions, 59, 61

B
Barbara Martin Agency, The
   beginning of (Wheeling, WV), 40–44
   end of, 57–58
   move to Nashville, 44–47
Barn Dance, The. *See* Casey Clark Barn Dance, The
Barton, Dave, 65–67, 69–70, 91–92, 117, 138
Belew, Carl, 27, 194–99
Betty Amos and the Rhythm Queens, 45, 46
Bluegrass Music Hall of Fame, 53, 320
Boatwright, Ginger Hammond, 217–30, 245–46
Bob Neal Agency, The, 91–93
booking
   becoming an agent, 33–36, 37–39, 40
   at fair conventions, 41–42
   post Gra-Mar, 57–58
Branscomb, Louisa, 170–89
Brooks, Garth, 62, 145
Brown, Jim Ed, 64, 65–66, 67, 85, 108
Buckhorn Music, 68
Buddy Lee Attractions, 61–62
Bushwhackers, The, 222

C
Canning, Michelle, 300–301
Casey Clark Barn Dance, The, 34, 64, 134, 201–2, 313
Cash, Johnny, 88, 143, 166
Cash, June Carter, 166
Cedarwood Publishing Company, 25, 26, 76
Clements, Cowboy Jack, 49, 143–44
CMT Television, 52, 290
Cooper, Stoney, 38, *200,* 201–2, 208–9, 267
Cooper, Wilma Lee, 38, *200,* 201–2, 204–7, 208–9, 210–16, 248, 267
Corrigan, John, 38, 39, 41, 57

348

Index

Country Music Association (CMA), 76, 78, 93, 123, 124, 285
Cousin Jody, 203, 207
Crook and Chase, 253–55
Crowe, J.D., 31–32, *310*, 314–17, 322

D
Darlene, Donna, 129–37
Davis, Jimmie, 35, 51, 87
Dean, Dixie, 53
Decca Records, 26, 45, 49, 126–27, 198
Denny, Bill, 76–77
Denny, Jim, 75–76
Denny, John, 57, 76, 77
Denny Music Group, 77
Derrick, Vernon, 167–68
Dillard, Doug, 222–25
D.J. Convention, 43–44, 64, 88
Don Light Talent Agency, 51
Doss, Colonel "Buster," *71*–73, 135
Dusty Road Tavern, 148–50, 151, 265–66

E
Emerson, Bill, 318–21
Emmons, Buddy, 129, 134

F
fair associations, 41–42, 58
Farm Aid, 62
Franks, Tillman, *32*, 33–34

G
Gaslight Theatre, The, 255–56
Gaye, Connie B., 54
Gene Johnson Promotions, 37–39
Gibson, Willowdeen Farmer, 131, 202
Glaser, Chuck, 102, 233–34
Glaser, Jim, 101, 235–36
Glaser Brothers, The, 27, 78, 123, 234
Glaser Publications, 101–2, 234
Gra-Mar Talent Agency, 26, *27*, 48–57
Grammer, Billy, 27, 47–49, 54–57, *111*, 263
Grammer, Ruth, 47, 110–11
Grand Ole Opry, 76, 190, 246–49, 257–58
   acts featured on the, 49, 55, 112, 200, 202, 235, 261
   Jimmy Martin and the, 43–44, 47
   union contracts, 279
Green, Bobby, 148, 149, 151, 265–66
Griggs, Elizabeth (Libby), 115–19

H
Haggard, Merle, 284–87, 291–92
Hall, Tom T., 271, 274
Harford, Betty, 95–105, 231, 232, 234
Harrell, Bill, 283, 284
Hartford, John, 95, 100–104, 234
Hawkins, Hawkshaw, 38
Hayride, The. *See* Lousiana Hayride, The
Helms, Don, *78*
Hitchcock, Stan, 49, *51*, 52, 290–91
Horton, Johnny, *32*, 33, 34
Hubert Long Talent Agency, 25, 64–70, 116–17
Hunter, Billy, 242–58
Husky, Ferlin, 118–19

Index

I
International Alliance of Theatrical and Stage Employees Local 46, 246, 247
International Bluegrass Music Association (IBMA), 181–82, 273

J
Jackson, Joyce, 106–14
Jackson, Leo, 108, 113
Jackson, Shot, 129, 132–35
Jim Denny Agency (Artist Bureau), 25, 53–54, 57, 74–77
Johnson, Gene, 37–39, 40
Johnson, Jerry, 43, 80–81, 200–207, 208–9, 210–11
Jones, George, 59, 64

K
Kahn, Mervin, 67
Kershaw, Doug, 131
Kershaw, Rusty, 131
Kilgore, Merle, 33, 164–69
Kristofferson, Kris, 68, 139, 143
Kuhn, C.C. "Buck," 225–30

L
Lanham, Charmaine and Marty, 264–68
Lavender, Shorty (Grover), 65, 117
Leary, Peggy, *200, 201,* 202–7, 209–10
Leary Family, The, *200,* 202, 208–9
Lee, Buddy, 59–*60,* 61–62
Lee, Larry, 178, 179
Lee, Rita, 59–61, 62
Lee Moore Show, The, 46

Light, Don, 49, *51*–52
Linebaugh's Restaurant, 107
Long, Earl K., 35
Long, Hubert, 25, 42, 54, 63–70, 116–18, 140–41, 143
Louisiana Hayride, The, 31–33, 73, 85, 165, 194
Lynn, Loretta, 27, 45, 54, 81, 82–83, 125, 126, 263
Lyric Mountain Retreats. *See* Woodsong Mountain Retreats

M
Martin, Jimmy
  bookings, 75, 135, 271
  and Elvis Presley, 85, 312
  friendship with Grant Turner, 190–91, 192
  and The Grand Ole Opry, 43–44, 47
  and The Osbornes, 310–14
  rift with Billy Grammer, 56–57
  and the Sunny Mountain Boys, 35, 40, 54, 220
Mauldin, Bessie, 178, 192, *193*
Maxwell, Sonja Light, *51*–52
Maxwell House Hotel, 191–92
McBride, Martina, 251
Miller, Jeff, 305–8
Moeller, Lucky, 25, 42, 53, *74,* 75
Monroe, Bill, 125, *193,* 250
Montgomery, Melba, 64
Moore, Lee, 39, 41
Moore, Scotty, *32,* 85
Morrison, DeLesseps Story, 35
Moss Rose Publishing Company, 67–68
music business today, the, 299–308

Index

musicians union, 40, 46–47. *See also* Nashville Musicians Union, the
Music Row, 53, 61, 62, 70, 73, 91
  changes in, 22–28, 119

N
Nashville Association of Talent Directors, 62
Nashville Musicians Union, the, 235, 276–79
Nashville Now, 249–52
Neal, Bob, 43, 44, 45, 54, 79, 84–93
Nelson, Willie, 62
Nightbeats, The, 66–67

O
Osborne, Bob, 18–20, 310–14
Osborne, Sonny, 309–14, 321–22
Osborne Brothers, The, 64, 81, 126, 284–86, 292–93
Owens, Bonnie, 286, 287

P
Parker, Colonel Tom, 70, 84, 86–88
Payne, Jimmy, 15, 28, 97, 98, 99, 100, 101, 231–41
phone rooms. *See* telephone rooms
Pickin' Parlor, The, 221, 222
Pierce, Webb, 28, *29,* 76, 122, 124, 165
Presley, Elvis, 27, 84–*86,* 87–88, 93, 312
promotion
  with Billy Grammer, 54–56
  the job of, 305
Pruitt, Jeanne, 67, 144, 210

R
Radio Dot and Smoky, 260–61
Rainwater, Cedric, 55–56
RCA Victor Studios, 24
Red, White & Blue(grass), 218–20, 221–22
Reeves, Jim, *106,* 107–12, 134
Reeves, Mary, 108–9, 110–14
Reno, Don, 45, 271, 280–83, *293*
Reno, Ronnie, 280–97
Reno Brothers, The, 288, *289*
retainer, importance of a, 75
Ric Records, 78, 123–25
R.O.P.E (Reunion of Professional Entertainers), 49, 77
Rushing, Jim, 138–46

S
Sawgrass Music, 178
Screen Door Songwriters Alliance, 171
Sho-Bud Guitars, 129, 134
Skaggs, Ricky, 145, 227
Slim Lay Show, The, 50
Smiley, Red, 271, 281–82
Smith, Birdie Lee, 148–62
Smith, Bob, 148–58, 162
Smith, Connie, 126, 210
Smothers Brothers Show, The, 102, 103
songwriter's night, 302–3
Spicher, Buddy, 130–31
Station Inn, The, 152–56, 266
Stephens, Chuck, 21, 22, 150–*51,* 161, 210
Summey, Sarah, 203, *206,* 207
Sure Fire Publishing Company, 78, 83, 125, 126
Swan, Dottie, 26, 259–63
Swan, Louis W. "Smoky," 260–61

Index

T
Taylor, Betty Gibson, 55–56, 132–33
TCB Enterprises, 93
telephone rooms, 54, 73
Terry, Gordon, 77
Tillis, Mel, 27, 53, 178–79
Tillis, Pam, 53, 178
Tree Publishing, 26
Turner, Grant, 190–93

U
USO shows, 43

V
Vanador, Lester, 123
Vandergrift Brothers, The, 45, 46–47
Vee-Jay Records, 234

W
Walker, Billy, 71–*72*
Walker, Jo, 78, 123–24
Wilburn, Doyle, 27, 63–64, *78*–79, 81, 82, 125, 207
Wilburn, Teddy, 27, 78, 81–82, 125
Wilburn Brothers, The, 54, 81, 124–25, 126
Wil-Helm Talent Agency, 26, 43, 44, 45, 78–83, 125
Wilkins, Marijohn, 68, 143
Williams, Audrey, 59, 167
Williams, Johnny and Jeanette, 269–75
Williams, Leona, 287
Williams, Paul, 31–*32*, 91, 315–16, 317
Williams Jr., Hank, 58, 59, 61, 166, 167

Wilson, Corky, 120–28
Wilson, Happy, 49–50
Wilson, Smiley, 54, *78,* 79–82, 83, 125
Wizard Records, 73
WMPS (radio station), 84–85
Woodsong Mountain Retreats, 180–81
Worth, Marian, 50
WWVA (radio station), 41, 42, 44
WWVA Jamboree, 36, 38–39, 40–41, 46, 57, 129–30, 202
Wynette, Tammy, 64

352

Printed in the USA
CPSIA information can be obtained
at www.ICGtesting.com
JSHW010012031224
74619JS00003B/4